Advanced Principles of Auditing

Advanced Principles of Auditing

Edited by Hugo Romero

CLANRYE INTERNATIONAL
www.clanryeinternational.com

Clanrye International,
750 Third Avenue, 9th Floor,
New York, NY 10017, USA

ISBN: 978-1-63240-937-9

Cataloging-in-Publication Data

Advanced principles of auditing / edited by Hugo Romero.
p. cm.
Includes bibliographical references and index.
ISBN 978-1-63240-937-9
1. Auditing. 2. Accounting. 3. Bookkeeping. I. Romero, Hugo.

HF5667 .A38 2020

657.45--dc23

For information on all Clanrye International publications
visit our website at www.clanryeinternational.com

CLANRYE INTERNATIONAL

Printed in China.

Contents

Preface

Over the recent decade, advancements and applications have progressed exponentially. This has led to the increased interest in this field and projects are being conducted to enhance knowledge. The main objective of this book is to present some of the critical challenges and provide insights into possible solutions. This book will answer the varied questions that arise in the field and also provide an increased scope for furthering studies.

The independent and systematic examination of books, accounts, documents statutory records and vouchers of an organization is known as auditing. It is done to ensure the fair representation of the financial statements and non-financial disclosures. It also ascertains that the accounts books are properly maintained by the organization. Auditing has become important in both public and corporate sectors. The process of auditing helps stakeholders in evaluating as well as improving the effectiveness of risk management. Financial audits are concerned with the validity and reliability of financial statements. Cost audit verifies the accuracy of cost accounts and records. This book elucidates the concepts and innovative models around prospective developments with respect to auditing. It includes some of the vital pieces of work being conducted across the world, on various topics related to this field. It will prove to be immensely beneficial to students and researchers of this field.

I hope that this book, with its visionary approach, will be a valuable addition and will promote interest among readers. Each of the authors has provided their extraordinary competence in their specific fields by providing different perspectives as they come from diverse nations and regions. I thank them for their contributions.

Editor

1

Determinants of the level of information disclosure in financial statements prepared in accordance with IFRS

Anna Białek-Jaworska[a1] and Anna Matusiewicz[a]

[a] *University of Warsaw, Faculty of Economic Sciences*

Abstract: This paper aims to identify the factors determining the extent of mandatory and voluntary information disclosure in financial reports of selected Polish listed companies. It is particularly important in the context of reporting standards harmonisation and the related process of IFRS coming into common use in consolidated accounts since 2005. We used the Polish Corporate Disclosure Index (PCDI), designed by the research team led by Świderska (2010), for non-financial companies. The PCDI index includes voluntary disclosures in financial statements, management reports and corporate social responsibility reports. Based on a panel study of factors determining the scope of information disclosed by 36 Polish public parent companies, forming capital groups, in the years 2005-2007 we demonstrated a negative correlation between the extent of mandatory and voluntary disclosure and the companies' financial performance (ROE) except for possitive relation with disclosure in management reports. Probably, managers prefer to show off good results in management reports (impression management theory). When the company profitability was lower, managers explained the financial standing in more detail (signaling theory). Auditor plays the important role in voluntary and corporate social responsibility disclosures, but not in mandatory ones. Bigger companies disclose more in each area, in accordance with agency theory.

Keywords: IFRS, Poland, mandatory disclosure, voluntary disclosure

---

[1] *Corresponding authors*: Department of Banking, Finance and Accounting, Faculty of Economic Sciences, University of Warsaw, Długa Str. 44/50, PL-00241 Warsaw, Poland, email address: abialek@wne.uw.edu.pl

1. Introduction

The mandatory adoption of International Financial Reporting Standards (IFRS) by EU publicly traded corporations, forming capital groups, in 2005, resulted in a significant change in consolidated financial reporting and disclosure practices in emerging economies of Europe, especially in Poland. Domestic GAAP shaped by local institutions and regulators and incorporated by national capital market were abandoned for a single set of principle-based accounting standards. One of the major intended purposes of the adoption of IFRS was to enhance financial reporting and mandatory and voluntary disclosure through the requirements of a set of 'high quality standards'. These problems seem even more complex to analyse if we compare the relatively restrictive specification of the required information disclosure provided by domestic GAAP with a certain freedom in case of IFRS in this respect. Earlier, in financial reports by domestic GAAP, the company presented data according to a specific pattern of the report with a list of information that should be given in the notes. Consequently, since 2005, under IFRS the extent of disclosure, especially voluntary, presented in financial statements, management reports and corporate social responsibility reports, has been much dependent on corporate management decisions. Because in emerging economies that adopted the IFRS, like especially Poland in 2005, corporations have been given a choice as to what information they wish to publish in consolidated reports, prepared according to IFRS. We examine how the adoption of IFRS influenced parent companies, forming capital groups, attitude to information disclosure, in particular shown by the extent and quality of mandatory and voluntary disclosure in financial statements, management reports and corporate social responsibility reports.

Therefore, we analyse the direction and significance of the impact of Polish public parent company characteristics like profitability, size, leverage, shareholding dispersion and auditor category, on the extent and quality of different information disclosure in the first years (2005-2007) following the introduction of compulsory consolidated reporting under IFRS. The information disclosure in financial reports of public companies is particularly important in the context of accounting standards harmonisation and the resultant requirement of companies in the European Union, including Poland, to use IFRS in their consolidated accounts since 2005. Understanding the factors that determine company disclosure decisions may be very beneficial for the bodies designing the reporting standards and for audit firms controlling the observance thereof. Exploring disclosure determinants is extremely important for guidance, focussing auditors activities intended to support businesses in reporting their financial standing in a trustworthy manner. Furthermore, this will enable them to identify the types of companies whose financial reports may potentially contain many frequent untruths or omissions.

This paper contributes to the literature on the effects of IFRS adoption and the information disclosures by providing empirical evidence of listed parent companies disclosure practices in reaction to the adoption for consolidated reporting in Polish setting, where less than 10% active companies (sole proprietorship including) do bookkeeping. However, it took only fifteen years to develop accounting from output-oriented communist accounting models to the adoption of IFRS in Poland. Though changes in accounting regulation and practice in Poland are very rapid, they concern only a small number of undertakings. The information asymmetry is an overall problem in the analysed emerging economy with accounting system based on tax law in case of over 90% entities. Consequently, this limits business sector growth. This severe information asymmetry settings clearly set out the originality of our research as information disclosure is crucial to the corporate access to funding sources.

The challenges in analysing of financial disclosures in transition economies stem from limited coverage in international financial databases and the limited availability of disclosure indexes, developed only in research projects. To mitigate the first problem we obtain data from local data providers, Notoria Service with support of data hand collecting from management reports and chartered auditor's opinions. The second problem limits our research to the sample contained 36 parent companies as only for them the PCDI index was calculated in the research project led by Świderska (2010). Quantification of the scope and quality of listed companies' notes conveyed in their financial statements enables the examination of the company disclosure decisions. However, analyses of the extent of disclosure in financial reports are impeded by the input of time and labour needed to manually collect data in purpose to measure the scope and quality of disclosure.

To identify the determinants of the level of information disclosure in consolidated financial statements prepared in accordance with IFRS we carry out five information disclosures regressions on a panel of annual consolidated financial statement data of parent companies listed at the Warsaw Stock Exchange over the period from 2005 to 2007. As dependent variables we use the PCDI index and its four components measured the extent and quality of mandatory, voluntary, management reports and corporate social responsibility disclosures. This approach has enabled us to compare the directions of the impact of analysed determinants on wide scope of information disclosures and allowed us test if the impression management theory, signalling theory and agency theory apply to attitude of Polish parent companies to information disclosures.

The rest of the paper is organized as follows. We begin with overview of the literature discussing the problems of disclosure in financial reports to develop our hypotheses. Then, we describe the research design including the Polish Corporate Disclosure Index (PCDI) structure. Next, in the empirical section, we employ panel regressions to identify the sign of estimated coefficients of parent companies characteristics after IFRS adoption. We discuss the implications of these results in the conclusion and suggest further research directions.

2. Literature review

Although differences in accounting rules across countries have diminished significantly in recent decade owing to the harmonisation efforts of the International Accounting Standards Committee/Board (IASC/IASB) and other organisations, according to Hope (2003a) there has not been a corresponding trend in the enforcement of accounting standards internationally. Holland (1998) argues that an overall aim of a firm's disclosure activities is to increase investor understanding of the firm's performance and future outlook, and to ensure that participants interpret firm-provided information in an informed and similar manner. Companies listed on international markets disclose more than those whose stocks are only available on their domestic stock of exchanges. Meek *et al.* (1995) analysed determinants of voluntary disclosures, based on a list of 85 items of strategic, non-financial and financial information published by 226 selected public companies from USA, Great Britain and Continental Europe (France, Germany, Netherlands) in their financial reports of 1989. The resultant disclosure index represented a ratio of information disclosed to the total number of items listed. In order to examine how various factors affect the extent of disclosure, four regressions were estimated depending on the category of information: strategic, financial and non-financial information, and the general level of information disclosed which comprised the three previous groups. As a result of the analysis, the significance of dependent variables was found to vary depending on the type of information. The most significant variables explaining the extent of voluntary disclosure included the company size, the region of its origin and whether the company is solely listed on its domestic stock exchange, or on foreign one, as well. Major companies clearly tend to disclose more information. Firms from Continental Europe seem to provide more information than those in Great Britain or USA, and those listed on international markets disclose more than firms whose stocks are only available on their domestic stock of exchanges (Meek *et al.*, 1995).

Based on annual financial statements of 135 Swiss listed companies for the year 1991, Raffournier (1995) developed a disclosure index for items specified in the Fourth and Seventh European Union's Directives and used it as a basis for examining disclosure determinants. The author obtained a considerably positive correlation between the disclosure index and the company size and scale of its international operations. Michad'lesco (1999) examined disclosure determinants based on the data of 100 French companies in the years 1991-1995. The extent of disclosure was measured by means of an index based on scoring sheets containing a list of disclosures with an adequate quality of information. The model proved that the domestic status and the fact of being additionally listed on foreign markets are the only variables having any statistically valid, positive effect on the disclosure index. The positive correlation seems obvious, considering the need to meet additional information requirements in order to obtain a positive reputation on the Paris stock exchange or to be able to be listed on a foreign market. The analysis covers major public companies, mainly due to the availability of reports needed for developing the disclosure index.

The analysis of disclosure measured by the Securities and Futures Institute ranking was conducted on a sample of 1028 observations from the years 2003 and 2004 of companies listed on the Taiwan Stock Exchange (Huang *et al.*, 2011). A logit model was adopted to accommodate the binary rating of transparency. The extent of control over companies was measured by binary variables reflecting the ownership structure in terms of supervisory board members, managers, government institutions and foreign investors participation and the proportion of independent members in the company management and in its supervisory board. Huang *et al.* (2011) took note of the electronics & IT industry with regard to its high share of venture capital financing as a factor potentially enhancing the extent of disclosure. The results suggest that the strict control of company activities reflected by the independence of members of its supervisory bodies and by the audit body size, has a positive impact on the information transparency. Financial leverage and the share of government institutions and foreign investors in the ownership structure had little significant effect on the level of transparency. Furthermore, the company scale was re-confirmed to influence the extent of disclosure and information transparency positively. Hope (2003a) documents that firm-level disclosures are positively related to forecast accuracy. Firms with higher information costs are less likely to issue public earnings forecasts (Bamber *et al.*, 2010).

Financial statements in some countries, including Poland, have historically been prepared to satisfy legal (often tax) requirements, rather than to inform investors. Reforms of accounting based on IAS/IFRS, that were recommended by the World Bank or the International Monetary Fund, manifested indeed in the 1990s in most of Central and South-Eastern European countries, but with variations in terms of how the reform was made, for what kinds of companies, and on which time horizon (Albu & Albu, 2014). Emerging economies embraced in many cases more rapidly than developed countries the international standards, because they expected benefits at the macro-economic level (Brown, 2011) due to the impact on equity markets. With the Accounting Act of 2000, Polish accounting shifted from tax-oriented system toward becoming a tool for decision making by implementing a “substance over form” principle (Dobija and Klimczak, 2010). The contemporary accounting and tax laws are two separate entities in the Polish legal system (Grabinski *et al.*, 2014) at least for limited liability companies and joint-stock companies (legal persons) that are obligated to bookkeeping without exceptions (Accounting Act). In 2001 a value of conformity of the national system to IFRS was 58 for Poland and 40 for Turkey, while the score was computed for 111 accounting items (Chen *et al.*, 2014). In Poland, Slovenia and Turkey starting with 2005, in Romania beginning from 2007, in Ukraine since 2012, IFRS as adopted by the EU were mandatory for consolidated financial statements of publicly traded companies (capital groups) (Albu & Albu, 2014). In 2005 in Poland only 8.3% of active enterprises did bookkeeping, including 90.3% of legal persons and only 1.57% of natural persons. Conversely, the rest conducted various form of registers for tax purpose. Most enterprises (61%) kept ledgers of revenue and expense and computed solely taxable income, recording revenue (sales of goods and services and other revenue items) and costs (categorised into trade goods and materials at purchasing prices, purchase-related costs and payroll-related expenses – in cash and in kind – and other cost items) and computing taxable income. The rest entities recorded only revenue for tax purpose (17%) or did not record any revenue nor cost (14%) due to pay tax in amount calculated by tax offices according to tax card (CSO, 2007; Białek-Jaworska & Gabryelczyk, 2015). Hope (2003b) showed that common law systems are associated with greater disclosure levels, whereas environments with a high ownership concentration have low disclosure levels. In countries that offer more choice among accounting methods firms disclose significantly more about their chosen accounting policies.

3. Hypotheses development

Understanding the factors that determine company disclosure decisions are extremely important in the context of financial reporting standards harmonisation. It may be very beneficial for the bodies designing the reporting standards and controlling the observance thereof (audit firms) to explore disclosure determinants for guidance, focussing their activities intended to support businesses in reporting their financial standing in a trustworthy manner. Furthermore, this will enable them to identify the types of companies whose financial statements may potentially contain many frequent untruths or omissions.

Since 2005, EU publicly traded companies have been required to prepare their consolidated financial statements in accordance with IFRS. The implementation of this requirement was a very important step towards the harmonisation of reporting standards, resulting in significant changes in reporting practices in Poland and Europe. Therefore, the paper analyses the factors affecting the extent of Polish public company information disclosure in the first years following the introduction of compulsory reporting under IFRS. As such, factors affecting the extent of disclosed information in this paper were analysed in the initial years in which consolidated financial statements of Polish listed companies were supposedly obligatorily to be drafted according to IFRS. Hence, a set of variables has been selected and research hypotheses advanced with this context as well as the literature overview, presented earlier in this paper, taken into consideration.

3.1. Profitability

The main focus here is on how ROE influences the extent of information disclosure. It seems that information asymmetry which characterises financial markets would strongly motivate well-managed companies to distinguish themselves from less profitable businesses and thereby raise capital on the best possible terms. According to the negative selection model described by Akerlof (1970), if more and less profitable companies (lemons) are treated by investors in exactly the same way, i.e. their shares are priced at a similar, averaged level, a situation may occur whereby more profitable companies will not be able to obtain satisfactory financing from the issue of shares and they will fall from the market. Increasing the extent of a firm's financial information disclosure and presenting the financial standing in a more specific manner is one way to raise its profile.

Furthermore, from the perspective of compulsory implementation of IFRS in Poland, these problems seem even more complex to analyse. The Polish Accounting Act provides a relatively restrictive specification of the information companies are required to disclose, whereas in case of IFRS a certain freedom is given in this respect, and, consequently, the extent of especially voluntary disclosure will be much dependent on company management. The requirement of preparing consolidated reports, according to IFRS, has therefore been a significant change for Polish corporations and, in a way, they have been given a choice as to what information they wish to publish. The higher level of disclosure which accompanies higher profitability seems to facilitate building an image of a proficient manager, thereby strengthening their position within the company, often reflected in their remuneration.

Mendes-da-Silva and Christensen (2004) noted that the implications of the theory and the results obtained in earlier studies on the relationship between disclosure of financial information and corporate performance constitute a mix. Investors generally perceive the absence of voluntary information disclosure as an indicator of "more news" about a firm. Thus, a better-performing company management would have an additional incentive to voluntarily disclose information (Lev & Penman, 1990; Lang & Lundholm, 1993; Clarkson *et al.*, 1994). Singhvi and Desai (1971) found a positive relationship between profitability indices and the quality of disclosure. Thus, a manager could be encouraged to release information when the rates of return are high as an indication of the high quality of administration. Conversely, Huang *et al.* (2011) detected a significant negative correlation between ROE and financial disclosure for Taiwanese firms. Bova and Pereira (2012) noticed that the positive relation between profitability and disclosure may not hold true for the other modes of financial reporting which largely involve discretionary decisions on management board. Despite the strong substantiation behind the positive impact of profitability on the extent of information disclosure in the theory of economics, empirical verifications do not provide any unambiguous results. Moreover, findings confirmed negative relation between industry profitability and voluntary disclosure (Hayes & Lundholm, 1996; Huang & Li, 2014; Günther, 2015). Furthermore, Günther (2015) showed that this negative relation is more pronounced for industry leaders. Vazquez and Nuñez-Nickel (2015) found an inverted U-shape relationship between corporate disclosure and a firm's abnormal profitability, which is suggestive of firms being reluctant to disclose when they are underperforming (outperforming) their rivals because of the fear of unveiling agency conflicts (raising proprietary costs). Specifically, a firm might be reluctant to disclose if it fears that rivals are able to use the released information to erode its relative competitive position (proprietary costs increase). This fear is increasing in the level of abnormal profits that the firm is earning in the industry, because those firms that are outperforming their competitors have more to hide from rivals than poor performers (Berger & Hann, 2007).

Because the Warsaw Stock Exchange is a young and relatively small market, that reacts in its pricing of corporate future earnings with a lag (Klimczak, 2011), we could expect results using Polish data to be different from results in the previous research for developed economies. Poland began its transition to a market economy in 1989. The Warsaw Stock Exchange was established in 1991 with only 9 companies, but by the year 2007 this number reached 326 in 2007 (*Table 1*). One reason for our expectation of the negative correlation between the profitability and mandatory or voluntary information disclosure by Polish companies, this may be that at the time after accession to the European Union and the adoption of IFRS, these earnings were highly uncertain. Another reason may be that the market does not efficiently price information (Klimczak, 2011) and companies behave in accordance with the signaling theory. Therefore, the following hypothesis can be advanced:

> H1: *The extent and quality of mandatory and voluntary information disclosure by Polish companies (in financial statements) decreases with profitability (measured by ROE).*

Results received by Klimczak (2011) indicate that the average impact of IFRS adoption was relatively small in Poland. Easy access to information and efficient processing of this information can serve as a substitute for more informative accounting standards and consequently it can result in lower market reaction. So we could expect that the management reports disclosures play more important role according to the impression management theory.

H1A: *The extent of information disclosure by managers (in management reports) increases with profitability (measured by ROE).*

3.2. Leverage

External financing appears in most studies examining determinants of the disclosure level referred to above, except in the analysis of German corporations. The quality of financial statements transparency may help solve the problem of information asymmetry between shareholders, managers and creditors.

Companies using external financing should feel motivated to reveal more in order to meet their creditors' information needs and to enhance trust. An approach like this reduces the cost of monitoring, which often affects the expenditure a company has to make to obtain financing. A creditor, when forced to bear a higher cost of monitoring the debtor's financial standing, will charge a higher interest rate on the loan or – in the best scenario – will expect the debtor to pay the extra cost of drawing up a complex contract, for example.

In Poland there is a negative correlation between profitability (the self-financing potential measured by operating cash flow) and debt-based financing for large firms, according to the pecking order theory, but a positive one for small and medium size companies, which supports the trade-off theory and the transaction costs theory. The negative correlation between quick ratio and leverage, regardless of the company size indicates that Polish firms' preferences in respect of debt financing follow the pecking order theory (Nehrebecka & Białek-Jaworska, 2015).

It could explain our motivation for carrying out this study on determinants of disclosures in Polish settings where large companies behave in accordance with pecking order theory. That is, we would expect results using Polish data to be different from results in previous research. We would receive negative correlation between use of external source of finance and information disclosure resulted from relational banking connections with creditors. However, we stated the following hypothesis:

H2: *The extent of information disclosure by Polish companies increases with external financing.*

Similarly, as in analyses carried out by Raffournier (1995) and Michad'lesco (1999), external financing was measured by a leverage factor equalling the debt to assets ratio. In this case, the debt item comprised financial liabilities to creditors, as well as debt securities issued.

3.3. Company size

Company size is another important determinant of information disclosure. On the one hand, it is relatively less costly to publish detailed data for major firms, as they usually prepare such reports for their internal purposes. Large companies are expected to have higher agency costs thus they are expected to disclose more information so as to decrease such costs. They generally have more resources to supply more information. So far the results support this conjecture since they find positive relation between size of the firm and the level of disclosure (Wallace *et al.*, 1994; Meek *et al.*, 1995; Zarzeski, 1996; Inchausti, 1997; Ahmed & Courtis, 1999; Hope, 2003b; Archambault & Archambault, 2003). On the other hand small firms may avoid disclosing information in order not to lose their competitive edge. Annual reports are a source of information for the competition, therefore smaller businesses will be reluctant to reveal all of their activities, fearing that this might compromise their competitive position (Wallace *et al.*, 1994). Therefore it is expected that

> H3: *The bigger the company, the more information it will disclose in its financial statements.*

Similarly Raffournier's (1995) study of Swiss companies, the sales logarithm was used for the Polish market analysis as a variable approximating the company size.

3.4. Ownership structure

Based on the literature overview (Raffournier, 1995; Michad'lesco, 1999; Huang *et al.*, 2011; Marston & Polei, 2004) it can be stated that ownership structure is also an important factor influencing the extent of corporate information disclosure. The approach presented in the analysis of the information practice of Polish companies is closer to studies of the situation in the European countries where special attention is paid to the degree of shareholding dispersion in the ownership structure. The frequent conflict of interests between management and shareholder (e.g. when management seeks to maximise profit, resulting in overly risky decisions) leads to a temptation of malpractice, thereby necessitating additional cost of monitoring the management action. The tendency to make decisions contrary to shareholder interest is stronger when the company is not controlled by a small group of major owners. Managers in companies with a dispersed ownership structure will be more motivated to disclose more information, as this will add transparency to their behaviour, thereby giving the shareholders a sense of control over the board's actions. Therefore, it is expected that:

H4: *The more dispersed the shareholding structure within the Polish companies (measured by the share of unknown shareholders), the greater the extent of information disclosure in reporting.*

3.5. "Big Four" auditors

The quality of control exercised over companies – mainly over that of management – is the last determinant to be analysed in terms of its impact on the situation in Polish corporations. This issue was discussed in studies of Swiss and Taiwanese businesses, where the audit firm size was used as a measure of control quality. Auditors play a particularly important role in the development of corporate disclosure policy. Major, renowned audit firms will be capable of persuading the auditee to increase the extent of disclosure, since they have stricter requirements concerning the quality of reporting. If the report does not meet these criteria, the auditor will be unable to issue a positive assessment to be used as an indicator of the quality of the report data, thereby building investor trust. The "Big Four" audit firms – Ernst&Young, KPMG, PricewaterhouseCoopers, and Deloitte – are regarded as the largest and frequently the most revered, therefore ensuring the highest quality of information. Furthermore, the role of auditors is especially important in the context of compulsory reporting under IFRS, which was introduced in 2005. In case of any doubt concerning the extent of information disclosure under IFRS, a chartered auditor might suggest modification of the final report. Hence, the following hypothesis has been advanced:

H5: *The extent of corporate disclosure by companies audited by the "Big Four" will be greater than that by companies examined by smaller audit firms.*

4. Research design

In the absence of an objective measure of the extent of disclosures in Polish company reports, we used the Polish Corporate Disclosure Index (PCDI), designed by the research team led by Świderska (2010), for 36 non-financial companies and 11 banks. The construction of the index was based both on the actual degree of mandatory disclosures (PCDI_1), as well as on the proposed disclosures (in the case of voluntary data) in the financial statements (PCDI_2), the management reports (PCDI_3) and the corporate social responsibility reports (PCDI_4).

$$PCDI = PCDI\_1 + PCDI\_2 + PCDI\_3 + PCDI\_4$$

where:

PCDI – the Polish Corporate Disclosure Index,

PCDI_1 – the PCDI index component in scope and quality of mandatory financial disclosures component,

PCDI_2 – the PCDI index component in extent and quality of voluntary financial disclosures,

PCDI_3 – the PCDI index component in level of disclosures in the management report,

PCDI_4 – the PCDI index component of corporate social responsibility disclosures.

The correlation among the PCDI index and its 4 components and among the 4 components is statistically significant and positive, the strongest between the PCDI index and its component of mandatory disclosures (*Table 6*). The coefficient of a correlation between the PCDI index and the management report disclosures (PCD_3) is bigger than between the PCDI index and its section of voluntary disclosures (PCDI_2). The weakest correlation is between the PCDI index and its part of corporate social responsibility disclosures and between the other segments of the PCDI index and the corporate social responsibility disclosures component, especially the voluntary disclosures part. The PCDI index includes areas such as general information (name, address, fiscal year-end), the completeness and quality of the accounting policy, with particular emphasis on those areas where accounting gives a choice regarding the valuation or disclosure; goodwill and other intangibles; risk management; fair value; hedge accounting; leasing; product and geographic segments and reserves. Each of the issues analysed in creating the PCDI index was evaluated by an expert, on a scale of 0 (no information or the issue has not occurred) to 4 (the highest possible level of disclosure). Based on whether a firm does not have the arrangement, the PCDI index varies up to 5 points, for maximum possible disclosure for the issue scored with a sheet containing the maximum number of questions. For instance variation of the PCDI index as a result of the lack of disclosure in terms of hedge accounting due to non-compliance its by the company in general ranges from 0.8 to 3 percentage points. The extent of disclosure of general data and the business environment, financial and non-financial, prospective data, information about management and the ownership structure, as well as information on intangible assets, were evaluated as part of the management statement. In Poland, the standards for the content and preparation of the management report sets out the Accounting Act and the Regulation of the Minister of Finance. Analysis of the corporate social responsibility disclosure has been made in terms of a voluntary disclosure of non-financial activities and results of the economic, social and environmental activity (see Appendix A).

Factors determining information disclosure in companies have been analysed in a breakdown by nature of disclosure and type of reports: mandatory or voluntary disclosure in the financial statement or information including in the management report or the corporate social responsibility report. The following panel model was used for analysing the impact of various company characteristics on the scope of disclosure:

$$Y_{it} = \beta_0 + \beta_1 X_{1,it} + \beta_2 X_{2,it} + \beta_3 X_{3,it} + \beta_4 X_{4,it} + \beta_5 D_{1,it} + u_i + \varepsilon_{it}$$

where:

Y – the rescaled PCDI index (in %) or the mandatory disclosure index (PCDI_1) or voluntary disclosure index (PCDI_2) or management report disclosure index (PCDI_3) or corporate social responsibility disclosure index (PCDI_4),

β_i – constant or coefficients of variables,

u_i – units' individual characteristics, non-observable, but constant over time,

ε_{it} – purely random error,

X_1 – profitability,

X_2 – company size,

X_3 – leverage,

X_4 – shareholding dispersion,

D_1 – the auditor category.

Table 4 describes variables definitions, constructions and sources of data. While we present the descriptive statistics of the variables for our sample in the Table 5.

5. Data and sample

The sample comprised 36 parent companies listed on the Warsaw Stock Exchange, for which consolidated financial reports following the IFRS were available for the years 2005-2007 (i.e. the first three years since the Polish public companies have been required to use IFRS in their consolidated accounts). The analysis cover data of all nonfinancial companies for which the team of researchers led by Świderska (2010) developed the PCDI index (in total 36 firms). The companies in the research sample represented the chemical industry (13 firms), media (7), food & beverage (12) and telecommunications (4), i.e. the sectors which are relevant in terms of the interests of households and are characterised by a relatively high share of intangible assets (Table 1). Due to limitations of our study resulting from the use of the PCDI index, it should be noted that this is a *non-random* sample and is therefore *non-representative*. Consequently, if any valid statistical conclusions are to be drawn, the results should be interpreted in the context of the analysed companies only. In the initial years following the implementation of IFRS, the mean value of PCDI for the analysed companies did not exceed 37.06 – the average level of disclosure (determined with an assumption that all questions used in the disclosure extent survey were scored 2 on a scale of 0 to 4, taking into account adopted by the Świderska (2010) weights for individual components of the PCDI index).

Table 1. Research sample characteristics and composition

Numbers of companies by different criteria	2005	2006	2007
companies and institutions listed on the WSE including:	275	308	326
banks	12	12	13
financial companies - non-adopters IFRS	11	10	12
insurance companies adopted IFRS	7	12	11
non-financial companies	**245**	**274**	**290**
including: companies - non-adopters IFRS	119	115	94
companies adopted IFRS	**126**	**159**	**196**
including: companies prepared only individual reports	363	332	248
capital groups prepared consolidated reports	**50**	**81**	**165**
sample companies analysed in this study	36	36	36
percentage of market coverage by the research sample	72%	44%	22%
including the chemical industry	13	13	13
food & beverage	12	12	12
media industry	7	7	7
telecommunications	4	4	4

In 2005, the lowest level of disclosure was 14.63, i.e. well below the threshold (meaning a poor quality of disclosure), in 2006 the lowest PCDI – 18.53 – was close to the threshold level, but did not exceed it, this only happening as late as 2007. In the period 2005-2007, the highest PCDI values exceeded 37.06, which implies an average degree of disclosure in the analysed sample, but the value representing a respectable degree of disclosure was achieved in 2007 (55.60, with all questions scoring 3 on a scale of 0 to 4, taking into account adopted by the Świderska (2010) weights for individual components of the index). In all years covered by the analysis, PKN Orlen (oil sector) achieved the highest value of the PCDI index (49.24 in 2005, 50.69 in 2006 and 58.63 in 2007). The company has been using IFRS since 2002. T

he basic statistics of the sample companies show that the level of mandatory disclosure grew during the first years following the compulsory implementation of IFRS. We used the Polish Corporate Disclosure Index as a dependent variable in our analysis of disclosure determinants in this paper. To make the results of the analysis more legible (clear and easier to interpret), we rescaled the PCDI values by the maximum possible value of the PCDI index, calculated taking into account adopted by the Świderska (2010) weights for individual components of the PCDI index. The maximum value of the PCDI index equals 74.13, that means the maximum level of disclosure. The basic descriptive statistics of the sample companies' PCDI show that the level of disclosure grew during the first years following the compulsory implementation of IFRS (Table 2). Figure 1 shows the PCDI's variation.

Table 2. Descriptive statistics of the sample companies' disclosure index PCDI

	Mean	Median	Min	Max	Standard Deviation	Variation Coefficient
2005	41.38	39.93	19.74	66.42	12.04	**29%**
2006	45.24	43.97	24.79	68.38	9.94	**22%**
2007	48.74	45.64	31.12	79.09	10.97	**23%**

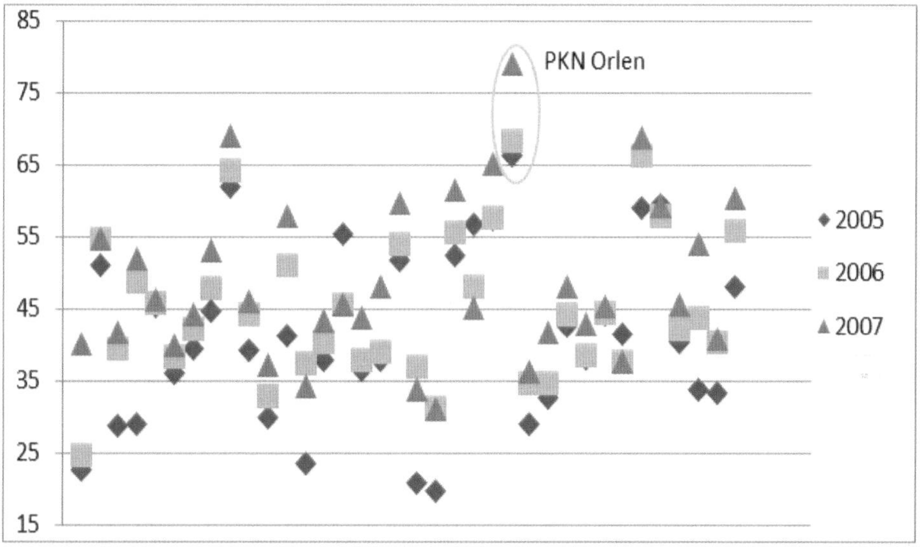

Figure 1. The sample companies' PCDI index variation (%) in 2005-2007

Finally, the disclosure measure that we used in our models had been estimated in percentages, with 100 indicated the maximum level of disclosures for real value of the PCDI index equals 74.13. Table 3 presents a complete description of variables used in the empirical analysis. The values of exogenous variables: profitability (return on equity ratio), the financial leverage estimated by the debt to assets ratio and the company size measured by the logarithm of sales were obtained for the sample companies from the Notoria data base based on their consolidated annual financial statements for the years 2005-2007. While the shareholding dispersion (measured by the share of unknown shareholders in the ownership structure) and the dummy variable indicating the auditor being a member of the "Big Four" were manually collected from management reports and chartered auditor's opinions. Before panel analysis, the descriptive statistics of variables has been determined (Table 4).

Table 3. Variables definitions and data sources

Variable name	Variable definition	Data source
PCDI	Polish Corporate Disclosure Index	
PCDI_1	a part of mandatory financial disclosures	
PCDI_2	a part of voluntary financial disclosures of PCDI	Świderska (2010)
PCDI_3	a part of management report disclosure of PCDI	
PCDI_4	corporate social responsibility disclosure	
Profitability	measured by return on equity (ROE)	consolidated annual
Firm size	measured by logarithm of sales	financial reports,
Leverage	equals to the debt to assets ratio	Notoria data base
Shareholding dispersion	ownership structure measured by the percentage of unknown shareholders in the ownership	manually collected from management reports
Auditor category	the dummy variable indicating the auditor being a member of the "Big Four", takes value 1 if a "Big Four" auditor and 0 in any other case	manually collected from chartered auditor's opinions

Table 4. Variables descriptive statistics

Variable	Observations	Mean	Std. Dev.	Min	Max
PCDI	108	0.4512194	0.1147442	0.1974	0.7909
PCDI_1	108	27.27009	7.254341	10.93	47.26
PCDI_2	108	4.186482	1.599415	0.82	8.43
PCDI_3	108	1.700926	0.7447744	0	3.24
PCDI_4	108	0.2862963	0.1576379	0	0.89
Profitability ROE	108	0.094067	0.4913213	-4.481321	0.7655
Company size	108	19.81837	2.024148	13.57598	24.87891
Leverage	108	0.4419018	0.172115	0.0743417	0.8383092
Shareholding dispersion	108	0.4006655	0.2066544	1.00e-05	0.9327
Auditor category	108	0.3611111	0.482562	0	1

The correlation between explanatory variables has been estimated. Detailed outcomes of Spearman's ranks correlation of the explanatory and explained variables (the PCDI index and its components) are presented in Table 5.

Table 5. Correlation of the explanatory variables and explained variables - the PCDI index and its components

	PCDI	PCDI_1	PCDI_2	PCDI_3	PCDI_4	ROE	Company size	Leverage	Shareholding dispersion	Auditor category
PCDI	1.000									
PCDI_1	0.978***	1.000								
PCDI_2	0.578***	0.414***	1.000							
PCDI_3	0.627***	0.573***	0.449***	1.000						
PCDI_4	0.511***	0.417***	0.323***	0.393***	1.000					
ROE	0.144	0.141	0.017	0.118	0.210**	1.000				
Company size	0.732***	0.686***	0.530***	0.641***	0.395***	0.29***	1.000			
Leverage	-0.067	-0.088	0.126	0.094	-0.206**	-0.122	0.087	1.000		
Shareholding dispersion	-0.112	-0.132	0.068	-0.163	-0.099	-0.278***	-0.277***	-0.257***	1.000	
Auditor category	0.680***	0.669***	0.409***	0.465***	0.261***	0.0872	0.607***	-0.104	-0.039	1.000

Note: Significance levels: * p<0.1, ** p<0.05, *** p<0.01.

6. Analysis and results

Tables 6-10 present the findings of: PCDI total disclosure index, mandatory disclosures, voluntary disclosures, management report disclosures and corporate social responsibility disclosures models estimation by means of the random effects estimator (RE) and the fixed effects estimator (FE) and results of tests that we conducted to choose the most appropriate estimator for our sample panel analyses. In order to determine which of the estimators: fixed effects or random effects estimator, is superior at estimating the values of parameters in this exercise, we applied the test of overidentifying restrictions (Sargan-Hansen test). The Hausman test often used for evaluating estimators for panel models, could not be applied in those cases (except voluntary information disclosure model in Table 8), as the assumptions for the method test are not satisfied here. Similarly as in the Hausman test, the possibility of a correct estimation of the model by means of the random effects estimator is assumed as a null hypothesis for the Sargan-Hansen test.

Table 6. Determinants of Information Disclosures Model estimation results, based on PCDI index (in total)

Variable	Coefficients			
	RE	FE	AMGLS1	AMGLS2
Profitability	-0.0295348** (0.01225)	-0.0587553*** (0.01453)	-0.0240677** (0.00913)	-0.0251048** (0.0111701)
Company size	0.0399581*** (0.00613)	0.0886087*** (0.01403)	0.0409922*** (0.00483)	0.0428274*** (0.0048531)

Variable	Coefficients			
	RE	FE	AMGLS1	AMGLS2
Leverage	-0.0064388 (0.04941)	0.0837837 (0.06294)	0.0002006 (0.02549)	-
Shareholding dispersion	0.0212616 (0.04170)	-0.0367418 (0.05525)	0.0083167 (0.02583)	-
Auditor category	0.0559708** (0.02183)	0.0310793 (0.02873)	0.0372689** (0.01647)	0.0296591* (0.01520)
Constant	-0.3637913 (0.11989)	-1.33286*** (0.27431)	-0.374609*** (0.09303)	-0.4037838* (0.09361)
Test of total insignificance of variables in the model	χ^2=93.43 p-value=0.000	F=9.24 p-value=0.000	χ^2=156.06 p-value=0.000	χ^2=130.92 p-value=0.000
Wald Test for significance of individual effects in FE	-	F=5.88 p-value=0.000	-	-
Sargan-Hansen Test	χ^2=23.689 p-value=0.0002		-	-
Wooldridge Test for autocorrelation	-	F=23.247 p-value=0.000	-	-
Modified Wald heteroscedacity test	-	χ^2=480000 p-value=0.000	-	-

Note: Significant at * 0.1, ** 0.05, *** 0.01. Standard deviations of coefficients are in brackets.

Based on the results of disclosure model estimation by means of the random effects estimator, we confirm the expected direction of correlations in the case of the company size, the shareholding dispersion (measured by share of unknown shareholders in the ownership structure), and the auditor category (except for disclosure in management reports as result of the insignificance of the auditor category variable presented in Table 9). Because the management report is not subject to audit by the auditor, this negative correlation is not surprising as a management report is prepared only by management board.

On the other hand, the negative estimation of leverage (measured by debt to assets ratio) coefficient indicate a correlation contrary to what was expected for information disclosure in total (Table 6). Yet when confine ourselves to a specific range of information, we noticed that we positively verified the hypothesis no. 2. for voluntary information disclosure (Table 8) and corporate social responsibility disclosure (Table 10). It should be noted however, that while independent variables are significant in total, only three of the independent variables are showing a statistically significant impact on the dependent variable in the case of total disclosures: profitability (ROE), company size and the auditor category (Table 6).

Table 7. Determinants of mandatory information disclosure model estimation results, based on PCDI_1

Variable	Coefficients			
	RE	FE	AMGLS1	AMGLS2
Profitability	-1.892536** (0.7814996)	-3.874839*** (0.9124489)	-1.825616*** (0.5682104)	-1.702823*** (0.6491381)
Company size	2.473816*** (0.4175426)	5.736527*** (0.8810683)	3.310747*** (0.3419168)	2.827606*** (0.192733)
Leverage	-1.660199 (3.258976)	2.764222 (3.951456)	1.618519 (1.131003)	-3.107033* (1.762108)
Shareholding dispersion	0.4065096 (2.750701)	-2.838261 (3.468596)	1.229309 (1.478694)	1.870704 (1.645391)
Auditor category	3.573438** (1.446484)	2.206036 (1.803746)	0.9543829 (0.9295617)	-
Constant	-22.29853*** (8.159616)	-86.93499*** (17.22222)	-39.50941*** (6.37918)	-28.15026*** (4.095885)
Test of total insignificance of variables in the model	χ^2=76.38 p-value=0.000	F=9.82 p-value=0.000	χ^2= 123.92 p-value=0.000	χ^2= 229.77 p-value=0.000
Wald Test for significance of individual effects in FE	-	F= 7.07 p-value=0.000	-	-
Sargan-Hansen Test	χ^2= 23.047 p-value=0.0003		-	-
Wooldridge Test for autocorrelation	-	F= 20.592 p-value=0.0001	-	-
Modified Wald heteroscedacity test	-	χ^2=4600000 p-value=0.000	-	-

Note: Significant at * 0.1, ** 0.05, *** 0.01. Standard deviations of coefficients are in brackets.

Moreover, it is worth noting that in the case of voluntary disclosure all independent variables are showing a statistically significant impact on the dependent variable and confirming hypotheses (Table 8). The results obtained using the fixed effect estimator allow for confirmation of the expected direction of correlations in case of the company size, the financial leverage ratio and the auditor category (Table 6). The share of unknown shareholders in the ownership structure seems to show a correlation which is opposite to the expected one. It should be noted that profiability (ROE) and the company size indicate a statistically significant impact on the disclosure index, the constant being of some significance too. Based on the test of overidentifying restrictions (Sargan-Hansen test in Table 6) we showed that the null hypothesis should be rejected and, in consequence, we chose the fixed effects estimator for model estimation in the further analysis.

Table 8. Determinants of voluntary information disclosure model estimation results, based on PCDI_2

Variable	Coefficients		
	RE	FE	GLS
Profitability	-0.4289655* (0.2237817)	-0.4070096 (0.2899029)	-0.39672** (0.1699088)
Company size	0.3637587*** (0.1093449)	0.2538109 (0.2799326)	0.5111586*** (0.0484167)
Leverage	1.817638** (0.8909261)	2.676022** (1.255455)	1.105989*** (0.4041481)
Shareholding dispersion	1.254285* (0.7519958)	0.5657289 (0.5730854)	1.239201*** (0.2812528)
Auditor category	0.595951# (0.3930325)	0.8511044# (0.5730854)	0.4896273*** (0.1447134)
Constant	-4.503243** (2.13953)	-2.521903 (5.471837)	-7.005471*** (0.8459624)
Test to the total insignificance of variables in the model	χ^2= 32.88 p-value=0.000	F=2.11 p-value=0.0753	χ^2= 307.80 p-value=0.000
Wald Test for significance of individual effects in FE	-	F= 4.67 p-value=0.000	-
Hausman Test	χ^2= 5.68 p-value=0.3391		
Wooldridge Test for autocorrelation	-	F= 6.401 p-value= 0.0161	-
Modified Wald heteroscedacity test	-	χ^2=63000000 p-value=0.000	-

Note: Significant at * 0.1, ** 0.05, *** 0.01. Standard deviations of coefficients are in brackets.

For the sake of correct statistical reasoning, we verified the assumptions regarding the random component's autocorrelation and homoscedacity. Based on the Wooldridge test for autocorrelation, we rejected the no-correlation thesis at 1% significance level. Therefore, we confirmed the presence of the first-order autocorrelation of random errors in the model. Furthermore, we conducted the modified Wald test and showed that the homoscedacity assumption appears not to be satisfied, either. At 1% significance level, we rejected the null hypothesis assuming homoscedacity of the random component. In case of a non-spherical random component, the estimator is inefficient in the model with fixed effects. Thus, in order to immunise the estimations of the model parameters against its heteroscedacity and autocorrelation, we used the Applicable Method of Generalised Least Squares (AMGLS), where the variance-covariance matrix is assumed to be unknown, therefore an estimated matrix is used. Tables 6 and 7 present the outcomes of regression analysis that we obtained using AMGLS and the final estimates that we obtained using Applicable Method of Generalised Least Squares after elimination of insignificant variables (AMGLS2), with the first order autocorrelation and heteroscedacity, in case of determinants of total disclosure model (Table 6) and mandatory information disclosure model (Table 7). Tables 8-10 show results of the final models estimates for voluntary information disclosure (Table 8), disclosure in management reports (Table 9) and corporate social responsibility disclosure (Table 10) that we obtained using Applicable Method of Generalised Least Squares, with heteroscedacity (GLS1, GSL2) (Tables 9-10).

Table 9. Results of model estimation of determinants influenced disclosure in management reports, based on PCDI_3

Variable	Coefficients			
	RE	FE	GLS1	GLS2
Profitability	0.0585353 (0.1243279)	-0.0645589 (0.1570835)	0.2008581* (0.1185912)	0.2270334** (0.1126961)
Company size	0.201884*** (0.0574187)	0.5367785*** (0.1516812)	0.1392832*** (0.0182706)	0.1417034*** (0.0071095)
Leverage	-0.5603818 (0.4785835)	0.5346711 (0.6802667)	-0.7428134*** (0.2152461)	-0.8189816*** (0.1862928)
Shareholding dispersion	0.0443376 (0.4042681)	-0.3744007 (0.5971395)	-0.1497116 (0.1421044)	-
Auditor category	-0.2604533 (0.2103502)	-0.7012892** (0.3105256)	0.0414579 (0.0955468)	-
Constant	-1.981671* (1.124757)	-8.764097*** (2.964908)	-0.6925222** (0.2870708)	-0.7738902*** (0.1664155)
Test of total insignificance of variables in the model	χ^2=18.41 p-value=0.0025	F=3.91 p-value=0.0036	χ^2= 339.76 p-value=0.000	χ^2= 399.02 p-value=0.000
Wald Test for significance of individual effects in FE	-	F= 4.04 p-value=0.000	-	-
Sargan-Hansen Test	χ^2= 14.598 p-value=0.0122		-	-
Wooldridge Test for autocorrelation	-	F= 7.493 p-value=0.0097	-	-
Modified Wald heteroscedacity test	-	χ^2=180000 p-value=0.000	-	-

Note: Significant at * 0.1, ** 0.05, *** 0.01. Standard deviations of coefficients are in brackets.

Summarizing, we showed that the extent and quality of mandatory and voluntary information disclosure by companies in Poland (in financial statements) decreases with profitability (measured by ROE). This findings support the H1 hypothesis. Besides, we also found that the more profitable companies in the sample analysed, the smaller the extent of information disclosure (in total). However, we confirmed that the extent of information disclosure by managers (in management reports) increases with profitability (measured by ROE). This result gives no reason to reject the H1A hypothesis. This shows that the analysed parent company managements like to show off good news and consequently they behave in accordance with *impression management theory*. We proved that the bigger the company, the more information it will disclose in its financial statements as at 1% significance level, the company size has a positive and statistically significant impact on the disclosure level in all area. Our results support the H3hypothesis.

Table 10. Results of model estimation of determinants influenced corporate social responsibility disclosure, based on PCDI_4

Variable	Coefficients			
	RE	**FE**	**GLS1 panels(hetero)**	**GLS2 panels(hetero)**
Profitability	-0.0252878 (0.0251158)	-	-0.0105422 (0.0138575)	
Company size	0.0466663*** (0.0095668)	-	0.0374578*** (0.0028293)	0.0363905*** (0.0027888)
Leverage	0.0693107 (0.084399)	-	0.0171612 (0.0154576)	0.0216553* (0.0118018)
Shareholding dispersion	-0.0048841 (0.0717537)	-	-0.0021794 (0.0212726)	-
Auditor category	0.0266661 (0.0366903)	-	0.047289*** (0.0081182)	0.0482123*** (0.007457)
Constant	-0.674477*** (0.1882818)	-	-0.4917853*** (0.0555183)	-0.4743381*** (0.0543564)
Test of total insignificance of variables in the model	χ^2= 48.94 p-value=0.000	-	χ^2= 272.91 p-value=0.000	χ^2= 259.37 p-value=0.000
Wald Test for significance of individual effects in FE	-	F= 2.01 p-value=0.0072	-	-
Sargan-Hansen Test	χ^2= 5.619 p-value= 0.3451		-	-
Wooldridge Test for autocorrelation	-	F= 1.074 p-value=0.3071	-	-
Modified Wald heteroscedacity test	-	χ^2=25000000 p-value=0.000	-	-

Note: Significant at * 0.1, ** 0.05, *** 0.01. Standard deviations of coefficients are in brackets.

We conformed that financial statements auditing by the "Big Four" auditor positive influences the quality and extent of total information disclosure, at 10% significance level. This is in accordance with the H5 hypothesis. Moreover, it increases voluntary information and corporate social responsibility disclosure. The extent of corporate disclosure by companies audited by the "Big Four" is greater than that by companies examined by smaller audit firms. We showed that the extent of information disclosure by companies listed on the Warsaw Stock Exchange increases with external financing, but only in the area of voluntary information and corporate social responsibility disclosure. However, consider mandatory information and management reports disclosure, we noticed that the extent of information disclosure by companies analysed decreases with their leverage. Hence we reject the H2 hypothesis for total disclosure based on its insignificance and for mandatory and management reports disclosure as the result of negative impact of leverage. We found some evidence that supports this H2 hypothesis for voluntary and corporate social responsibility disclosures. Finally, we noticed that shareholding dispersion matters only for voluntary information disclosure, where the more dispersed the shareholding structure within the companies, the greater the extent of voluntary disclosure in reporting. This result supports the H4 hypothesis only in scope of voluntary disclosures. The constant in our models is of some significance too.

7. Conclusions

Considering the estimation findings presented in tables 6-10, two of the hypotheses formulated earlier should be rejected. The financial leverage and the shareholding dispersion do not have any statistically significant effect on the extent of corporate information disclosure (in total) within the research sample. Hence, the intention to satisfy creditors' information needs seem not to influence information disclosure decisions in non-financial companies, with the exception of disclosure in the area of voluntary information and corporate social responsibility. Similarly, as in our exercise for the PCDI disclosure index treated as whole, neither the Swiss nor the French analyses (Raffournier, 1995; Michad'lesco, 1999), confirmed the impact of the financial leverage on the extent of information disclosure in total. In France firms have high block holder concentration and high debt financing complemented by regulations that require better disclosure when debt levels are higher. There is low intent and capacity of major financiers to monitor external financial reporting quality (Rahman *et al.*, 2010).

Level of compliance with IFRS is higher in Switzerland than in France (Street & Gray, 2001). It is worth to be noting that value added of our research are significant findings of the positive impact of leverage on voluntary information disclosure and corporate social responsibility disclosure, as well. In contrary to Raffournier (1995) and Michad'lesco (1999), we noticed that the public companies (included in the sample) aim to increase the dispersed shareholders' sense of control by increasing the extent of voluntary disclosure. Given the similarities of institutional features of the Central and South-Eastern European countries, the results are likely to contribute to strengthening the protection of investors in the capital markets of emerging economies.

The exercise results supported the hypothesis regarding the impact of company size or the audit firm category on the extent of information disclosure. The logarithm of sales approximating company size has a positive, statistically significant effect on the disclosure index. Attention should be given to the fact that major companies have larger financial and accounting departments as a rule, as well as better qualified staff and these factors may have a positive impact on the extent of information disclosure. Furthermore, preparing detailed reports is less costly for major companies, as they typically collect such data for their internal purposes, regardless. It should also be noted that smaller companies are less motivated to reveal their activities, fearing that the competition might take advantage of such information. These findings are consistent with the agency theory and the conclusions drawn by other researchers (Berger & Hann, 2007; Vazquez & Nuñez-Nickel, 2015). The positive correlation between company size and the scope of disclosure was confirmed by Meek *et al.* (1995), Huang *et al.* (2011), Larran and Giner (2002), Marston and Polei (2004), as well as Raffournier (1995), who approximated this determinant by the logarithm of sales, similarly as we ourselves.

Furthermore, the findings shows that the average disclosure index was by 2.96 percentage points higher among companies audited by the "Big Four" firms as compared with companies audited by other providers of such services. This supports the thesis presented earlier. With the strict quality requirements imposed by the "Big Four" firms on financial reporting, the scope of information disclosed there is greater. Besides, it should be noted that the analysed period covered the first three years following the introduction of compulsory reporting under IFRS for public companies. Therefore, the role of an audit firm might be even more significant in disclosure practices, also in other emerging economies. The renowned "Big Four", with their better trained staff and experience in the application of IFRS could provide more effective support to their customers, as far as disclosure required by the standards was concerned.

The results of the estimation show that the company profitability measured by ROE has a negative statistically significant impact on the extent of corporate information disclosure in total and in the scope of mandatory and voluntary information disclosure, as well. These findings correspond with the conclusions drawn by Huang *et al.* (2011) – the authors demonstrated a negative impact of ROE on the transparency of Taiwanese companies. However, we confirmed the positive correlation between profitability and information disclosed in management reports. Our findings support the impression management theory. In accordance with Gassen (2015) findings, investors, when analysing financial statements, focus largely on company bottom lines, mainly income, paying less attention to any other information. Hence, companies generating more profit will not find it necessary to disclose much information, since they are attractive to investors due to their financial performance. Managers, therefore, are less motivated to present a company's standing, in the scope of mandatory and voluntary information disclosure in financial statements, in a more detailed manner when a satisfactory profit is being generated. This results are in accordance with the signaling theory. The study has proved that the companies covered by the analysis decided to disclose more when their profitability was lower. It seems to common practice among Polish firms to increase the extent of disclosure upon a decline in financial performance to assuage shareholders, particularly if earnings are insufficient to justify the payment of a dividend. This may result from an intention to maintain investors confidence in the company and its board of directors. This is also confirmed by the results received by Gassen (2015) that 63% of investors surveyed investigate industry, market and product data and 42% of investors also analyse information from management, apart from income. As pointed out by Grabinski *et al.* (2014), IFRS implementation improves companies' image, increases confidence in their activities and improves the quality of profits. In this light, the obtained results are also important for emerging economies, implementing IFRS. Since the main limitation of the study is the small research sample, directions for future research will focus on a separate analysis of the short- and long-term effects of IFRS adoption on extent and quality of information disclosures, measured at different scope of information and different types of reports, and the extension of the sample in quantity and time.

References

Ahmed, K. & Courtis, J.K. (1999) "Associations between corporate characteristics and disclosure levels in annual reports: A meta analysis", *British Accounting Review,* vol. 31, no. 1: 35-61

Akerlof, G. (1970) "The market for lemons: Quality uncertainty and the market mechanism", *Quarterly Journal of Economics*, vol. 84: 488-500

Albu, N. & Albu, C. N. (2014) "Editorial - IFRS application in Central and South-Eastern European countries", *Accounting and Management Information Systems*, vol. 13, no. 2: 182–197

Archambault, J.J. & Archambault, M.E. (2003) "A multinational test of determinants of corporate disclosure", *The International Journal of Accounting,* vol. 38, no. 2: 173-194

Bamber, L.S., Jiang, J. & Wang, I.Y. (2010) "What's my style? The influence of top managers on voluntary corporate financial disclosure", *The Accounting Review*, vol. 85, no. 4: 1131-1162

Berger, P. & Hann, R. (2007) "Segment profitability and the proprietary and agency costs of disclosure", *Accounting Review,* vol. 82: 869-906

Białek-Jaworska, A. & Gabryelczyk, R. (2015) "Stimulating entrepreneurship by teaching accounting: concept and implementation", *World Review of Entrepreneurship, Management and Sustainable Development*, vol. 11, nos. 2/3: 137–155

Bova, F. & Pereira, R. (2012) "The Determinants and Consequences of Heterogeneous IFRS Compliance Levels Following Mandatory IFRS Adoption: Evidence from a Developing Country", *Journal of International Accounting Research*, vol. 11, no. 1: 83–111

Brown, P. (2011) "International Financial Reporting Standards: what are the benefits?", *Accounting and Business Research*, vol. 41: 269-285

Chen, C.J.P., Ding, Y. & Xu, B. (2014) "Convergence of accounting standards and foreign direct investment", *The International Journal of Accounting*, vol. 49: 53-86

Clarkson, P.M., Kao, J.L. & Richardson, G.D. (1994) "The voluntary inclusion of forecasts in the MD&A section of annual reports", *Contemporary Accounting Research*, vol. 11: 423-450

Dobija, D. & Klimczak, K .K. (2010) "Development of accounting in Poland: Market efficiency and the value relevance of reported earnings", *The International Journal of Accounting*, vol. 45: 356–374

Gassen, J. (2015) "Professional investors and the objectives of financial reporting", Symposium 3, the 38th European Accounting Association Annual Congress, 28-30.04.2015, SEEC, Glasgow, Scotland, UK

Grabinski, K., Kedzior, M. & Krasodomska, J. (2014) "The Polish accounting system and IFRS implementation process in the view of empirical research", *Accounting and Management Information Systems*, vol. 13, no. 2: 281-310

Greene, W.H. (2008) *Econometric Analysis*, 7 th Edition, Prentice Hall, Upper Saddle River, New Jersey

Güntherl, J. (2015) "Providing Disclosure in the Face of Competition: An Analysis of Financial Statements in Imperial Germany", the 38th European Accounting Association Annual Congress, 28-30.04.2015, SEEC, Glasgow, Scotland, UK

GUS (2007), Działalność przedsiębiorstw niefinansowych w 2005 r., Warszawa (Central Statistical Office (2007), Non-financial corporate activity in 2005, Warsaw)

Hayes, R.M. & Lundholm, R. (1996) "Segment Reporting to the Capital Market in the Presence of a Competitor", *Journal of Accounting Research*, vol. 34, no. 2: 261-279

Hope, O.K. (2003a) "Accounting policy disclosures and analysts' forecasts", *Contemporary Accounting Research*, vol. 20, no. 2: 295-321

Hope, O.K. (2003b) "Disclosure practices, enforcement of accounting standards, and analysts, forecast accuracy: An international study", *Journal of Accounting Research*, vol. 41, no. 2: 235-272

Huang, S.H., Huang, S.Y., Chang, F. & Fu, C. (2011) "Impact of Information Disclosure and Transparency Rankings System (IDTRS) on Investors in Taiwan", *International Research Journal of Applied Finance*, vol. 2: 770-807

Huang, Y. & Li., N. (2014) "Market Competition and Voluntary Disclosure: Evidence form Industry", Research Reports, *Working paper*, Available at: ssrn.com.

Inchausti, B.G. (1997) "The Influence of company characteristics and accounting regulation on information disclosed by Spanish firms", *The European Accounting Review,* vol. 6, no. 1: 45-68

Klimczak, K.M. (2011) "Market reaction to mandatory IFRS adoption: Evidence from Poland", *Accounting and Management Information Systems*, vol. 10, no. 2: 228-248

Lang, M. & Lundholm, R. (1993) "Cross-sectional determinants of analyst ratings of corporate disclosures", *Journal of Accounting Research*, vol. 31, no. 2: 246–271

Larran, M. & Giner, B. (2002) "The use of the internet for corporate reporting by Spanish companies", *The International Journal of Digital Accounting Research*, vol. 2: 53-82

Lev, B. & Penman, S. (1990) "Voluntary forecast disclosure, nondisclosure and stock prices", *Journal of Accounting Research*, vol. 28: 49-76

Marston, C. & Polei, A. (2004) "Corporate reporting on the Internet by German companies", *International Journal of Accounting Information Systems*, vol. 5: 285-311

Meek, G., Roberts, C. & Gray, S. (1995) "Factors influencing voluntary annual report disclosures by U.S., U.K. and Continental European multinational corporations", *Journal of International Business Studies*, vol. 26: 555-572

Mendes-da-Silva, W. & Christensen, T.E. (2004) "Determinants of voluntary disclosure of financial information on the internet by Brazilian firms", Available at: ssrn.com.

Michaďlesco, C. (1999) "The determinants of the quality of accounting information disclosed by French listed companies", paper presented at the 22nd Annual Congress of the European Accounting Association, 5-7 May 1999, Bordeaux, France, available at: http://hal.archivesouvertes.fr/docs/00/54/ 05/70/PDF/EAA_1999.pdf (accessed 16 February 2014).

Nehrebecka, N. & Białek-Jaworska, A. (2015) "Determinants of Polish companies' debt financing preferences", *Social Sciences*, vol. 87, no. 1: 19-32

Raffournier, B. (1995) "The determinants of voluntary financial disclosure by Swiss listed companies", *The European Accounting Review*, vol. 4: 261-280

Rahman, A., Yammeesri, J. & Perera, H. (2010) "Financial reporting quality in international settings: A comparative study of the USA, Japan, Thailand, France and Germany", *The International Journal of Accounting*, vol. 45: 1–34

Singhvi, S. & Desai, H. (1971) "An empirical analysis of the quality of corporate financial disclosure", *The Accounting Review*, vol. 46: 129-138

Street, D.L. & Gray, S.J. (2001) "Observance of International Accounting Standards: Factors explaining non-compliance", Council of the ACCA

Świderska, G.K. (2010) *Wpływ zakresu ujawnianych informacji na poprawę ochrony inwestorów oraz pozycję konkurencyjną emitentów papierów wartościowych.* Warszawa

Accounting Act of 29 September 1994, Journal of Laws of 2013, points 330 and 613

Torres-Reyna, O. (2007) *Panel Data Analysis Fixed and Random Effects using Stata* (v. 4.2), http://www.princeton.edu/~otorres/Panel101.pdf

Vazquez, M.F.M. & Nuñez-Nickel, M. (2015) "Multidimensional competition and corporate disclosure", the 38th European Accounting Association Annual Congress, 28-30.04.2015, SEEC, Glasgow, Scotland, UK

Wallace, R.S., Naser, K. & Mora, A. (1994) "The Relationship between the comprehensiveness of corporate annual reports and firm characteristics in Spain", *Accounting and Business Research*, vol. 25, no. 97: 41-53

Zarzeski, M.T. (1996) "Spontaneous harmonization effects of culture and market forces on accounting disclosure practices", *Accounting Horizons,* vol. 10, no. 1: 18

2

The effectiveness of internal audit in Jamaican commercial banks

Delroy Chevers[a,1], Devon Lawrence[a], Arlene Laidlaw[a] and Dane Nicholson[a]

[a] *The University of the West Indies, Jamaica*

Abstract: Banks play a vital role in every economy as they hold the savings of the public, provide a means of payment for goods and services, and finance the development of businesses. The financial sector experienced a meltdown, which some critics argued was the result of inadequate regulatory oversight from regulatory bodies and the auditing function. This highlights the ever-increasing attention which should be placed on internal control systems and the critical role being played by the internal audit function in ensuring that weaknesses are minimized and that exposures to risks are adequately identified and managed. Banks in developing countries and especially those in Jamaica might find it difficult to absorb such failures due to severe resource constraints. As a result, this study seeks to investigate the factors that influence the effectiveness of the internal audit function in Jamaican commercial banks. The study found that the quality of audit investigation, organizational independence, professional proficiencies and management support have a significant impact on internal audit effectiveness. It is imperative that the various stakeholders and policy makers understand the important role internal audit plays in the financial viability and financial health of any financial institution.

Keywords: Commercial banks, internal audit, internal controls, Jamaica.

---

[1] *Corresponding authors*: Mona School of Business and Management, The University of the West Indies, Mona P.O., Jamaica; email addresses: delroy.chevers@uwimona.edu.jm, larrodev@yahoo.com, arlene32law@gmail.com, danenicholson@yahoo.com

1. Introduction

Banks play a critical role in every economy as they hold the savings of the public, provide a means of payment for goods and services, and finance the development of business and trade (Siddiqui & Podder, 2002). The importance of banks is further supported by Latibeaudiere (2002) who posits that a well-functioning and efficient financial system is vital for achieving robust economic performance and that integrity and confidence are the fundamental tenets on which the operations of the financial system rests.

The rapid technological advancements, dynamic and challenging business environment, allegations of corruption and fraudulent financial reporting, and the global financial crisis have caused some financial institutions to experience financial woes and closures. Some critics argue that the global financial crisis is due mainly to inadequate regulatory oversight from the regulatory bodies and the audit function. In a single case at the Canadian Federal Government Sponsorship Program, as much as $50 million of the $338 million allocated to the program went missing (Neu *et al.*, 2013). Other local examples in Jamaica are the Trafigura Beheer incident, Manat, Phelps and Phillips case and the closure of Century National Bank. These cases highlight the ever-increasing attention which should be placed on internal control systems and the critical role being played by the internal audit (IA) function in ensuring that weaknesses are minimized and that exposures to risks are adequately identified and managed (Karagiorgos *et al.*, 2009).

The internal audit department is critical to the process of ensuring efficiency and effectiveness in the financial sector (Latibeaudiere, 2002). Thus, the role of an internal auditor of a bank is very crucial (Siddiqui & Podder, 2002). The internal auditor's role has been revolutionized from performing traditional internal audit functions to focusing on value adding services in organizations such as reporting irregularities, identifying business risks and advising management on the internal control environment (Cashell & Aldhizer, 2002; Leung *et al.*, 2004; Mautz, 1964).

The aftermath of the global financial crisis and the vigorous regulatory activity have most financial institutions, especially banks, grappling to strike a balance among risk management, maximization of profits, and achieving regulatory compliance. While at the country level, Jamaica, an island in the English-speaking Caribbean has a heavy debt to GDP ratio of over 113% (Williams and Jones, 2010). The country has a fragile economy in which most of its foreign exchange is earned from tourism, remittances and the declining bauxite/alumina industry. The Jamaican economy faces serious problems with high interest rates, growing internal debt, increased foreign competition, a downward sliding exchange rate, a huge trade deficit and large-scale unemployment. As a result, the economic and social measures in Jamaica could be improved when compared to other countries in the English-speaking Caribbean and the wider developing countries/emerging economies.

However, within the western hemisphere, the United States of America (USA) is considered a reference point or baseline for social and economic measures. As a result, the comparative analysis below specifically explores the differences between Jamaica, a developing country in the English-speaking Caribbean and the United States of America, a developed country. In terms of social measure, Jamaica was ranked 85 out of 175 countries based on its corruption index, while the United States of America was ranked 17th in the same report (Ugaz, 2014). Other key measures reported in 2012 as distilled by the Department of Economic and Social Affairs (2014) report are:

Measure	Jamaica	United States
Corruption index	85/175	17/175
GDP per capita (current US$)	$5,343.1	$51,163.3
Exchange rates (national currency per US$)	92.56	---
Balance of payments (million US$)	-$1,905	-$440,423
Consumer price index (2000=100)	319	133
Unemployment (% of labour force)	13.9%	8.1%

Based on the social and economic measures above, it is evident that Jamaica needs to improve in five areas. These are corruption, GDP per capita, exchange rate, consumer price index and its unemployment rate in relation to the USA. These improvements can be achieved through an effective internal audit function. The internal audit function can play an important role in building solutions that help organizations achieve the right balance among risk management, maximization of profits and achieving regulatory compliance, by conducting internal control environment assessments, and recommending process improvements. This claim is supported in prior studies which have shown a positive relationship between internal audit resources and internal audit effectiveness (Ramachandran and Subramanian, 2012). Other studies have highlighted the various benefits that can be gained through the implementation of international financial reporting standards. These benefits include the production of higher quality financial statements and reduced costs of capital (Grabinski *et al.*, 2014). These positive gains by firms can lead to growth and development of nations.

However, there is very few academic studies on the effectiveness of the internal audit function (Cohen & Sayag, 2010), with relatively little research in this domain in Jamaica. However, such studies are important for banks in developed and developing countries and especially those in Jamaica who might find it difficult to absorb such failures due to severe resource constraints (Chevers, 2014). It is expected that the findings of this study will better equip bank managers to make more informed and better decisions. These decisions can create the opportunity for banks to not only to survive but to strive. This can increase the ability of banks to offer loans and finance developmental projects, which can lead to economic growth and development, and nation building.

As a result, this study seeks to investigate the factors that influence the effectiveness of the internal audit function in Jamaican commercial banks. Prior studies discovered that professional proficiency, organizational independence, quality of audit work and support from top management were determinants of internal audit effectiveness (Al-Twaijry *et al.*, 2003; Chambers *et al.*, 1988; Cohen & Sayag, 2010; Courtemanche, 1986; Fernandez & Rainey, 2006; Glazer & Jaenike, 1980). These determinants were confirmed by internal audit experts in Jamaica. As a result, in this study these four determinants were used to assess the effectiveness of the internal audit function in Jamaica. It is considered important that the various stakeholders and policy makers understand the important role the internal audit plays in the financial viability and financial health of any financial institution.

The remainder of the paper is organized as follows: The next section reviews the relevant literature, this is followed by the details regarding the research method, and this is followed by the findings and discussion and finally the conclusion.

2. Literature review

Today's financial institutions are faced with a dynamic and challenging environment in which they must address the needs of all stakeholders by remaining competitive, while responding to the demands of regulatory bodies, technological advancement, corporate governance concerns, and expanded product and service offerings. These developments have caused some financial institutions to experience financial woes, with Jamaica being no exception. The Jamaican commercial banking sector has experienced significant contraction over the last two decades, in response to the financial meltdown of the 1990's. During the period December 1990 to June 2014 there has been a decline in the number of commercial banks from thirteen to seven.

In responding to the financial crisis some critics argue that it was the result of inadequate regulatory oversight from the regulatory bodies (Bernanke, 2012; Olson & Wessel, 2015). They further posited that this inadequate oversight contributed to the poor corporate governance structure within financial institutions. Globally, the collapse of companies such as Enron and WorldCom due to fraudulent financial reporting and most recently, the global financial crisis of 2007, have sparked considerable interest in assessing the effectiveness of internal controls, internal audit and audit committees (Karagiorgos *et al.*, 2009). This has led many firms to strike a balance among risk management, maximization of profits and achieving regulatory compliance. It is widely accepted that the internal audit function plays an important role in building solutions that help organizations achieve the right balance by conducting internal control environment assessments, and recommending process improvements for enterprise risk management.

Against this background, in an effort to strengthen the supervisory and regulatory framework for deposit taking institutions and responding to numerous banks failures, the Bank of Jamaica, the central bank of Jamaica, issued in July 2008, the standard of best practice for effective corporate governance of deposit-taking entities (including commercial banks). This stipulated that all commercial banks put in place an adequate internal control system. Internal control systems and as such, the internal auditor (IA) has a critical role to play in ensuring that weaknesses are minimized and that exposures to risks are adequately identified and managed. There is reference to mandatory adoption of international standards on accounting quality by some firms in an effort to minimize fraudulent acts and behaviour (Ahmed *et al.*, 2013), which by extension can increase the quality of financial reporting (Dehaan *et al.*, 2013). It is also believed that having a sound internal audit function within the banks was one of such control mechanism (Lament, 2013).

It is important to note that the auditing profession has witnessed substantial and rapid change since the 1990's. This is as a result of the accelerating growth in world economies and deepening financial crisis. According to Porter *et al.* (2005), present-day auditing has developed into new processes that build on a business risk perspective of their clients. They stated that since the early 1990s, the audit profession began to adopt increased responsibility to detect and report fraud and to assess, and report more explicitly, doubts about an auditee's ability to continue in conformance with society's and regulators' increasing concern about corporate governance matters.

The roles and functions of internal auditors and by extension the audit committee have evolved from an assurance and compliance function to a value added and forward looking one. Traditionally, the internal audit function was seen as transaction based; that is, it was developed to protect the company's assets, monitor performance against adherence to policies and procedures and to ensure that the controls were working effectively. Cashell and Aldhizer (2002) stated that internal auditors have seen their role revolutionized from performing traditional internal audit functions to focusing on adding value services to the organization, such as reporting on irregularities, identifying business risks and advising management on the internal control environment.

This position is endorsed by Cosserat (2004) who stated that currently, internal auditors are expected not only to enhance the credibility of the financial statement, but also to provide value-added services. Similarly, Leung *et al.* (2004) claimed that the role of internal auditors has moved from mere conformance to a more convergence role (p. 23). In addition it is evident that the paradigm of independent auditing has shifted over the years. It is believed that these trends will continue in the future.

Internal Audit is considered a key pillar in the corporate governance framework and is very essential, given its independent role in assessing organizations' internal control framework. In June 1999, the Institute of Internal Auditors (IIA) offered a definition of the internal audit function as "an independent, objective assurance and consulting activity designed to add value and improve an organization's operations". In essence, it seeks to assist organizations to accomplish their objectives by bringing a systematic, disciplined approach to evaluating and improving the effectiveness of risk management, control and governance processes. As a result, it is important that the Internal Audit Department be placed at a sufficiently senior level in the organization (Hedley & Ben-Chorin, 2011), and internal auditors be given a high level of independence in reporting their findings (Fiolleau *et al.*, 2013).

From as early as the late 1980's researchers began to explore the role of internal audit in the banking sector. In a study sponsored by the Institute of Auditing, aimed at evaluating the effectiveness of internal audit departments by Albrecht *et al.* (1988), where they identified fifteen (15) criteria that were used to assess internal audit effectiveness by thirteen (13) private organizations. They concluded that among other things, management support for the internal auditing team, the fit between the auditing work and the goals set by managers and the qualifications of the internal auditor were the main drivers that determined internal audit effectiveness.

In another early study, Celal (1989) examined the function of internal audit in the banks of Turkey and concluded that the importance of internal audit in the banking sector is increased by the usage of computer and the international extension of banks. They went further to make the point that the size of the internal audit team was in direct proportion to the size of the bank and highlights the growing importance of internal auditing in business success. Furthermore, Bou-Raad (2000) argued that the strength of an IA department must be assessed with respect to the level of independence it enjoys from management and from operating responsibilities. Chambers *et al.* (1988) differentiate between organizational independence, based on organizational support and individual factors. They argue that organizational independence is very crucial to the effectiveness on internal auditors, as it protects the internal auditor from pressure or intimidation, and increases the objectivity of the auditing work.

In a study looking at both organizational and individual factors, Nassir *et al.* (2001) found that interpersonal skills, internal auditor's commitment, audit performance and integrity, internal competencies, internal auditor's knowledge on company's business operation and industry, internal auditor's independence, support from the audit committee and Board of Directors, and the audit department efficiency were important attributes of a quality internal audit function.

In a more recent study, Ussahawanitchakit and Intakhan (2011) stated that audit effectiveness is the outcome of the internal auditors' activities, duties, professional practices and responsibilities through a high commitment with audit standards, goals, objectives, policies and procedures. Internal audit plays a key role in monitoring a company's risk profile and identifying areas to improve risk management. Also, Ramachandran and Subramanian (2012) examined the effectiveness of the internal audit function in Tanzanian commercial banks, adopting the Arena and Azzone (2009) model. The results of their study concluded that there is a positive relationship between internal audit resources and competencies and internal audit effectiveness in Tanzanian commercial banks. This suggests that an increase in the level of internal audit resources will also result in an increase in the level of internal audit effectiveness in these banks.

Similarly, Dhamankar and Khandewale (2003) examined the effectiveness of Internal Audits, given the numerous corporate governance failures in the United States of America and other parts of the world. The study found that internal audit is an important constituent of good corporate governance and effective internal auditing would be a strong tool in the hands of the management.

In terms of banking irregularities, Augustine *et al.* (2013) examined the internal control system and quality of audit work in the Nigerian Banking Sector, and posited that the main cause of banking fraud is the lack of an effective internal control system. They concluded that the management of every bank should create and establish a standard internal control system, strong enough to stand against the wiles of fraud to promote continuity of operations, ensure the liquidity, solvency and going concern of the bank, as well as to facilitate quality audit work within the bank.

In addition, Hedley and Ben-Chorin (2011) claimed that internal auditing and monitoring activities help uncover fraud, because it is an important function in highlighting potential organizational weaknesses before they become costly or public crises. They went on further to state that an effective audit function typically reports to top management and have direct communication with the audit committee of the board of directors, because an unbiased perspective is important in an audit function. A major issue such as senior managers' willingness to disclose financial information can be enhanced with good governance structure and effective audit function (Damak-Ayadi & Klibi, 2015).

In another study Coram *et al.* (2008) examined a population of 324 Australian and New Zealand organizations and concluded that those with an internal audit function are more likely than those without such a function to detect and self-report fraud through misappropriation of assets. Given, those finding, it is clear that an effective internal audit unit helps to keep the organization in check and could lead to improve organizational performance. Despite numerous studies being conducted on internal audit effectiveness, there is the call for further research into this domain. Badara and Saidin (2013), suggest that more research should be conducted on internal audit effectiveness both in the public and private sectors.

Similar studies have been conducted on the effectiveness of internal audit in various countries, but no such research has been conducted in the Jamaican or the English-speaking Caribbean context. Given the importance of internal audit in the corporate governance structure, it is imperative that the various stakeholders and policy makers understand the important role internal audit plays in the financial viability and financial health of Jamaican financial institutions in the English-speaking Caribbean and the wider developing countries/emerging economies contexts.

Emerging economies are countries that have some characteristics of developed countries, but do not meet the standard to be classified as a developed country. The five largest emerging economies are Brazil, Russia, India, China and South Africa, commonly called 'BRICS'. They collectively hold an estimated $4 trillion in foreign reserves and represent one-third of the world's six billion population (Marquand, 2011). The five countries have a combined nominal GDP of US$16 trillion, which comprise 20% of the gross world product. Table 1 provides further details regarding various social and economic measures between Jamaica and the 'BRICS' countries.

Table 1. Social and economic measures between Jamaica and the 'BRICS' countries for year 2014

Measure	Jamaica	Brazil	Russia	India	China	South Africa
Corruption	85/175	69/175	136/175	85/175	100/175	67/175
GDP per capita (current US$)	$5,343.1	$11,346.8	$14,177.7	$1,516.3	$6,069.7	$7,336.2
Exchange rate (national currency per US$)	92.56	2.05	30.37	54.78	6.29	8.50
Balance of payment (million US$)	-$1,905	-$54,246	$72,016	-$91,471	$193,139	-$20,016
Consumer price index (2000=100)	319	214	---	217	133	198
Unemployment (% of labour force)	13.9%	5.5%	5.5%	---	2.8%	25.1%

(*Source*: Department of Economic and Social Affairs (2014) and Ugaz (2014))

Again, just like the comparison with the USA, Jamaica needs to improve its performance in about four measures. These are GDP per capita, exchange rate, consumer price index and its unemployment rate in relation to the 'BRICS' countries. However, it is important to note that China's corruption index is the lowest among the six countries, and India's GDP per capita and balance of payment are the lowest.

In looking closer in the English-speaking Caribbean of which Jamaica is a member, a similar comparison was done between Jamaica and five other member countries. The English-speaking Caribbean refers to members of the Caribbean Community and Common Market (CARICOM) whose first language is English (Duggan & Virtue, 2004). The comparison produce a similar result in which Jamaica is low in all six measures, as shown in Table 2. The measures are corruption, GDP per capita, exchange rate, balance of payment, consumer price index and unemployment. Hence, Jamaica needs to improve its performance in all these social and economic measures.

Jamaica's social and economic measures are low when compared to the United States of America, or the 'BRICS' countries or five English-speaking Caribbean countries. This is coupled with the fact that Jamaica's commercial banking industry accounts for over 75% of the deposits held by the country's deposit-taking institutions and these comprise only seven banks (Harriott *et al.*, 2010). The larger banks have consistently secured 75% of the revenue generated in the industry. In fact, the two largest banks – National Commercial Bank and Bank of Nova Scotia – collectively operate 85 of the 130 branches (65.4%) throughout the island and account for over 75% of the industry's revenue (Harriott *et al.*, 2010). Hence, the smaller banks exert relatively little competitive pressure on the larger banks. Against this background, it is important for Jamaica to understand the determinants of effective internal audit, with the hope that this knowledge can increase the likelihood of improving the country's social and economic measures.

Table 2. Social and economic measures between Jamaica and the ESC for year 2014

Measure	Jamaica	Antigua & Barbuda	Bahamas	Barbados	St. Vincent & the Grenadines	Trinidad &Tobago
Corruption	85/175	---	24/175	17/175	29/175	85/175
GDP per capita (current US$)	$5,343.1	$13,207.2	$21,623.9	$16,004.3	$6,348.8	$17,365.2
Exchange rate (national currency per US$)	92.56	2.70	1.00	2.00	2.70	6.43
Balance of payment (million US$)	-$1,905	-$79	-$1,500	-$218*	-$216	$2,899
Consumer price index (2000=100)	319	131	129	170	154	206
Unemployment (% of labour force)	13.9%	---	---	11.6%	---	5.9*

(*Source*: Department of Economic and Social Affairs (2014) and Ugaz (2014))
Note * = 2010 figure

It is widely felt that commercial banks play a critical role in every economy as they hold the savings of the public, provide a means of payment for goods and services, and finance the development of business and trade (Siddiqui & Podder, 2002). As a result, this empirical study assessed the effectiveness of internal audit in Jamaican commercial banks. The research questions seek to evaluate the following.

1. What is the relationship between quality of audit work and internal audit effectiveness in Jamaican Commercial Banks?
2. What is the relationship between organizational independence and internal audit effectiveness in Jamaican Commercial Banks?
3. What is the relationship between professional proficiency and internal audit effectiveness in Jamaican Commercial Banks?
4. What is the relationship between top management support and internal audit effectiveness in Jamaican Commercial Banks?

Hence the four hypotheses emerging from these research questions are:

H1: There is a positive relationship between quality of audit work and internal audit effectiveness.

H2: There is a positive relationship between organizational independence and internal audit effectiveness.

H3: There is a positive relationship between professional proficiency of internal auditors and internal audit effectiveness.

H4: There is a positive relationship between management support and internal audit effectiveness.

These hypotheses are similar to those used in Cohen and Sayag (2010) study, which evaluated the determinants of internal audit effectiveness in Israeli organizations. It is hoped that this study will assist in unearthing meaningful information regarding the factors with the greatest influence on internal audit effectiveness, as well as stimulate other researchers to conduct further research in this domain.

3. Methodology

This was a quantitative study in which the unit of analysis was the firm. The study sought to determine the extent to which internal audit is considered effective in Jamaican commercial banks. The study is considered relevant given the relative importance placed on the role and function of internal auditors and the mandate for commercial banks to have a permanent internal audit structure.

A questionnaire was used to collect data from the selected respondents using closed-ended questions. According to Bird (2009) questionnaires are considered stable, consistent, free of variations, uniform, and demonstrate high levels of reliability and validity when used in surveys. A pilot study was conducted to ensure that the research instrument was well understood. This pilot study was conducted at JMMB Merchant Bank in Jamaica. A sample of twenty five (25) persons was selected from various departments to answer the questionnaire. This institution was selected because it had similar characteristics to the commercial banking sector. Upon completion of the pre-test the questions were deemed to be straightforward and simple in language to prevent ambiguity in responses. The questionnaire was developed using a five point Likert scale measuring from Strongly Agree (5) to Strongly Disagree (1). All questions were arranged in one direction and all the constructs were operationally defined. Three methods of distribution were used for the questionnaire: (a) Facsimile (b) E-mail and (c) Personal delivery.

One hundred and fifty (150) questionnaires were distributed to employees in three commercial banks in Jamaica that were willing to participate in the survey. Survey responses were sought from persons working in the treasury, finance, operations, and risk management departments. The questionnaires were administered to supervisors, middle management and senior management who have been in direct contact with the internal auditors during an audit of the various sections of the three commercial banks surveyed. A convenience sampling technique was used to collect the data. In addition, given the absence of research on this area in Jamaica, preliminary discussions were held with internal auditors in the local commercial banking sector and one of the leading auditing firms in Jamaica, to identify what factors they considered relevant in measuring internal audit effectiveness in the local context.

Based on the interviews conducted, it was derived that the quality of the internal auditor's work, the evaluations of the auditees and the added contribution of IA were found to be the three most appropriate dimensions that encompass the concept of internal audit effectiveness; this was supported by a study conducted by Cohen and Sayag (2010). Hence, the dependent variable - internal audit effectiveness - which is the ability of the internal auditors to achieve established objective of the internal audit function, was measured by these three indicator variables. The four independent variables were adopted from a study conducted by Cohen and Sayag (2010), as well as discussions with the Chief Internal Auditors from the three (3) commercial banks that participated in the survey. The variables are professional proficiency, quality of audit work, organizational independence and top management support (as shown in Table 3).

The data from the survey was analyzed using Statistical Package for Social Scientists (SPSS) – version 20. The output included, descriptive statistics (means, standard deviation, frequencies and factor analysis), and inferential statistics (correlations and regressions).

Table 3. Variables and reliability result

Indicator Variable	Cronbach Alpha
Professional Proficiency	0.744
Quality of Audit Work	0.774
Organizational Independence	0.891
Top Management Support	0.640
Audit Quality	0.609
Auditees' Evaluation	0.811
Added Contribution of IA	0.683

To ensure accuracy, consistency, completeness and reliability of the instrument was established using Cronbach's coefficient Alpha test. It is widely accepted that reliability is established at 0.7 and above, but values of 0.6 to 0.70 is considered the lower limit of acceptability (Hair, Black, Babin and Anderson, 2010). Based on this threshold reliability is established as all the readings were above 0.6 as shown in Table 3.

4. Findings

Out of the one hundred and fifty (150) questionnaires that were issued, one hundred and thirty (130) were returned which lead to a response rate of 86.7%. But out of the 130 questionnaires that were collected, eleven (11) questionnaires were incomplete and therefore rejected for the purpose of analysis. This makes the remaining one hundred and nineteen (119) responses which represent the valid response rate of 79.3%. According to Hair et al. (2010), a response rate of 30% is acceptable for survey.

The majority of the respondents were female (64%) while male constituted the remaining 36%. Most responses were received from middle managers (45.4%), followed by supervisors (31.9%) and senior management (22.7%). In terms of duration of employment with the organization, the majority of the respondents (37%) had been employed by their respective employer for over 10 years, followed by those between 1 – 5 years constituting 30.3%, 6 – 10 years accounting for 29.4% and 3.3% being employed for less than one year. The result revealed that the majority (64.5%) of the respondents were between 21 – 40 years of age, with those between 41 – 60 years accounting for 35.5%. There were no respondents below 20 years and above 60 years old.

The result of the descriptive statistics is shown in Table 4. The analysis is done on the basis of the 1 – 5 scale, where 1 is strongly disagree and 5 is strongly agree. The results in table 4 was populated and sorted in descending order of mean using information from the independent variables (Professional Proficiency, Quality of Audit Work, Organization Independence and Management Support). The results from the table revealed that internal auditors understanding of the business (4.51), participation in training and development by the internal auditors (4.38) and the focus of the audit plan (4.28) were the most important factors based on mean values, while follow up by the internal audit department was considered the least important with mean values of (3.77). The weighted score for independent variables (factors that expected to influence internal auditing effectiveness) ranged from 3.77 to 4.51 (75.4% to 90.2%) out of five, indicating that the respondent almost agree that the selected independent variables influencing internal audit effectiveness.

Table 4. Descriptive statistics

Survey Items	N = 119 Min	Maxi	Mean	Standard Deviation
Internal Auditors should understand the business well enough to be able to look beyond the apparent facts, and identify root cause of problems.	1	5	4.51	.862
The organisation allows internal auditors to participate in training and development programs in order to maintain their skills and keep up to date in the field.	1	5	4.38	.736
The annual audit plan focuses on areas relevant to the organisation's stakeholders	2	5	4.28	.700
Management is sufficiently aware of the needs of IA, as demonstrated in the budget allocation to the department.	1	5	4.20	.850
The audit results will be useful in enhancing the overall effectiveness of the organisation's controls, policies and procedures.	1	5	4.10	.796
The Internal Auditors displayed technical competence and proficiency whilst conducting the review.	1	5	4.09	.725
Top management provides IA with the support needed	1	5	4.06	.773
IA operates totally independent and can audit area of the organisation it considers in need of auditing	1	5	4.06	.773
The areas to be audited are decided after identifying risks, quantifying them and determining appropriate risks levels.	2	5	3.95	.790
Adequate human resources are provided to the IA department and are sufficient given the amount of work required.	2	5	3.95	.757
The employment and termination of the Chief Internal Auditor requires approval from the Audit Committee, and/or the Board of Directors.	2	5	3.95	.757
IA has access to the organisation's information, records and locations.	2	5	3.95	.757
The audit work performed was consistent with the initial scope and objectives conveyed during the planning meeting.	2	5	3.95	.769
The audit scope and objectives were clearly communicated and agreed on during the planning phase of the audit.	2	5	3.93	.851
The audit team kept you informed of key issues identified during the audit.	2	5	3.90	.877
All organizational data pools are accessible to the Internal Auditor	2	5	3.89	.779
Regular and direct working relations with the Audit Committee, strengthen independence	2	5	3.89	.779
Detailed Budget proposals are included in the Audit Plan	2	5	3.87	.853
There is regular follow-up by the IA Department to examine actions taken to address audit findings.	1	5	3.77	.934

4.1 Correlation analysis

The correlation analysis of the variables under study was subjected to a two-tailed test of statistical significance at $p<0.01$ level. Table 5 below shows that the correlations between all variables under study were statistically significant at $p<0.01$ level. Pearson correlation test was employed to establish the relationship between the independent and dependent variables. The results are detailed below:

Table 5. Results of the hypothesis test

Hypotheses	Variable	Result
H1	Quality of audit work	Supported***
H2	Organizational independence	Supported***
H3	Professional proficiency	Supported***
H4	Management support	Supported***
Note: *** $p \leq 0.001$		

4.2 Multiple regression analysis

Linear regression estimates the coefficients of the linear equation, involving one or more independent variables that best predict the value of the dependent variable. Table 6 presents the results of the regression analysis.

Table 6. Results of multiple regression analysis at 5% significant level

Dependent Variable	Independent Variable	Adjusted R Square	Durbin-Watson	F-stats	Sig.	Constant	β	VIF
IA Effectiveness	Quality of Audit Work	0.797	1.511	117.14	.000	11.518	.226	2.473
	Organizational Independence						.855	2.405
	Professional Proficiency						.339	1.485
	Management Support						.530	1.251

- The adjusted R^2 was 79.7%, which reflects the explanatory power for the independent variables to explain about 79.7% of the changes in the dependent variable - Internal Audit Effectiveness (IAE).
- Durbin-Watson statistic (which was 1.511) indicates that there is no serial correlation (autocorrelation) in the dependent variable, since it is so close from the optimal value (2).

- F-statistic and its significant denote the goodness of fit. In other word, f-statistic indicates that the model is properly specified to reflect the effect of independent variables on the dependent variable. In this study, the significance test value is less than (<0.001) than the critical value of 0.05, which means that at 5% type 1 error rate or at 95% confidence interval, the model fits well in explaining the relationship that exist among the factors. The regression model which is used to explain the relationship among the factors is as follows:
  $IAE = \alpha + \beta_1$ *Organizational Independence* $+ \beta_2$*Professional proficiency* $+ \beta_3$*Quality of audit work* $+ \beta_4$*Management Support* $+ \epsilon$
- Finally the, variance inflation factor (VIF) was low for all independent variables, indicating the absence of multi-collinearity problem.

The findings revealed that quality of audit work, organizational independence, professional proficiencies and management support significantly contribute to internal audit effectiveness at a 5% significant level.

5. Discussion

The study was designed to assess the factors that influence internal audit effectiveness in Jamaican commercial banks. Internal audit effectiveness was measured by quality of audit work, auditees' evaluation and added contribution of IA, while the independent variables were quality of audit work, organizational independence, support from top management and professional proficiency. The study confirmed the notion that the internal audit function is revolutionized from performing the traditional internal audit role of compliance and monitoring to focusing on value adding services. This claim is made based on the fact that all four hypotheses were found significant.

In addition, the findings are consistent with prior studies in which it was discovered that there is significant relationship between:

- Professional proficiency and internal audit effectiveness in the Jamaican commercial banks, ($r = 0.339$, $p<0.01$). Hypothesis 1 (H1) was supported and the findings were consistent with Al-Twaijry et al. (2003) and Cohen and Sayag (2010) studies. This finding means that internal auditor's knowledge on company's operation, interpersonal skills and integrity are key influential factors on audit effectiveness in Jamaica.
- Organisational independence and internal audit effectiveness in Jamaican commercial banks, ($r = 86.4$, $p< 0.001$). Hypothesis 2 (H2) was supported and the findings were in alignment with those of Courtemanche (1986), Chambers et al. (1988), Bou-Raad (2000), Nassir et al., (2001) and Cohen and Sayag (2010). This finding supports the notion that internal auditor's

should be empowered and given the associated authority to seek compliance to the recommendations in their reports.

- Quality of audit work and internal audit effectiveness in Jamaican commercial banks, ($r = 0.744$, $p < 0.001$). H3 was consistent with Glazer and Jaenike (1980), who argued that performing auditing work in line with the auditing standards contributes significantly to the effectiveness of auditing. Based on this finding it is evident that the internal auditor's function should add value and improve efficiency in the operations of Jamaican banks.
- Top management support and internal audit effectiveness in Jamaican commercial banks, ($r = 0.526$, $p < 0.001$). The findings (H4) were thus consistent with the findings of Fernandez and Rainey (2006), who postulated that top management support and commitment to change play a crucial role in organisational renewal, as senior managers can mobilize the critical mass needed to follow through on efforts launched by one or two visionary thinkers.

The findings of this research are somewhat similar to the study conducted by Cohen and Sayag (2010). The regression results in this study revealed a positive relationship between quality of audit work, organizational independence, management support and professional proficiency on internal audit effectiveness in Jamaican commercial banks. This implies that increase in the level of quality of audit work; organizational independence; management support and professional proficiency will also result in an increase in the level of internal audit effectiveness. This high level of performance is critical in Jamaica who is plagued with resource constraints, as do most developing countries. Based on the constraints being experienced by Jamaican commercial banks it is important that operational weaknesses are minimized and risks are adequately identified and managed. Banks in Jamaica might find it difficult to absorb such failures due to resource constraints.

6. Conclusion

The study found that the quality of audit investigation, organizational independence, professional proficiencies and management have a significant impact on internal audit effectiveness. It was expected that both organizational and individual factors could influence the effectiveness of the internal audit function.

The findings of this study will contribute to the internal audit literature and also provide insight to enhance internal audit effectiveness in Jamaican commercial banks. These insights can strengthen corporate governance structure of these institutions. However, the findings of this study are not generalizable. They are limited to the scope of commercial banks in Jamaica.

Although limited in scope, a few recommendations are made in the context of Jamaica. Policies makers, such as the Central Bank of Jamaica, can use the research to access the impact internal audit have on the efficient operation of the banking sector. Other financial institutions and the commercial banks that did not participate in the can also use the findings of this study to design and implement a system to assess the effectiveness of internal audit as a governance tool. Internal auditors should seek to maintain professional proficiency, organisational independence and the quality of work performed to maintain internal audit effectiveness. Future research could be conducted on the effectiveness of internal audit in other sectors, both public and private. In addition further study should concentrate on the examination of other factors that contribute to internal audit effectiveness which were not included in this study.

References

Ahmed, A., Neel, M., & Wang, D. (2013) "Does mandatory adoption of IFRS improve accounting quality? Preliminary evidence", *Contemporary Accounting Research,* vol. 30: 1344-1372

Albrecht, W. S., Howe, K. R., Schueler, D. R. & Stocks, K. D. (1988) "Evaluating the effectiveness of internal audit departments", Altamonte Springs, FL.: Institute of Internal Audit

Al-Twaijry, A. A. M., Brierley, J. A., & Gwillian, D. R. (2003) "The development of internal audit in Saudi Arabia: An institutional theory perspective", *Critical Perspectives on Accounting*, vol. 14: 507-553

Arena, M., & Azzone, G. (2009) "Identifying organizational drivers of internal audit effectiveness", *International Journal of Auditing,* vol. 13: 43-60

Augustine, O. E., Chijioke, M., Sadiq, O. A., & Francis, A. O. (2013) "Internal control system and quality audit work", *Research Journal of Finance and Accounting*, vol. 4: 100-105

Badara, M. S., & Saidin, S. Z. (2013) "The journey so far on internal audit effectiveness: A calling for expansion", *International Journal of Academic Research in Accounting, Finance and Management Sciences*, vol. 3: 340-351

Bernanke, B. S. (2012) "Some reflections on the crisis and the policy response", In A. S. Blinder, A. W. Lo & R. M. Solow (Eds.), *Rethinking the financial crisis* (pp. 3-13). New York: Russell Sage Foundation

Bird, D. K. (2009) "The use of questionnaires for acquiring information on public perception of natural hazards and risk mitigation - A review of current knowledge and practice", *Nat. Hazards Earth Syst. Sci.,* vol. 9: 1307-1325

Bou-Raad, G. (2000) "Internal auditors and a value-added approach: The new business regime", *Managerial Auditing Journal,* vol. 15: 182-186

Cashell, J. D., & Aldhizer, G. R. (2002) "An examination of internal auditors' emphasis on value added services", *Internal Auditing*, vol. 9: 117-127

Celal, K. (1989) "Internal auditing in the Turkish Banking sector", Unpublished manuscript, Izmir, Turkey

Chambers, A. D., Selim, G. M., & Vinten, G. (1988) "Internal auditing", Australia: CCH Australia

Chevers, D. A. (2014) "Key factors of process maturity in English-speaking Caribbean firms", *RAE - Revista de Administracas de Empresas,* vol. 54: 322-329

Cohen, D., & Sayag, G. (2010) "The effectiveness of internal auditing: An empirical examination of its determinants in Israeli organizations", *Australian Accounting Review*, vol. 54: 296-307

Coram, P., Ferguson, C., & Moroney, R. (2008) "Internal audit, alternative internal audit structures and the level of misappropriation of assets fraud", *Accounting and Finance*, 543-559

Cosserat, G. (2004) "Modern auditing", New York: John Wiley & Sons

Courtemanche, G. (1986) "The new internal auditing", New York: John Wiley & Sons

Damak-Ayadi, S., & Klibi, E. (2015) "Impact of executives' profile on the extent of voluntary financial disclosure: The case of Tunisian companies", *Accounting and Management Information Systems,* vol. 14: 655-684

Dehaan, E., Hodge, F., & Shevlin, T. (2013) "Does voluntary adoption of a clawback provision improve financial reporting quality", *Contemporary Accounting Research,* vol. 30: 1027-1062

Department of Economic and Social Affairs. (2014). *World statistics pocketbook - 2014 Edition*. New York: United Nations

Dhamankar, R., & Khandewale, A. (2003) "Effectiveness of internal audit", *The Chartered Accountant*, 275-279

Duggan, & Virtue, G. (2004). Bridging the Digital Divide in Caribbean Group Decision-Making. *The Electronic Journal on Information Systems in Developing Countries, 17*(5), 1-23

Fernandez, S., & Rainey, H. G. (2006) "Managing successful organizational change in the Public Sector", *Public Administration Review,* vol. 66: 168-176

Fiolleau, K., Hoang, K., Jamal, K. & Sunder, S. (2013) "How do regulatory reforms to enhance auditor independence work in practice?", *Contemporary Accounting Research,* vol. 30: 864-890

Glazer, A. S., & Jaenike, H. R. (1980) "A framework for evaluating an internal audit function", Altamonte Springs, FL.: Institute of Internal Auditors

Grabinski, K., Kedzior, M., & Krasodomska, J. (2014) "The polish accounting system and IFRS implementation process in the view of empirical research", *Accounting and Management Information Systems,* vol. 13: 281-310

Hair, J., Black, W. C., Babin, B. J., & Anderson, R. E. (2010) *Multivariate analysis*, New Jersey: Pearson Educational International

Harriott, K., Amonde, T., & Grant, K. (2010) "Nature and extent of competition in the commercial banking sector", *Jamaica Fair Trading Commission*, pp. 1-58

Hedley, T. P. & Ben-Chorin, O. (2011) "Auditing and monitoring activities help uncover fraud and assess control effectiveness", *The CPA Journal*, pp. 68-71

Karagiorgos, T., Drogalas, G., Gotzamanis, E. & Tampakoudis, I. (2009) "The contribution of internal auditing to management", *International Journal of Management Research and Technology,* vol. 3: 417-427

Lament, M. (2013) "Audit as a control mechanism used by insurance companies", *Scientific Quarterly,* vol. 4: 105-119

Latibeaudiere, D. (2002) "Internal audit for banks", *Bank of Jamaica*, 1-3

Leung, P., Coram, P., Cooper, B. & Richardson, P. (2004) *Modern auditing & assurance service*, Australia: John Wiley & Sons.

Marquand, R. (2011) "Amid 'BRICS' rise and 'Arab Spring', a new global order forms", *The Christian Science Monitor*, p. 1-6

Mautz, R. K. (1964) *Fundamentals of Auditing*, New York: John Wiley & Sons

Nassir, A., Abdul Hamid, M. A., Mohamed, S. H. & Sori, Z. M. (2001) "Effectiveness of the internal auditor in Malaysian listed firms", *Malaysian Institute of Accountants,* vol. 14: 30-33

Neu, D., Everett, J., & Rahaman, A. (2013) "Internal auditing and corruption within government: The case of the Canadian Sponsorship Program", *Contemporary Accounting Research,* vol. 30: 1223-1250

Olson, P. & Wessel, D. (2015) "Kohn calls U.S. systemic regulation inadequate, urges learning from U.K", *Up Front*, p. 1-3

Porter, B., Simon, J. & Hatherly, D. (2005) *Principles of external auditing*, Chichester, West Sussex, UK: John Wiley & Sons

Ramachandran, J. & Subramanian, R. (2012) "Effectiveness of internal audit in Tanzanian Commercial Banks", *British Journal of Arts and Social Sciences,* vol. 8: 32-44

Siddiqui, J., & Podder, J. (2002) "Effectiveness of bank audit in Bangladesh", *Managerial Auditing Journal,* vol. 17: 502-510

Ugaz, J. (2014) Corruption perceptions index 2014, *Transparency International*, pp. 1-12

Ussahawanitchakit, P. & Intakhan, A. (2011) "Audit professionalism, audit independence and audit effectiveness of CPA's in Thailand", *International Journal of Business Research,* vol. 11: 1-11

Williams, D. & Jones, O. (2010) "Factors associated with longevity of small, family-owned firms", *International Journal of Entrepreneurship,* vol. 14: 37-56

3

The relevance of financial information and contents of the new audit report for lending decisions of commercial banks

Marina Trpeska[a1], Atanasko Atanasovski[a] and Zorica Bozinovska Lazarevska[a,]

[a] *University Ss Cyril and Methodius, Faculty of Economics-Skopje, Macedonia*

Abstract: This research study examines the importance of financial information and information contained in the ISA's New Audit Report effective from 2016 for lenders as capital providers. We base our findings on a survey conducted in September of 2016 with corporate loan officers for medium-large corporate clients in Macedonia. The results show that the annual report of the company, except for the management report and notes to the financial statements, has consistently high importance and usability for respondents' decision making. Various accounting ratios related to liquidity, financial stability and profitability of the company are considered very important and regularly used in credit analysis. However, respondents were not consistent in their shared perceptions regarding high importance of projected profits and historical information on operating cash flows. All loan officers gave high importance to the information found in existent auditor's report format regardless of the form of expressed opinion. Also, information on key audit matters, additional information on going concern and related auditor's judgement, procedures related to fraud risk were considered of high importance. Lenders rated as less important the disclosure of the name of engagement partner, auditor's statement on independence and compliance with ethical requirements and the level of materiality used in the audit.

---

[1] *Corresponding authors*: Department of Accounting and Audit, University Ss Cyril and Methodius in Skopje; Goce Delcev 9V, Skopje; email addresses: marinas@eccf.ukim.edu.mk; atanasko@eccf.ukim.edu.mk; zoricab@eccf.ukim.edu.mk

Keywords: importance of audit, new auditor's report, survey, lenders, lending decisions

1. Introduction

This study examines the importance and use of accounting information and accounting ratios for lending decisions, as perceived by corporate loan officers and heads of corporate loan departments. The study also focuses on perceived importance of information contained in the existent audit report format according to ISA's requirements and incremental information content of ISA's New Auditor's Report as effective from December, 2016.

The importance and usage of accounting information and accounting ratios in lending decisions is extensively investigated in the literature and remains an important topic in financial reporting since creditors as capital providers are considered key users of financial statements (Hines, 1982; Bartlett & Chandler,1997; Berry & Robertson, 2006). Researchers also reported changes in traditional importance of certain accounting information and accounting ratios over time, such as shifts from balance sheets and income statements to cash flow statements and increased use of projected financial statements and management accounts (Berry & Robertson, 2006). One of the main motivations of our study was to investigate how traditional are banks in Macedonia in the use of accounting information for lending decisions and whether they tend to rely more on official and historical accounting information for reliability reasons or give more value to management projections and unaudited financial information.

Many researchers provided empirical evidence on the relevance of certain information in the audit report for the decision making of investors and creditors (Gay & Schelluch, 1993; Miller *et al.*, 1993; Bamber & Stratton, 1997; Bartlett & Chandler,1997; Berry & Robertson, 2006; Guiral-Contreras *et al.*, 2007). However, there were critics, both in academia and practice, on the usefulness of auditor's report for capital providers in dynamic business environment where entities are exposed to more risky and complex transactions.

The first big change of the audit report content was in 1993 as a result of the researches that bankers, analysts and shareholders confuse the relative responsibilities of management and auditors for the financial statements. There were a lot of misconceptions of the auditor's role and responsibilities. Some research studies provided evidence that bankers placed greater responsibility for the completeness and accuracy of the financial statements on auditors than on management (Nair & Rittenberg, 1987). Bankers also felt in the past that audited financial statements were less reliable most likely because bankers were unfamiliar with the procedures employed by the independent auditors (Rankin, 1982). Even more, it was reported that the responsibility of the auditors is to prevent all major fraud and error (Gay & Schelluch, 1993). Despite of these misconceptions and unfamiliar understandings of audit report in the very early years of audit report usage, accounting scandals in recent past and the world economic and financial crises have imposed larger importance for the audit profession.

The implications and usages of audit report are different in many areas of business environment. With the latest changes of ISA 700 and implementation of extended audit report, many questions were raised about its usefulness, its value added to different stakeholders and their decisions. The main purpose of our study was to evaluate perceptions of lenders about the importance of incremental information to be found in future audit reports in respect of, among the rest, key audit matters, going concern assumptions and material uncertainties, materiality used in the audit and procedures applied by auditor in respect of fraud in financial statements. We performed a survey among bank loan officers and heads of corporate loan departments involved in lending decisions with medium-large companies.

The results of the study show that historical accounting information and accounting ratios are very important for lending decisions in Macedonian banks. Loan officers give more importance to traditional and published financial information, in comparison to projected profits, historical cash flow information or the Management report part of the Annual report. Also lenders rely on information from the standard audit report, and gave equal importance weight to all types of auditor's opinion. Regarding the incremental information contained in the New Auditor's Report, lenders value most information on key audit matters, existence of material uncertainty and auditor's judgement for the going concern and auditor's procedures related to risk of fraud in the financial statements.

The reminder of the paper is structured as follows. The next section provides a literature review and presents the objective of the research and research hypotheses. The third section explains the research methodology, the empirical results are then presented, and a final section providing concluding remarks.

2. Literature review

Financial institutions loan millions of dollars to companies daily relying mainly on financial statements. This is one of the reasons why loan officers are considered among the principal users of financial information who are most affected by the credibility of audit reports and their interpretation in loan granting decisions (Guiral-Contreras *et al.*, 2007). But bankers and loan officers reported different importance and usage of accounting information and audit report through the time. It is common conclusion from the academic papers, and practice too, that audited financial statements continue to be the most important single source of information for the lending decisions. Balance sheets and income statements are still important for credit analysis and loan decisions (Hines, 1982). Bartlett and Chandler (1997) highlighted shifts to cash flow statements as well as directors' report. Besides these changes in frequency of use of "traditional" statements and reports, there is noticed increased frequency of use of management accounts and projected financial statements (Berry & Robertson, 2006). Also financial indicators have changed ranking and importance through the time. For example, profitability ratios are not any more the most important, but the prime importance is given to liquidity ratios in accordance with previous finding for increased importance of cash flow statement (Berry & Robertson, 2006).

Long ago capital markets were not such developed like nowadays and independent auditor's report was significantly different from the one proposed in the latest ISA's. Up until now, it can be argued that standardized and predefined wording was used. Many researchers investigated the usefulness of the standard form of the audit report (Miller*et al.*, 1993; Gay & Schelluch, 1993). According to Epstein and Pava (1992) the auditors' report is considered more important than it used to be, but according to other researchers there is decreasing importance or extend of reading of the audit report despite the fact that it was considerably extended in 1993 (Anderson & Epstein,1995; Bartlett & Chandler,1997; Berry & Robertson, 2006). The explanation for decreased importance of audit report could be found in increased complexity in accounting and audit profession that makes audit reports and published financial statements difficult for understanding outside the profession, for people such as loan officers.

The main changes in the current audit report were in 1993 when SAS600 (later on in 2004 replaced with ISA700) was primarily focused on identifying responsibilities of the management and the auditor (Masters, 2015). In this audit report introductory paragraph is included which specifically addresses relative responsibilities of management and auditors. Also, the scope paragraph of this audit report from 1993 was expanded to include a brief description of an audit and terms like "reasonable assurance" and "materiality" were introduced for the first time (Miller *et al.*, 1993). The extended audit report significantly improved users' perception of the purpose and procedures of the audit as well as the responsibilities of the management and auditors (Gay & Schelluch, 1993).

In between the big change of audit report content in 1993 (1988 in USA) and the latest big change about expanding audit report content there were changes adopted in 2006 that include a greater discussion on the auditor's responsibilities, a note that the auditor has complied with ethical requirements, a note that the audit evidence obtained is "sufficient and appropriate" to provide a basis for the audit opinion and an explanation as to why the auditor evaluates internal control (IAASB, 2003). The main critics about this revised ISA 700 were (Gray *et al.*, 2011): not quantifying level of assurance, materiality and sample sizes and not imply anything about the quality of internal controls nor explicitly say anything about fraud. Similar findings about expectation gap between auditors and users are identified by Asare and Wright (2012) too.

IAASB and AICPA, aware for the existence of the expectation gap between users' understanding and the intended meaning of the standard audit report, have consulted many research papers to identify and evaluate this gap (Gray *et al.*, 2011; Asare & Wright, 2012; Gold *et al.*, 2012). IAASB exposure draft of ISA 700 released in 2013 initiated many researches about the perception of auditors and other users of new proposed changes. In these studies respondents have supported the IAASB's proposed reforms addressing the expectations, information and communication gaps (Simnett & Huggins, 2014). Recent studies indicate that participants give attention to the supplementary information presented in the auditor's reports and that the matters mentioned in the report affect the participants' information acquisition in a way that users paid higher attention to the information mentioned in the key audit matters in auditor's report. Furthermore, the number of matters mentioned in the report also has an effect on information acquisition by users (Sirois *et al.*, 2014).

Academics and practitioners are consistent about the increased requirements for audit quality and better communication through the audit report. Triggered by the recent financial crises, new regulation and revised ISA 700 suggest expansion of the audit report in order to decrease the expectation gap which is characterized with continuous existence. The main feature of the new audit report is the introduction of Key Audit Matters where additional information and explanation about the audit process will be included. The very first researches of the effects of the expanded audit report reported that the presence of the quite extensive ISA 700 explanations does not affect the expectation gap (Gold *et al.*, 2012; Boolaky & Quick, 2016). Only the future will show whether KAM will really be valuable for users of audited financial statements (Kohler *et al.*, 2016).

Auditors following the new audit format should be very careful in choosing what to report in key audit matters since there is evidence that users might to perceive the level of audit quality to be lower especially if there is only one matter mentioned in the auditor's report (Sirois *et al.*, 2014). However, new audit report provides a roadmap that helps users navigate complex financial statements and focus on matters highlighted by the auditor (Sirois *et al.*, 2014) although this could have bias effect on distracting the users' focus from other information presented in financial statements and in a way increase the expectation gap.

Many of the research studies about extended new audit report also are focused on loan officers. For example, preliminary effects and perceptions are that loan officers have the highest audit expectation gap and place significantly higher value on additional information about the audit process and information about the entity (Litjens *et al.*, 2015).

Regarding the standard audit report that was in force till 2015, the loan officers were better able to identify the responsibilities assumed for the financial statements by both management and the independent auditor (Miller *et al.*, 1993) than from the previous format of the audit report where only the audit opinion was expressed. Furthermore, the modified audit report influenced the loan officers' risk assessment, the interest rate premium and the decision whether or not to grant the loan (Bamber & Stratton, 1997). The bankers granted loans less often to a company with a modified report than a company with a standard report, and assigned higher interest rate premiums to the former company. Elias and Johnston (2001) in another study investigated whether the explanatory paragraph about going concern has any information content. The results showed that explanatory paragraph indicating going concern uncertainty appeared to convey no additional information content, i.e. bankers receiving modified report did not feel significantly less confident of their decision than those receiving the standard report.

Regarding the audit opinion expressed in audit report, loan officers give no importance to an unqualified audit report if they receive other financial information that is unfavourable towards the client requesting credit, or they are prepared to change a previously favourable attitude when faced with adverse opinions expressed by the auditors (Guiral-Contreras *et al.*, 2007). In later situation, audit report act as 'red flag' that only alerts the loan officers to be more critical and severe in the conditions imposed on a loan when it contradicts the a priori favourable attitude by the loan officers vs. modified or adverse audit report. But there are research studies that do not support the prediction that modified opinions have impact on credit availability possibly because lenders use other kinds of data for their loan decisions (Niemi & Sundgren, 2012). Other authors go in more details and connect the audit opinion with the internal control opinion describing situation where auditors express unqualified overall opinion but also express adverse internal control opinion that weakens the importance of financial statements and consider the auditors' opinion about internal controls as relevant for their decisions for granting loans (Schneider & Church, 2008). In other words, even when an auditor provides an unqualified opinion on financial statements, loan officers may view material weaknesses of internal controls and adverse opinion on them as bad news and as a basis for decision to do not grant loan. But very interesting fact about the user of financial statement audit and fact in front of which we cannot slur over is that users of audit report value audit, but do not read entire auditor's report, or even more they cannot assign a measurable value to the audit (Gray *et al.*, 2011). They will more preferably rely on quantitative data or independent analysis. In order to address the existent expectation gaps of different users, audit profession should start thinking about innovative and tailor created audit reports that can meet the expectations and needs of different users (Litjens *et al.*, 2015). It means that although additional information are proposed to be included in the new audit report, it is not guarantee that expectation gap will be outmatch.

We decided to conduct a survey study to analyse the perceptions on importance and usage of certain financial information and accounting ratios when deriving at corporate loan decisions. Furthermore, we aim to investigate what importance has for lenders information provided in the independent auditors report according to the old audit report format. The perceptions of lenders as capital providers about the information content of the new audit report is the main purpose of this study, so therefore our survey includes statements on information contents of the new audit report format and asked respondents to evaluate the importance. We were also curious to find whether there is additional information that lenders consider important but not required to be reported under the requirements of ISA's new audit reporting standards. By analysing this, we expect to be able to provide evidence on possible residual audit expectation gap from lenders perspective after implementation of the enhanced audit report in practice.

3. Research methodology

The research was carried out with corporate loan officers and heads of corporate loan departments with the banking sector in Macedonia. The online survey was conducted in September 2016 covering in total 114 identified corporate loan officers and heads with 15 banks in the country. Only loan officers and heads involved in disbursement of corporate loans to medium and large companies at least were considered for the sample. The reason is that small and micro companies in Macedonia are not legally required to perform statutory audit on their financial statements, in addition, size thresholds for companies applicable in the country are considered low and there are rare cases of small companies engaging auditors for cost efficiency reasons. The first letter and request to participate in the study was sent early in September 2016, directly through e-mails to all heads of corporate loan departments. In total 18 respondents completed the online survey after the first request, two weeks after the first request a second request was sent and 31 completed online survey questionnaires were considered for the analysis. Table 1 below shows the response statistics for the survey instrument.

Table 1. Survey response statistics

Focus group	Population	Mailed	Incomplete	Responses	Response rate
Corporate loan officers and heads	114	114	2	31	27.2%

The response rate based on completed surveys without omissions is 27.2 per cent and is considered as satisfactory since online surveys are usually considered inferior to other survey data gathering methods (Owen & Jones, 1994). The survey questionnaire was composed of four parts, containing statements on the following:
Part I: Data on respondents' characteristics (i.e. gender, relevant experience);
Part II: Importance of main statements in companies' annual report;
Part III: Statements on the use and importance of certain accounting ratios in deriving at lending decision;
Part IV: Statements designed to examine the importance of auditors' opinion and other information provided in accordance with the old and new format of the audit report.

The questions were made in closed-ended format in form of a statement that is easier to answer. Likert scale was used for the answer options, ranging from being not important (1) to being very important (5) and accordingly for the extent of reliability in lending decision analysis where the answer options were ranging from never (1) to always considered (5). We conducted focused interviews with four loan officers in the process of constructing the questionnaire in order to achieve reliable understandability for the statements related to the new information that is part or considered desirable in the audit report. In the next section we provide the descriptive statistics for the perceived importance and extent of use of financial information and audit report information by corporate loan officers. We have performed non-parametric Chi-square test in order to test whether there is equal probability for any importance to be given by respondents to the investigated financial or auditor's information, in other words whether our respondents were consistent in assessing the surveyed information as important or not for their lending decisions.

4. Results

Most of the respondents were female and had more than 6 years of experience in corporate lending decision making. Cumulatively more than 70% of the respondents were between 31 and 40 years old (see Table 2). The second part of the questionnaire was designed to investigate perceived importance of the component parts of companies' annual report and the extent of use when evaluating loan proposals. It was expected that loan officers will undoubtedly perceive balance sheet and income statement as very important, but we didn't expected that loan officers will give only medium importance to the Management report. Although, respectively 11 and 10 of the 31 respondents perceived the Management report as considerably important and used very often in their analysis, there were also respondents that viewed the report as not important and never used for their decisions. This contradicts the findings of Berry and Robertson (2006) who provided evidence of increased use of projected financial statements and management accounts in lending decision making.

Table 2. Respondents' characteristics

Gender	Frequency	Percent	Experience	Frequency	Percent
Female	20	64.5	less than 3	2	6.5
Male	11	35.5	3-5	4	12.9
Total	31	100	6-10	11	35.5
			more than 10	14	45.2
			Total	31	100

Age	Frequency	Percent
23-30	7	22.6
31-35	15	48.4
36-40	8	25.8
40-	1	3.2
Total	31	100

In respect of disclosed accounting policies and the notes to the financial statements most of the respondents (18 out of 31) considered the information as very important and always used in the analysis, however considerable number of respondents perceived medium or no importance and usability.

Table 3: Descriptive Statistics and Chi square test for the Components of the Annual Report

		Importance (1- not to 5-very important)				Use (1- never to 5-always)				
Components of Annual Report	N	Mean	S.D	Chi square	Sig.	Mean	S.D	Chi square	Sig.	
Balance sheet	31	5.00	0			5.00	0			
Income Statement	31	5.00	0			5.00	0			
Cash flow Statement	31	4.87	.341	17.065	.000	4.65	.755	46.032	.000	*
Management report	31	3.87	.957	5.516	.138	3.48	1.262	6.258	.181	
Accounting policies & other notes to financial statements	31	4.35	.839	8.581	.014	4.13	1.118	28.839	.000	*
Auditor's report	31	4.90	.301	20.161	.000	4.68	.702	46.806	.000	*

*Significant at 1 per cent level

The third part of the questionnaire focuses on perceived importance of selected accounting ratios and suggested type of analysis that uses historical or prospective accounting information. The descriptive statistics and respective Chi-square test results are presented in table 4 below. We conclude that respondents were consistent in evaluating the high importance and usage of liquidity and financial stability ratios. However, respondents were not consistent when they evaluated the importance of projected figures for company's profitability, although this information is very often used in lending decision making. Similar perceptions loan officers have regarding the importance of historical operating cash flow information. Most of the respondents considered it little less important than other surveyed information (mean of 4.41 for importance and 4.28 for use).

Table 4: Descriptive Statistics and Chi square test for Accounting information and Ratios

		Importance (1- not to 5-very important)				Use (1- never to 5-always)				
Ratios	N	Mean	S.D.	Chi square	Sig.	Mean	S.D.	Chi square	Sig.	
Liquiduty										
Current ratio	31	4.68	.653	27.161	.000	4.81	.543	40.323	.000	*
Quick ratio	31	4.61	.667	20.194	.000	4.71	.643	31.326	.000	*
Working capital trend analysis	31	4.45	.810	25.129	.000	4.32	1.045	35.290	.000	*
Financial stability										*
Interest coverage	31	4.84	.374	14.226	.000	4.81	.543	40.323	.000	*
Total debt/equity	31	4.87	.428	45.355	.000	4.84	.583	45.355	.000	*
Interest bearing debt/equity	31	4.45	.888	27.968	.000	4.35	1.082	40.774	.000	*
Long-term debt maturity analysis	31	4.74	.445	7.258	.007	4.52	.811	20.194	.000	*
Profitability										*
Profit margins (i.e. gross, oper., net)	31	4.90	.301	20.161	.000	4.97	.180	27.129	.000	*
Historical trends in profitability	31	4.68	.599	24.065	.000	4.71	.588	27.548	.000	*
Projected future profitability	31	4.35	.755	5.871	.053	4.16	1.068	17.387	.001	*
Cash flows										*
Planned cash flows	31	4.84	.454	40.516	.000	4.65	.755	46.032	.000	*

Long-term debt maturity analysis and planned future cash flows	31	4.81	.402	11.645	.001	4.55	.768	32.871	.000	*
Historical cash flows from operating actitivities	31	4.42	.765	8.968	.011	4.32	1.045	35.935	.000	*
Planned cash flows from operating activities against all loans	31	4.68	.599	24.065	.000	4.52	.890	32.871	.000	*

*Significant at 1 per cent level

Our research shows interesting results for the primary focus of the study, the importance of information contained in the audit report for lending decisions as perceived by corporate loan officers and heads of corporate loan departments. We also wanted to assess the views on newly required information according to new and revised ISA's on audit reporting (Tables 5 and 6). In order to obtain data on lenders' perceptions whether the New Audit Report will satisfy needs of creditors in respect of audit information, we deliberately introduced statements for additional information that could be considered important for creditors but is not required under new ISA's on audit reporting (Table 6).

Corporate lenders rated the importance of main statements in the standard audit report as very high, and these perceptions were consistently shared among all 31 respondents (from 22 to 28 on 6 different statements). This is consistent with the findings of Epstein and Pava (1992), but contradicts the findings of Berry and Robertson (2006) and Bartlett and Chandler(1997) who provided evidence of decrease importance of the audit report.

Table 5: Descriptive Statistics and Chi square test-Audit Report in the old format

		Importance (1- not to 5-very important)				
Statements	N	Mean	S.D.	Chi square	Sig.	
The Auditor stated he is independent or highlighted conditions that threat his independence.	31	4.71	.643	28.323	.000	*
The Auditor expressed an opinion that financial statements give true and fair view of financial condition and results.	31	4.65	.608	20.968	.000	*

The Auditor has identified in his opinion existence of material misstaments in the financial statements	31	4.90	.301	20.161	.000	*
The Auditor expressed unqualified opinion, however emphasized on the going concern of the entity.	31	4.65	.755	46.032	.000	*
The Auditor could not perform appropriate procedures and has given a disclaimer.	31	4.61	.844	46.032	.000	*
The Auditor expressed opinion that financial statements do not give a true and fair view of financial condition and results of the entity.	31	4.84	.523	45.355	.000	*

*Significant at 1 per cent level

Interestingly, our analysis showed the highest mean result (4.9 in table5) for the statement "*The Auditor has identified in his opinion existence of material misstatements in the financial statement*". This can be interpreted that corporate lenders expect to see qualified audit reports for certain financial statements' positions for which material misstatement have been identified. In that sense the audit report is more valuable to lenders and financial information provided in financial statements is more credible for usage in lending decisions.

We continue our analysis in respect of perceived importance of new information content of the Audit Report as required by new and revised ISA's on audit reporting. As shown in table 6 below, loan officers perceived information related to going concern assumption and any material uncertainties for the assumption as highly important for lending decision process, and they were consistent in their evaluation. This contradicts the findings of Elias and Johnston (2001) who found no evidence of information content differences attributable to auditors' explanatory paragraph for going concern in addition to notes disclosure.

Table 6: Descriptive Statistics and Chi square test for the New Audit Report

	Importance (1- not to 5-very important)				
Information content	Mean	S.D.	Chi square	Sig.	
*Information **required** by new ISA's on audit reporting*					
Description of procedures used by auditor to assess whether the entity is a **going concern**.	4.13	.957	13.258	.004	*
Separate information section whether the entity is **going concern** when material uncertainty exists.	4.58	.720	19.806	.000	*
Information on key matters considered during the audit related to most risky and complex areas that can result in material misstatements in financial statements.	4.65	.798	51.452	.000	*

	Importance (1- not to 5-very important)				
Information content	Mean	S.D.	Chi square	Sig.	
Information how the auditor addressed key audit matters.	3.97	1.048	6.548	.088	
The name of the partner of the audit firm responsible for the audit engagement.	3.55	1.261	6.258	.181	
Affirmative statement about the **auditor's independence** and fulfillment of relevant **ethical responsibilities**	3.77	1.359	18.839	.001	*
Information disclosed for the level of **materiality** used during the audit.	3.77	1.087	1.903	.593	
Description of **auditor's procedures** related to the **risk of fraud** in the financial statements.	4.32	.909	20.226	.000	*
*Information **not required** by new ISA's on audit reporting*					
Information in the Audit report for **identified misstatements** been corrected and misstatements for which financial statements are not corrected	4.52	.811	31.839	.000	*
Information on effectiveness of internal controls related to **the process of producing financial information.**	4.10	.978	14.290	.003	*
Information on effectiveness of internal controls related to the **overall operations of the entity.**	4.13	.922	10.935	.012	*
Information on **entity's breach of covenant provisions in loan agreements** related to required financial results and condition.	4.61	.803	45.774	.000	*
*Significant at 1 per cent level					

Also, loan officers considered information on audit procedures related to risk of fraud in financial statements and disclosed information on key matters for auditors as very important. Key audit matters disclosed in the audit report were also perceived as very important and this is consistent with the findings of Sirois *et al.* (2014) and opposite to the findings of Boolaky and Quick (2016). However, less important is the information for the name of the audit partner in the engagement and the level of materiality used. Different loan officers were also inconsistent when evaluating the importance of this type of information disclosed in the audit report (chi-square at 1% significance level).

Concerning information that is not required to be disclosed by the auditor in the audit report prepared according to the requirements of new and revised ISA's on audit reporting, loan officers gave consistently high importance to information related to identified misstatements for which financial statement were corrected or not corrected (mean 4.52). Also, considerably high importance is perceived for disclosed information on entity's breach of debt covenants related to required financial condition and performance. Loan officers were consistent when evaluating information on internal controls related to financial reporting as important but less important than above mentioned information (mean 4.10). Considering information on internal controls related to the overall operations of the entity, respondents gave inconsistent assessments for the importance resulting in a mean result for high importance (mean 4.13).

5. Conclusion

Based on the results from the survey study discussed, we can conclude that published accounting information and traditional accounting ratios remain very important for lenders when arriving at lending decisions. Management information on projected profitability or the Management Report part of the Annual Report is less important when bank loan officers evaluate loan proposals of their clients, which contradicts the findings of recent studies on usefulness of financial information to lenders (Berry & Robertson, 2006). The balance sheet and income statement are considered more important than information on accounting policies used or other information provided in the notes to the financial statements.

Lenders perceive the standard audit report as valuable source of information for lending decisions, regardless of the type of the auditor's opinion. However, lenders are keener to see qualifications in the auditors' reports regarding material misstatements in the financial statements, finding supported in other studies as well (Guiral-Contreras *et al.*, 2007). Most of the incremental information in the New Auditor's Report is perceived as very important, such as information on key matters for the auditor, existence of material uncertainty and auditor's judgement for the going concern and auditor's procedures related to risk of fraud in the financial statements. However, there is still important information that could be provided by auditors, as per lenders perceptions, but disclosure of such information is not required under ISA's new and revised audit reporting standards effective from 2016. Lenders expect to see information on effectiveness of internal controls related to financial reporting. In other jurisdictions, such as US lenders judgments have been also affected by auditor's report on effectiveness of internal controls (Schneider & Church, 2008). Also, information on identified misstatements during the audit for which financial statements were corrected, as well as misstatements for which statements are not being corrected is considered very important. As usually evidenced by researchers of bankers' preferences for financial and audit information, details on eventual breach of debt covenants provided in the audit report are very important.

Similarly to other survey studies, this study has limitations deriving from the method employed in terms of possible non-response bias (Sax *et al.*, 2003). Also, on-line surveys do not provide large samples in comparison to other ways of gathering survey data. Although we have taken appropriate steps while constructing questions and statements to measure the variables, statements bear certain degree of subjectivity. The study does not go into indebt analysis of lenders understanding of certain type of information found or to be found into auditor's report, nor their ability to use and interpret such information in order to improve lending decisions. Respondents of the study have no practical experience with the New Auditor's Report, so future survey research performed on the same focus group could provide evidence of different views for the importance of incremental information provided in the New Auditor's report.

Nevertheless, the study contributes the limited literature so far investigating the impact of the information contained in the New Auditor's Report on lenders decision making and general perceptions in the public about the quality of the audit report of the future and audit expectation gap.

Acknowledgements: the authors thank the reviewer and participants at the 12thAccounting and Management Information Systems (AMIS) International Conference held at the Bucharest University of Economic Studies (June 7-8 2017) and the editor of the Journal of Accounting and Management Information Systems for guidance and support in revising the paper.

References

Anderson, R. & Epstein, M. (1995) "The usefulness of annual reports", *Australian Accountant*, Issue April: 25-28

Asare, S. & Wright, A. (2012) "Investors', auditors', and lenders' understanding of the message conveyed by the standard audit report on the financial statement", *Accounting Horizons*, vol.26(2): 193-217

Bamber, E. M. & Stratton, R. A. (1997) "The information content of the uncertainty-modified audit report: evidence from bank loan officers", *Accounting Horizons*, vol.11(2): 1-11

Bartlett, S. & Chandler, R. (1997) "The corporate report and the private shareholder: Lee and Tweedie twenty years on", *British Accounting Review*, Issue September: 245-261

Berry, A. & Robertson, J. (2006) "Overseas bankers in the UK and their use of information for making lending decisions: Changes from 1985", *British Accounting Review*, vol. 38: 175-191

Boolaky, P. K. & Quick, R. (2016) "Bank directors' perceptions of expanded auditor's report", *International Journal of Auditing*, vol. 20: 158-174

Elias, R. Z. & Johnston, J. G. (2001) "Is there incremental information content in the going concern explanatory paragraph?", *Advances in Accounting*, vol. 18: 105-117

Epstein, M. & Pava, M. (1992) "How useful is the statement of cash flow", *Management Accounting*, vol.74 (1): 52-55

Gay, G. & Schelluch, P. (1993) "The effect of the longform audit report on users' perceptions of the auditor's role", *Australian Accounting Review*, vol.3(2): 2-11

Gold, A., Gronewold, U. & Pott, C. (2012) "The ISA 700 Auditor's report and the audit expectation gap: do explanations matter?", *International Journal of Auditing*, vol. 16: 286-307

Gray, G., Turner, J., Coram, P. & Mock, T. J. (2011) "Perceptions and misperceptions regarding the unqualified auditor's report by financial statement preparers, users and auditors", *Accounting Horizons*, vol. 25(4): 659-684

Guiral-Contreras, A., Gonzalo-Angulo, J. & Rodgers, W. (2007) "Information content and recency effect of the audit report in loan rating decisions", *Accounting and Finance*, vol. 47: 285-304

Hines, R. (1982) "The usefulness of annual reports: the anomaly between the efficient market hypothesis and shareholder surveys", *Accounting and Business Research*, Issue Autumn: 296-309

IAASB (2003) "The independent auditor's report on a complete set of general purpose financial statements", New York: IAASB.

Kohler, A. G., Quick, R. & Willekens, M. (2016) "The new European audit regulation arena: discussion of new rules and ideas for future research", *International Journal of Auditing*, vol.20: 211-214

Litjens, R., Buuren, J. & Vergoossen, R. (2015) "Addressing information needs to reduce the audit expectation gap: evidence from Dutch bankers, audited companies and auditors", *International Journal of Auditing*, vol.19: 267-281

Masters, C. (2015) ACCA [Online] Available at: http://www.accaglobal.com /pk/en/student/sa/news/the-audit-report-evolution.html [Accessed 15 11 2016].

Miller, J. R., Reed, S. & Strawser, R. (1993) "Bank loan officers' perceptions of the new audit report", *Accounting Horizons*, vol.7(1): 39-52

Nair, R. & Rittenberg, L. (1987) "Messages perceived from audit, review and compilation reports: extension to more diverse groups", *Auditing: A Journal of Practice and Theory*, vol. 7 (Fall): 15-38

Niemi, L. & Sundgren, S. (2012) "Are modified audit opinions related to the availability of credit?: Evidence from Finnish SMEs", *European Accounting Review*, vol.21(4): 767-796

Owen, F. & Jones, R. (1994) *Statistics*, London: Pitman

Robertson, J. C. (1988) “Analysts' reactions to auditors' messages in qualified reports”, *Accounting Horizons*, vol.2: 82-89

Sax, L.J., Gilmartin, S.K. & Bryant, A.N. (2003) “Assessing response rates and nonresponse bias in web and paper surveys”, *Research in Higher Education*, vol.44 (4): 409-432

Schneider, A. & Church, B. (2008) “The effect of auditors' internal control opinions on loan decisions”, *Journal of Accounting and Public Policy*, vol.27: 1-18

Simnett, R. & Huggins, A. (2014) “Enhancing the auditor's report: to what extend is there support for the IAASB's proposed changes?”, *Accounting Horizons*, vol.28(4): 719-747

Sirois, L., Bedard, J. & Bera, P. (2014) “The informational value of key audit matters in the auditor's report: evidence from an Eye-tracking study”, Available at *SSRN 2469905*

4

Determinants of demand and supply of accounting and audit services in SMEs

Semiu Babatunde Adeyemi[1,a], Sunday Obah[a] and Ini Etete Udofia[a]

[a] *University of Lagos, Nigeria*

Abstract: The study investigated the factors that determine the demand and supply of accounting and audit services in small and medium enterprises (SMEs), with evidence from Lagos, Nigeria. It also sought to know whether accounting and audit services contribute to the success of SMEs. The study made use of survey design. Using a structured questionnaire, evidence was collected from 380 respondents comprising of 300 SME owner-managers and 80 accounting firms. The data collected were analysed using both the descriptive and inferential statistics. The research findings indicated that owner-managers' characteristics, legal structure, education of managers, possession of accounting skills by managers and capital structure influence demand, while legal structure, attitude towards marketing, Government policy and owner-managers' characteristics influence supply of accounting and audit services. Findings also indicated that services of accountants and auditors have significant influence on the success of SMEs. The study recommended that owner-managers of SMEs should be given proper orientation on the importance of accounting and audit services to the success of their business. It was also recommended that Government should make the preparation and filing of audited accounts of SMEs mandatory, especially in order to render financial assistance to SMEs with a view to enhancing their socio-economic relevance. Accountants were also advised to take their services to the SMEs rather than waiting for the SME owner-managers to voluntarily call for their services.

Keywords: SMEs, accounting and auditing services, theory of inspired confidence, agency theory, Nigeria

---

[1] *Corresponding author:* Semiu Babatunde Adeyemi, Department of Accounting, Faculty of Business Administration, University of Lagos, Nigeria, E-mail: sadeyemi@unilag.edu.ng

1. Introduction

Accounting and audit services are essential to the life of any business that involves the use of financial and human resources. The professional accountant has long been regarded as a trusted and competent business adviser for clients because they provide high quality professional services to meet a wide range of client needs (Keune & Keune, 2015). Blackburn and Jarvis (2010) described Small and Medium Scale Enterprises (SMEs) as heterogeneous groups possessing different size, age, sector, location and growth profiles as well as run by owner-managers with different capabilities and motivations. The SMEs in Nigeria play a significant role in sustaining socio-economic development of the country. Seventy per cent of all job opportunities and wealth formation have been linked with SMEs (Shehu *et al.*, 2013). However, they are filled with challenges such as low level of entrepreneurial skills, poor management policies, constrained access to capital markets, vulnerability to market imperfections, low equity participation from the promoters, shortage of skilled manpower, societal and attitudinal problems, among others (Shehu *et al.*, 2013; Kamyabi & Devi, 2012).

SMEs can improve their operations by engaging the services of professional accountants because the professional accountant can assist SMEs operating in a competitive environment to harmonise operational considerations within long-term plans to enhance their survival (Shehu *et al.*, 2013). However, most SMEs owner-managers often times, do not see the need for these services as they may not be bothered by the issue of information asymmetry. Moreover, they lack basic accounting knowledge and do not see any need to hire professional accountants. They probably regard the amount paid to the accountants for their services as a waste of resources that has the effect of depleting business profits (Dyer & Ross, 2007). Often, these owner-managers wholly provide the business capital, which keeps the firms under no pressure to prepare audited financial statements. They believe that engaging accountants to handle their financial affairs will amount to exposing their businesses to outsiders unnecessarily.

The accountants, on their own part, have not shown keen interest in taking their services to the SMEs. The apathy shown by the SME owner-managers is construed by the accountants as a sign that these owner-managers may not appreciate the value of professional services, and as such, may not be willing or able to patronise their services or they do not have the in-house resources to provide the range of services required (Blackburn & Jarvis, 2010).

Most SMEs are managed by their owners, who do not see the need for proper financial record keeping. They do not understand the control environment in which these SMEs operate. They believe that, as owners, they oversee the daily operations of their businesses and, as such, the possibility of fraud occurring is very remote. Most of them even lack the basic accounting knowledge needed for effective financial management. There is this feeling that, since they manage the affairs of these companies, there is no fear of information asymmetry. They see themselves as both the principal and agent and so, do not see the need for any audit. Expenses on accounting and audit services are seen as financial drains that have the effect of depleting business profits. Moreover, most SME owners provide their business capital without resorting to borrowing. As a result, there is hardly any external pressure for transparency and accountability. To some of them, there is no legal requirement that makes their audit compulsory. This makes it optional for them to engage the services of accountants. As such, these owner-managers are likely to prefer the option of ignoring these services. Also, most employees of SMEs are relations of the owner-managers, which in turn, make the job of auditing the financial statements very tasking. Not minding these problems, researchers have not deemed it worthy to ascertain what brought about this apparent neglect and the possible panacea from the perspective of Nigeria.

Several studies in developed countries have examined the effect of professional accountants' services on SME performance but no research has investigated what determines demand for and supply of accounting and audit services among SMEs in Nigeria. Accounting scholars appear to have neglected this very important issue of the determinants of demand and supply of accounting and audit services in SMEs. As a result, the current study finds relevance in bridging this research gap. The study also sought to know whether the services of accountants contribute to the success of SMEs, and also, whether the owner-managers of SMEs appreciate the importance of these services. The study also investigated the internal and external factors that could cause SME owner-managers to seek the services of accountants and also, those factors that could influence accountants to willingly render their services to SMEs.

The study specifically pursued the following objectives: (1) ascertain the determinants of demand for accounting and audit services among SMEs in Lagos, Nigeria; (2) ascertain the determinants of supply of accounting and audit services among SMEs in Lagos, Nigeria; and (3) determine whether accounting and audit services have significant effect on the success of SMEs in Lagos, Nigeria.

This study reveals several factors that make owner-managers of SMEs to seek or not seek the services of accountants and auditors in their businesses. The recommendations made in this work are expected to improve the demand and supply of accounting and audit services in SMEs and improve the working relationship between accountants and SME owner-managers. With the findings of the study, the owner-managers and operators of SMEs will probably change their perception about the importance of accounting and audit services to the life of their business. The study may also sensitise accountants and auditors to make efforts at making the owner-managers and operators of SMEs see the value of professional accountancy services to the life of their businesses.

The following research questions are formulated to guide the study: (1) Which external and internal factors determine the demand for accounting and audit services among SMEs in Lagos, Nigeria?; (2) To what extent do external and internal factors determine the supply of accounting and audit services among SMEs in Lagos, Nigeria?; (3) What is the significance of accounting and audit services on the success of SMEs in Lagos, Nigeria?

This study was carried out in Lagos, Nigeria focusing accountants in practice and SME owner-managers. The target SMEs include restaurants, pure-water bottling factories, soap and detergents factories, woodwork factories, leather products factories, textiles mills, computer software firms, tailoring and fashion designing outfits, printing presses, fabrication outfits, cassava processing mills, block moulding factories and consultancy services firms. This study focused on small and medium scale enterprises employing between five (5) and fifty (50) full time staff with annual turnover not exceeding five million naira (₦5m) and a total assets investment of less than one million naira (₦1m).

2. Literature review

Evidence from literature reveals that there is no universally agreed definition of an SME across all academic disciplines. This is because no single definition can capture all the dimensions of a small and medium-sized entity, nor can be expected to reflect the differences between entities in different industrial sectors or countries at different levels of development (Nelson & Onias, 2011). The definition of small firm varies from country to country and what may be referred to as small firms in developed economies (such as US, UK and Australia) is classified as medium or even larger firms in developing economies (Padachi, 2012). Different people see SMEs from different perspectives. Ademola *et al.* (2012) reported that Central Bank of Nigeria defined small scale enterprises as all businesses with a total assets investment of less than one million, an annual turnover of less than one million and with a total number of employees of less than fifty.

In Nigeria, the National Economic Reconstruction Fund (NERFUND) sets a maximum limit for small scale industries at 10 million Naira, while Section 37b(2) of the Companies and Allied Matters Act (CAMA, 1990) defined a small scale company as one with an annual turnover of not more than 1 million Naira only, Yahaya *et al.* (2011). The EU has begun to standardize the concept. Its current definition categorizes companies with fewer than 10 employees as “micro”, those with fewer than 50 employees as “small”, and those with fewer than 250 as "medium" (Samson *et al.*, 2012). International Accounting Standards Board (IASB) also described Small and medium-sized entities for the scope of the IFRS for SMEs application as entities that (a) do not have public accountability, and (b) publish general purpose financial statements for external users. Examples of external users include owners who are not involved in managing the business, existing and potential creditors, and credit rating agencies. Small and medium enterprises, in the context of this study is defined as firms employing between five (5) and fifty (50) full time staff, with annual turnover not exceeding five million naira (₦5m) and a total assets investment of less than one million naira (₦1m).

2.1 Importance of SMEs to the Nigerian economy

The importance of SMEs to any economy has severally been documented by many scholars. In the words of Padachi (2012), SMEs are the backbone of an economy as they are a major contributor of job creation and play an important role as efficient providers of intermediate goods and services to large firms. Samson *et al.* (2012) opined that small businesses are important to the Nigerian economy. They are of the view that, as a developing economy, the investment of vast wealth and resources in small businesses and the auditing of their business are very crucial to the financial growth and prosperity of the economy. They further stated that if Nigeria is to reach its full potential in terms of economic and social development, it cannot afford to ignore the importance of quality audit and other relevant accounting services for its indigenous small enterprises. According to Ita (2013), micro, small and medium-sized enterprises (MSMEs) are a key source of employment and economic growth especially in developing countries. It has been recognized that small and medium-sized enterprises (SMEs) play an important role in the economic growth and sustainable development, not only in developing, but also in developed countries (Shehu, 2013).

The role of SMEs in promoting grass root economic growth and equitable and sustainable development is significant. To effectively play this role however, requires that all their activities are properly accounted for by employing the services of accountants and auditors. Ita (2013) posited that there is a positive relationship between the relative size of the SMEs sector and economic growth. SMEs are generally regarded as the engine of economic growth and equitable development in developing economies. They are also perceived as the key to Nigeria's economic growth, poverty alleviation and employment generation. But their unimpressive performance in employment generation in recent years has generated a lot of research interests regarding their challenges and prospects (Mba & Cletus, 2014). Given the position occupied by the SMEs in the Nigerian industrial sector, it is expected that the success of the Nigerian economy would be partly dependent on the success of the SMEs (Onaolapo & Adegbite, 2014).

To ensure that all these positive comments on the importance of SMEs to the growth and development of an economy translates to improved standard of living for the populace, the finances of the SMEs must be properly managed and accounted for. This is better achieved by employing the services of competent finance managers, such as accountants, to assure investors' confidence and guarantee accountability. Moreover, considering that some SME managers are agent-managers, the services of accountants and auditors will serve to lend credibility to the financial statements prepared by management in the minds of the principals and other stakeholders. It will also allay the fear rightfully expressed by the principals and other stakeholders as to whether the managers are acting in their best interest.

2.2 Relevance of accounting and audit to SMEs

Accounting is the measurement, statement or provision of assurance about financial information primarily used by managers, investors and other stakeholders or decision makers to make resource allocation decisions within companies, organizations, as well as public agencies. Accounting is also the process of measuring, communicating and interpreting financial activity (Jayamalathi & Murali, 2009). These researchers opined that typical accounting functions play an important role in businesses to maintain competitive advantages, but that however, some SMEs face problem in handling their accounting functions. A financial audit is a thorough analysis of a firm's past and current financial position designed to verify and evaluate the effectiveness of its financial operations and compliance with management policies. It can help management detect circumstances that could lead to financial problems in the future. A management audit is much broader in scope than a financial audit. A management audit aims at detecting potential managerial problems in the small enterprise that threaten its existence (Samson *et al.*, 2012). Audit in SMEs by small audit companies and individual auditors has its specifics; it is recognized by international and domestic audit regulators (Libuse *et ul.*, 2011).

Accounting systems provide a source of information to owners and managers of SMEs operating in any industry for use in the measurement of financial performance (Belal, 2013). While the performance levels of small businesses have traditionally been attributed to general managerial sectorial factors, such as manufacturing, marketing and operations, accounting systems also have a strong impact on the survival, growth and success of SMEs (Shehu, 2013; Kamyabi & Devi, 2012). A large number of business failures have been attributed to inability of financial managers to plan and control properly the current assets and the current liabilities of their respective firms (Padachi, 2012).

Accounting plays a critical role in the success or failure of contemporary business institutions (Mohammed *et al.*, 2011). Onaolapo and Adegbite (2014) concluded that there is a strong positive relationship between accounting record keeping and performance of small scale enterprises. Accounting records keeping is essential for decision making which invariably affects the performance of SMEs. The importance of internal and external accounting as a source of information for owners and managers of small enterprises and their different stakeholders is steadily growing (Ita, 2013). He also asserted that, though MSMEs play a vital role in economic development, majority of them do not keep complete accounting records to prepare financial statements with some not preparing any financial statements at all because of lack of accounting skill and knowledge and weakness of regulatory enforcement. Nelson and Onias (2011) revealed that SMEs do not keep complete accounting records because of lack of accounting knowledge and the cost of hiring professional accountants. They recommended that the regulators should come up with some SME-specific accounting guidelines and provide a template for capturing accounting information by SMEs. They further recommended that record keeping in SMEs must be made mandatory to improve their accounting practices and increase chances of them formalizing their business operations.

A small enterprise can improve its business operations internally and externally by engaging the services of a professional accountant that may include the auditor to audit the business (Samson *et al.*, 2012). Audits of small and medium scale enterprises have proven to be among the most worrisome for professional accountants because of the inadequacy of the internal controls. The small businesses may not even have kept any records at all but for tax purposes, (Olatunji, 2013). He recommended that accountants involved in the audit of small and medium scale enterprises should adopt methodologies that adequately capture the accounting and reporting needs of the enterprises and comment on their peculiarities, if necessary, in the audit report. Very few of these small businesses have managers who understand a control environment, basic accounting systems, and control procedures. In addition, they typically employ family members in key positions, thereby presenting unique challenges for the auditor (Samson *et al.*, 2012).

By providing accounting system as a business infrastructure, it is supposed to assist small business for achieving competitive advantage (Haryani, 2012). But many entrepreneurs think that employing capable hands to keep adequate data of business operations is the concern of the big business only. Little did they know that good accounting services can help keep their business in sound state (Ademola *et al.*, 2012).

Majority of owners of SMEs do not follow proper accounting procedures in their day to day transactions (Yahaya *et al.*, 2011). The small business owners' perception of business in this regard is very critical. They need not undermine or disregard the inherent advantages of engaging professional services of accountants and auditors if their financial performance is to be guaranteed and public confidence in their business attained (Samson *et al.*, 2012).

The need for an audit stems for the delegation of the authority to manage a business by the principals (owners) to agents (managers). The problem which emerged when owners begin to delegate the running of an entity in which they had invested to managers, and thus sacrificed any involvement in the day-to-day control of the organization, is: can the owners believe the financial report prepared by their managers (Millichamp & Taylor, 2012)? The authors asserted that the report may contain errors; not disclose fraud; be inadvertently misleading; be deliberately misleading; fail to disclose relevant information; and fail to conform to regulations. They also opined that owners of companies must be protected from unscrupulous management who would use the owner's investment for their own benefit and not that of the owner; and abuse of limited liability where companies are deliberately set up for speculative or high risk ventures because the initial investors have very little to lose, and the managers perhaps nothing at all apart from their employment. If later investors are not aware of company activity they could be induced to invest in a project which carries a much greater level of risk than the rewards they might achieve would warrant. Audit helps to reduce these agency costs by helping to protect investors from the actions of predatory managers. The solution to the problem of credibility in reports and accounts lies in appointing independent professionals to investigate the contents of the financial statements and report on their findings.

The purpose of an audit therefore is to enhance the degree of confidence of intended users in the financial statements through the expression of an opinion by the auditor on whether the financial statements are prepared, in all material respects, in accordance with an applicable financial reporting framework. In the case of most general purpose frameworks, that opinion is on whether the financial statements are presented fairly, in all material respects, or give a true and fair view in accordance with the framework (Millichamp and Taylor, 2012).

2.3 Determinants of demand for accounting & audit services in SMEs

For many SME owner-managers, especially those of micro-firms, their business life is often lonely and isolated, and owner-managers seek a confidante to provide advice (i.e., intangible services), but this confidante is not necessarily the accountant (Blackburn *et al.*, 2010). If this is considered to be true, we then, need to ascertain the reason for that and strive to encourage the owner-managers to seek confidante in the accountant, as doing so will guarantee their financial performance and also guarantee public confidence in their affairs.

One of the major issues currently confronting CPAs and SME clients is the lack of authoritative guidance involving the reporting and assurance processes for sustainability reporting (Kimberly *et al.*, 2012). Kamyabi and Devi (2012) reported that the lack of necessary financial skills and resources to perform accounting functions internally increases demand for accounting and audit services by SMEs. Blackburn and Jarvis (2010) found that the inability of SME owners to access expert and specialized knowledge in regulatory matters, decision-making and control, accounts for the demand for outsourcing of accounting and audit services by SMEs.

The growth of the SMEs has a significant impact on the demand for Accounting professionals and their services. Banham and He (2014) conducted a study on the services provided by accounting professionals to SMEs and found that accounting firms rely heavily on services generated from SMEs and vice versa. This implies that as SMEs grow, the demand for accounting services from public practitioners is also expected to increase. In a study by the Accounting and Corporate Regulatory Authority in Singapore on the decline in revenue by Small and Medium practices, it was identified that intense competition from within the profession and from non accountants was a key reason for decline in demand for accounting and audit services in Small and Medium Professional Accounting Practices (SMPs) (ACCA, 2011).

The cost of service, shortage of time, ignorance on the availability of service providers and the range of support services available to them and their benefits were identified as the obstacles influencing SMEs demand for external services (Ismail & King, 2007; Banham & He, 2014; Watson, 2003; Devi & Samujh, 2010).

Some researchers have also suggested that SME owners fear of loss of autonomy and independence when they seek advice or technical information from an external business advisor (Curran & Blackburn, 2000). Shaw (2006) identified that the psychology of owner-managers to avoid showing weakness, the opportunity cost and financial cost of taking on advices were some of the reasons for low demand of audit and accounting services. Dyer and Ross (2008) also identify legal and statutory compliance for most startup businesses, makes it compulsory for SMEs to demand the services of auditors and accountants. Blackburn and Jarvis (2010) conducted a study on the role of SMPs in providing business support to SMEs and identified three major motivations and reasons for SMEs' use of Accountants as Business Advisers as: technical competency of the accountant/ auditor, trust in the owner-manager accountant/auditor relationship, and proximity and responsiveness of the accountant/ auditor.

2.4 Determinants of supply of accounting and audit services to SMEs

The service quality and availability of manpower and skill that will satisfy SMEs needs has significant impact on the supply of accounting and audit services (ACCA, 2011). This need creates a burden on the professional accountant, because in order to provide comprehensive services to SMEs, there must be sufficient staff skilled in the areas of other business functions other than accounting (Devi & Samujh, 2010). The satisfaction of SMEs needs also requires that the accounting curriculum in academic institutions, continuous professional education and development by the professional bodies and other regulatory institutions is comprehensive enough to have a positive impact on the expertise and skills of the Accounting professional (Banham & He, 2014). Diversification of operations and business models/ services, shift to more profitable clients and change of strategy were identified by respondents in Singapore as some of the factors that boost successful revenue and supply of audit and accounting services to SMEs (ACCA, 2011).

2.5 Theoretical framework

The relevant theoretical frameworks adapted to explain the issues in accounting, which could be used to explain and extend existing knowledge are the Limperg's theory of inspired confidence and agency theory.

2.5.1 Limperg's theory of inspired confidence

In 1926, Professor Theodore Limperg of the University of Amsterdam developed a theory known as the Theory of Inspired Confidence, which, eventually became known as the Theory of Rational Expectations (Millichamp and Taylor, 2012). The theory holds that the value of the auditor's report derives from the expert nature of the auditor as an independent, competent professional. It holds that as the business community changes, so the expectation it has of the auditor's function also changes. Limperg held that the work carried out by the auditor should be governed by the rational expectations of those who use their reports so auditors should not disappoint those expectations. Further, auditors should not seek to raise those expectations by any more than the work they do justify. Limperg's theory further states that the usefulness of the auditor's opinion is based on the general understanding society has about the usefulness of audit. Legal considerations aside, the necessity and cost of an audit is borne by the companies because of the need of investors and lenders for reliable information to aid their decision making. If the audit process changed so that it ceased to inspire a uniform level of confidence in society, but instead, inspired different levels of confidence in different users, society's confidence in audit process would decline as the social usefulness of the audit is reduced (Millichamp & Taylor, 2012).

2.5.2 Agency theory

Jensen and Meckling (1976) define an agency relationship as a contract under which one or more persons (the principal(s)) engage another person (the agent) to perform some service on their behalf which involves delegating some decision-making authority to the agent. Agency relationships occur when the principals hire the agent to perform a service on the principals' behalf. Principals commonly delegate decision-making authority to the agents. Problems can arise due to agency operation because of inefficiencies and incomplete information. Consequently, agency theory addresses two fundamental problems.

Dilemma exists because sometimes the agent is motivated to act in his own best interests rather than those of the principal. Problem also arises where the two parties have different interests and asymmetric information (the agent having more information), such that the principal cannot directly ensure that the agent is always acting in its (the principal's) best interests, particularly when activities that are useful to the principal are costly to the agent, and where elements of what the agent does are costly for the principal to observe. Moral hazard and conflict of interest may arise. Indeed, the principal may be concerned with the possibility of being exploited by the agent that he chooses not to enter into a transaction at all, when that deal would have actually been in both parties' best interests. The agency theory is useful for this study because to clear the concerns of the principal, and forestall the differences that could arise as a result of information asymmetry, the services of accountants and auditors are very essential.

Figure 1 (Appendix A) conceptualizes what the demand and supply of accounting and audit services in small and medium enterprises entail. The parties involved in the demand and supply of accounting and audit services in SMEs are the SMEs, who demand the services of accountants and auditors, and the accountants, who supply their services to SMEs. Since it is the SMEs that demand for the services of accountants and auditors, the owners and managers of SMEs are therefore in a better position to supply information on why they do or do not demand such services. Also, since accountants are the people that have the services, they are in a better position to provide information on why they do or do not supply their services to the SMEs. However, a review of existing literature points to various factors that could determine the demand and supply of accounting and audit services in SMEs are the SMEs. The researchers regard these as internal and external factors. The identified factors were statistically tested to ascertain how significantly they influence the demand for the services of accountants and auditors; and the supply of accounting and auditing services to SMEs in Lagos, Nigeria.

3. Research methodology

3.1 Research design

Cross-sectional survey design was adopted for this study. The researchers made use of primary data to arrive at their conclusions. The data used for this study were obtained through the administration of purposely structured questionnaire to respondents. Simple random sampling method was used in selecting the test sample of 380 respondents, in Lagos State of Nigeria, comprising 80 Accounting firms and 300 SME operators. The questionnaire was structured in such a manner as to be able to elicit responses to the items capturing the determinants of demand for accounting and audit services, and the determinants of supply of accounting and audit services, respectively. It also sought to know how significant the services of accountants and auditors are to the success of SMEs in Lagos, Nigeria and whether the managers and owners of SMEs appreciate the importance of accounting and audit services to the life of their business. While the accountants were required to respond to items on the determinants of supply of accounting and audit services, the operators of small and medium scale enterprises were made to respond to items on the determinants of demand for accounting and audit services. To ensure depth in the distribution of the questionnaire, judgment sampling method was used, so that responses could be from experts in SME operations and professionals in the field of accounting and audit profession and give the prospective respondents equal chance of being selected. Copies of the questionnaires were completed by owner-managers of the firms or their appointed representatives. The data collected were summarized using descriptive statistics, such as frequency distribution tables and percentages.

Seven independent variables (owner-managers' characteristics, legal structure of SMEs, experience of managers, level of education of SME owner-managers, possession of accounting skills by SME owner-managers, lukewarm attitude towards audit and capital structure of SMEs) were included on the determinants of demand, while four independent variables (legal structure of SMEs, Accountants' attitude towards marketing, Government policy; and owner-managers' characteristics) were measured as the determinants of supply of accounting and auditing services.

According to Yomere and Agbonifoh (1999), the population of a study is the universe or the totality of the elements of the research from which the researcher draws his sample. In line with this definition, this study made use of two populations which are: (1) the universe or the totality of Small and Medium-Scale Enterprise Operators, and (2) the universe or the totality of professional accounting firms in Lagos, Nigeria. There are 37,531 chartered accountants and 5,290 Small and medium practicing Audit firms (ICAN Annual Report, 2013). The actual

SMEs figures were not officially available as at the time of this study. From the two populations samples were drawn comprising of 80 Accounting firms and 300 SME operators.

This study made use of judgemental sampling technique in arriving at the samples used for the research work. To achieve this, a sample of 80 respondents was selected from all the accounting firms in Lagos, Nigeria and another sample of 300 respondents from the operators of small and medium scale enterprises (SMEs).

The questionnaire was structured in the form of a five-point likert type scale ranging from "strongly agree" to "strongly disagree" as follows: (5 = strongly agree, 4 = agree, 3 = Neutral, 2 = disagree, and 1 = strongly disagree. The respondents were required to indicate the extent of their agreement or disagreement with each of the items on a scale of one (1) to five (5). On this scale, a score of 5 or 4 indicates that the item is perceived to significantly contribute to the demand or supply of accounting and audit services in SMEs in Lagos, Nigeria. A score of 3 or 2 indicates that the item is perceived to slightly contribute to the demand or supply of accounting and audit services in SMEs in Lagos, Nigeria, but not essential, while a score of 1 indicates that the item could be disregarded as being unimportant. Similar scales have been used by Courtis (1992) and were found suitable.

Preliminary tests were carried out by the researcher for the instrument validation. The research instrument was subjected to content validity test to ensure that the content measures the attributes investigated in the research. To achieve this, the initial draft questionnaire was subjected to the constructive inputs of two doctoral degrees and professional accountants in academia who possess at least five (5) years' experience in academic research. This was done to ensure that the information in the questionnaire conveyed the intended meanings and connotations. The comments of these experts were taken into cognizance in preparing a second draft which was subsequently placed on scrutiny and independent critique by two other practicing professional accountants. Afterwards, necessary amendments were incorporated into what became the final instrument.

After the preliminary and expert tests and the required amendments were done, it became imperative to pilot test the instrument to assess the questions and items, the overall questionnaire and the process proposed for its administration. That is, the pilot test was used to finalize the questionnaire. In the preliminary pilot testing, twenty (20) copies of the instrument were administered to SME operators and Accountants in practice who responded to the items as providers and users of accounting and audit services, respectively. The 20 copies of the instrument were retrieved and analysed. Accountants in practice and operators of SMEs were considered relevant because they possess the relevant knowledge for this study.

For the purpose of this study in which a multi-item scale was used, the relationship between constructs and their indications were assessed via the reliability instrument used. The test used for the assessment includes individual item reliability (factor loading) and composite reliability (internal consistency). In order to measure both convergent and discriminant validity, the use of Pearson correlation coefficient was employed. All coefficients exceeded 0.60, an indication that there is appropriate internal consistency of measurement items (Fornell & Larcker, 1981). Bartlett's Test of sphericity was 0.000 which indicates that the correlation among variables is strong and therefore suitable for further analysis. The Cronbach Alpha statistics is 0.743 for 12 items. The result was considered satisfactory for the study.

3.6 Model development and statistical tools of analysis

The dependent variable in this study is accounting and audit services while the independent variables are demand related and supply related. If the independent variables are represented by ''X'' and the dependent variable by ''Y'', then, the relationship between an independent variable (X) and a dependent variable (Y), can be represented by the formula below:

$$Y = \beta_0 + \beta_1 X + u \quad \ldots (1)$$

Where

- Y = Accounting and Audit Services (Bookkeeping, Audit, Taxation, Cost and Management Accounting)
- X = demand of accounting and auditing services;
- S = supply of accounting and auditing services
- β_0 = the level of demand and supply without any external influence;
- β_1 = the effect of any external influence on demand and supply with changes on each independent variable;
- u = the "noise" term reflecting other factors that influence demand and supply.

$$Y = \int(\beta_0 + \beta_1 X_i + \beta_2 S_i + u) \quad \ldots (2)$$

Where:

β_0 = the intercept

X = Independent variables of demand, comprised of:

1. Owner-managers' Characteristics (X_1);
2. Legal Structure (X_2)
3. Experience of managers (X_3)
4. Education of managers (X_4)
5. Possession of accounting skills by managers (X_5)
6. Capital Structure (X_6)
7. Lukewarm attitude towards audit (X_7)

S = independent variables of supply, comprising:

1. Legal structure (S_1)
2. Attitude towards marketing (S_2)
3. Government policies & regulations (S_3)
4. Owner-managers' Characteristics (S_4)

$$Y = \beta_0 + \beta_1 (X_1) + \beta_2 (X_2) + \beta_3 (X_3) + \beta_4 (X_4) + \beta_5 X_5 + \beta_6 X_6 + \beta_7 (X_7) + ...U_i \quad ... (3)$$

$$Q = \beta_0 + \beta_1 (S_1) + \beta_2 (S_2) + \beta_3 (S_3) + \beta_4 (S_4) + \ ...U \quad ... (4)$$

3.7 Statistical tools/analytical procedure

Both the descriptive and inferential (analytical) statistics were used for the purpose of this study. The descriptive statistical tools used are frequency distribution tables, descriptive statistics tables and percentages. The tables were used to depict the distribution of respondents along age, sex, grade level, educational qualifications, knowledge of the need for accounting and audit. They were also used to depict the frequency of the various responses. Also, the inferential statistical tool used is regression analysis. Finally, using Statistical Package for Social Sciences (SPSS) version 20, an analysis of the responses to items in the questionnaire was made.

4. Results analysis

Primary data were used for this analysis. Copies of the structured questionnaire were distributed to three hundred and eighty (380) respondents. Of this number, three hundred and twenty six (326) were validly completed and returned. Two hundred and sixty two (262) of these respondents (SMEs) answered questions relating to the demand for accounting and audit services, while sixty four (64) respondents (accounting firms) answered questions on the supply of accounting and audit services.

4.1 Demographic information

Information about respondents' gender, academic qualifications, membership of professional bodies, working experience and positions held by respondents in their various organizations were collected and summarized in frequency tables as follows:

Table 1. Gender

	Frequency	Percent	Valid Percent	Cumulative Percent
Male	197	60.3	60.3	60.3
Female	129	39.7	39.7	100.0
Total	326	100.0	100.0	

Table 1 shows the distribution of respondents according to their gender. It shows that 197 respondents, representing 60.3% were males, while 129 (39.7%) were female respondents.

Table 2. Academic qualification

	Frequency	Percent	Valid Percent	Cumulative Percent
BSc	230	70.6	70.6	70.6
MSc	75	23.0	23.0	93.7
Others	21	6.3	6.3	100.0
Total	326	100.0	100.0	

Table 2 depicts the academic qualifications of respondents. It indicates that two hundred and thirty (230) of the respondents, representing 70.6% had first degree, seventy five of the respondents (23%) had second degree, while the remainder had other qualifications such as first school leaving certificate, SSCE, etc.

Table 3. Descriptive statistics for the demand of accounting services

	N	Min.	Max.	Mean	Std. Deviation
Demand_for_accounting_services	262	40.00	44.00	42.7290	1.05366
Characteristics_determine_demand	262	40.00	44.00	42.7863	1.02091
Legal_structure_determines_demand	262	40.00	44.00	42.8435	.97592
capital_structure_determines_demand	262	40.00	44.00	42.9160	.97900
experience_of_manager_influences_demand	262	40.00	44.00	42.7176	1.03038
education_of_manager_affects_demand	262	40.00	44.00	42.7786	1.03049
accounting_skills_affect_demand	262	40.00	44.00	42.7634	1.09217
lukwarm_attitude_affects_demand	262	40.00	44.00	42.8053	.95306
The services of Accountants and Auditors have significant effect on the success of SMEs.	262	40.00	44.00	42.7863	1.02091
Audited Financial Statements increase the confidence of stakeholders in management's stewardship	262	40.00	44.00	42.8435	.97592
SME owner-managers know the importance of accounting & audit services	262	40.00	44.00	42.9160	.97900
Audit assures the reliability of information contained in the financial statements.	262	40.00	44.00	42.7176	1.03038
Valid N (listwise)	262				

Table 3 depicts the descriptive statistics for the demand for accounting and audit services. It indicates that 44 respondents, believe that owner-managers' characteristics, legal structure of SMEs, level of education of SME owner-managers, possession of accounting skills by SME owner-managers, capital structure of SMEs and lukewarm attitude towards audit by SME owner-managers determine the demand for accounting and audit services, in Lagos, Nigeria. On the average, 43 respondents share this believe. 1% deviation can occur among the respondents, either positively or negatively.

The table further shows that 44 respondents believe that the services of accountants and auditors will positively affect the success of SMEs; that audited financial statements increase the confidence of stakeholders in management's stewardship; that SME owners and managers know the importance of accounting and audit services; and that audit assures the reliability of information contained in the financial statements. Also, 1% deviation can occur among the respondents, either positively or negatively. On the average, 43 respondents share this belief.

Table 4. Descriptive statistics for the supply of accounting services

	N	Min.	Max.	Mean	Std. Deviation
Supply_of_accounting_services	64	40.00	44.00	42.6563	1.07229
Audit fees affect supply of accounying & audit services	64	40.00	44.00	42.5938	1.12290
Lack of proper marketing affects supply of accounting & audit services	64	41.00	44.00	42.8125	.94070
Owner-managers' characteristics affect supply of accounting & audit services	64	40.00	44.00	42.9844	.89960
Legal structure affects suppy of accounting & audit services	64	40.00	44.00	42.9063	.83035
Valid N (listwise)	64				

Table 4 represents the descriptive statistics for the supply of accounting and audit services to SMEs in Lagos, Nigeria. It shows that 44 respondents believe that audit fees, lack of proper marketing, owner-managers' characteristics, and legal structure of SMEs affect the supply of accounting and audit services to SMEs in Lagos, Nigeria. Averagely, 43% of the respondents have this belief. 1% deviation can occur among the respondents for audit fees, 94% for lack of proper marketing, 90% and 83% deviations for owner-managers' characteristics, and legal structure of SMEs, respectively.

In order to respond to the first research question concerning Which internal and external factors determine the demand for accounting and audit services by SMEs in Lagos regression analysis is employed, and the results are reported in Table 5.

Table 5. Regression result on demand for accounting and auditing services

PANEL A

Regression Statistics	
Multiple R	0.86242
R Square	0.74376
Adjusted R Square	0.71054
Standard Error	20.68263
Dublin-Watson	1.729
Observations	262

PANEL B

ANOVA

	Df	*SS*	*MS*	*F*	*Sig. F*
Regression	30	67048.746	9578.392	22.391	0.0000
Residual	228	23099.641	427.771		
Total	258	90148.387			

PANEL C

	Coefficients	*Standard Error*	*t Stat*	*p-value*	
Intercept	82.2526	32.8070	2.5072	0.0152	*
Owner-managers characteristics (X1)	30.8383	7.3298	4.2073	0.0001	**
Legal Structure affect the demand (X2)	21.0861	7.7829	2.7093	0.0090	**
Experience of Managers affects demand (X3)	2.9845	8.2413	0.3621	0.7187	NS
Education of Managers affects demand (X4)	23.1043	6.3965	3.6120	0.0007	**
Accounting Skills affects their demand (X5)	18.1954	7.6685	2.3727	0.0212	*
Capital Structure affect their demand (X6)	22.3874	6.1926	3.6152	0.0007	**
lukewarm Attitude towards Audit (X7)	-16.1131	5.9489	-2.7086	0.0090	**

Table 5 presents the result of the linear regression analysis of demand for accounting services as dependent variable (Y), with Owner-managers characteristics (X_1), Legal Structure affect the demand (X_2), Experience of Managers affects demand (X_3), Education of Managers of affects demand (X_4),

Accounting Skills affects their demand (X_5), Capital Structure affect their demand (X_6) and lukewarm Attitude towards Audit (X_7) as independent variables. The estimated linear model then is as follows:

$$Y = 82.2526 + 30.8383X_1 + 21.0861X_2 + 2.9845X_3 + 23.1043X_4 + 18.1945X_5 + 22.3874X_6 - 16.1131X_7 \quad ...(5)$$

Table 5 shows that all the independent variable, except the lukewarm Attitude towards Audit, had positive coefficients. The F–statistics was significant at a probability level of less than 1%, implying that the specified independent variables significantly contributed jointly to the demand for accounting and auditing services. Specifically however, all the independent variables except Experience of Managers had significant effect on the demand for accounting and audit services. The R-Square shows that the independent variables account for 74% of changes in the demand for accounting and audit services. Experience of managers had a p-value of 0.7187, therefore did not have significant effect on the demand for accounting and audit services.

Table 5 shows that all the independent variable, except the lukewarm attitude towards audit, had positive coefficients. The F–statistics was significant at a probability level of less than 1%, implying that the specified independent variables significantly contributed jointly to the demand for accounting and auditing services. Specifically however, all the independent variables, except Experience of Managers, had significant effect on the demand for accounting and audit services.

The finding in this study agrees with that in Samson *et al.* (2012), which states that the wrong perception and inexperience of small business owners, operators and managers on the audit of a business constitute negative impact on auditors in providing accounting and audit services for small scale businesses in Nigeria. Also, the findings of Nelson and Onias (2011) that SMEs do not keep complete accounting records because of lack of accounting knowledge supports our finding that possession of accounting skills and education of managers affect the demand for accounting and audit services by SMEs in Lagos, Nigeria. Furthermore, our position that 'educational level of Owner-managers' affect their demand for accounting and audit services agrees with the position of Padachi (2012) that important variables which discriminate between firms having accounting systems and firms with minimal accounting systems are the education level of owner-managers.

In order to respond to the second research question regarding the extent do internal and external factors determine the supply of accounting and audit services to SMEs a regression analysis is also performed.

Table 6. Regression result on supply of accounting and auditing services

PANEL A

Regression Statistics	
Multiple R	0.6735
R Square	0.6476
Adjusted R Square	0.6441
Standard Error	9.9118
Dublin-Watson	1.734
Observations	64

PANEL B
ANOVA

	Df	*SS*	*MS*	*F*	*Sig. F*
Regression	4	104889.528	26222.382	266.9101	0.0000
Residual	59	5796.4097	98.2442		
Total	63	110685.938			

PANEL C

	Coefficients	*Standard Error*	*t Stat*	*p-value*	
Intercept	247.8359	8.0151	30.9210	0.0000	**
Legal structure (S_1)	-10.1979	2.9229	-3.4890	0.0009	**
Attitude towards market (S_2)	24.0076	3.1714	7.5700	0.0000	**
Government policy (S_3)	19.6009	5.3613	3.6560	0.0005	**
Owner-managers characteristics (S_4)	16.1675	2.8879	5.5983	0.0000	**

Table 6 presents the result of the linear regression analysis of supply of accounting services as dependent variable (Q), with Legal structure (S_1), Attitude towards market (S_2), Government policy (S_3) and Owner-managers characteristics (S_4) as the independent variables. The estimated linear model then is as follows:

$$Q = 247.8359 - 10.1979 S_1 + 24.0076 S_2 + 19.6009 S_3 + 16.1675 S_4$$

Table 6 (Panel A) shows that all the independent variable, except the legal structure of SMEs, had positive coefficients. The F–statistics was significant at a probability level of less than 1%, implying that the specified independent variables significantly contributed jointly to the supply of accounting and auditing services.

Specifically however, all the independent variables, with p-value of less than 1%, had significant effect on the supply of accounting and auditing services among the firms studied. The R-Square was 0.6476, indicating that the independent variables had approximately 65% contribution to the changes in the supply of accounting and auditing services.

Table 6 (Panel C) shows that all the independent variables, except the legal structure of SMEs, had positive coefficients. The F–statistics was significant at a probability level of less than 1%, implying that the specified independent variables significantly contributed jointly to the supply of accounting and auditing services. Specifically however, all the independent variables, with p-value of less than 1%, had significant effect on the supply of accounting and auditing services among the firms studied.

Based on the regression result, the findings are consistent with *Samson et al.* (2012) which posited that the fear of audit is also a major characteristic of small business owners that inhibit possible audit of small businesses. Also, our finding that attitude towards marketing affects the supply of accounting and audit services agrees with the position of Robert (2011) that in order to respond to the increasing demand for specialized services, and adding value beyond compliance services to their SME clients, it may be argued that accountants need to create an opportunity to enable them capture the market share that is available through the pre-existing relationship of trust.

The tests for the third research question regarding the significance of accounting and audit services success of SMEs are conducted as to exam the following hypothesis: Accounting and audit services do not have significant effect on the success of SMEs in Lagos, Nigeria.

Table 7. Regression result on importance of accounting and audit services

Panel A

Regression Statistics	
Multiple R	0.94342
R Square	0.88876
Adjusted R Square	0.88554
Standard Error	12.38114
Dublin-Watson	1.693
Observations	262

PANEL B

ANOVA	*df*	*SS*	*MS*	*F*	*Sig. F*
Regression	8	68.204	34.102	234.754	0.0000
Residual	249	8.571	0.145		
Total	257	76.774			

PANEL C	*Coefficients*	*Standard Error*	*t Stat*	*p-value*
Intercept	52.2256	27.7270	3.6042	0.0093
Accounting services have sig effect on success (a_1)	33.2383	7.5214	1.1023	0.0001
Audit increases shareholders' confidence(a_2)	13.0861	5.6329	0.8075	0.0070
SME owners know importance of Audit (a 3)	6.5545	7.4313	0.2547	0.5717
Audit assures information reliability (a 4)	18.7053	3.2565	3.5520	0.0006

Table 7 presents the result of the linear regression analysis of demand for accounting services as dependent variable (Y), with Services of Accountants have sig effect on success (a_1), Audit increases shareholders' confidence(a_2), SME owners know importance of Audit (a_3), Audit assures information reliability (a_4), as independent variables. The estimated linear model then is as follows:

$$Y=52.2256+33.2383a_1+13.0861a_2+6.5545a_3+18.7053a_4$$

The Table shows that all the independent variable had positive coefficients. The F–statistics was significant at a probability level of less than 1%, implying that the specified independent variables significantly contributed jointly to the importance of accounting and auditing services. Specifically however, all independent variables with the exception of SME owners know the importance of audit (a3), with p-value of less than 1%, had significant effect on the importance attached to accounting and auditing services among the firms studied. The R Square was 0.88876, indicating that the independent variables had approximately 89% contribution to the amount of importance attached to accounting and auditing services.

Table 7 shows that services of accountants had significant effect on SME success, since it had a positive coefficient of 33.2383. The F-statistics was significant at a probability level of less than 1%. The p-value was also less than 1%, implying that accounting and audit services did significantly contribute to the success of the firms studied. Based on the regression output, the null hypothesis is rejected and the alternative retained. This finding is consistent with Samson *et al.* (2012) that the role of accounting and audit is crucial to the well-being of small business entities. It also agrees with Onaolapo and Adegbite (2014) who concluded that there is a strong positive relationship between accounting record keeping and performance of small scale enterprises. They further stated that the finding implies that accounting record keeping affects performance of small scale businesses. According to them, accounting record keeping increases the chances of businesses operating and achieving success. Olatunji (2013) also concluded that an effective accounting system in small and medium scale enterprises has profound impact on the corporate performance. In the same vein, the findings of Mohammed *et al.* (2011) shows that good accounting and control system could assist in evaluating the performance of an organization and its managers. SMES with proper books of accounts are often capable of attracting external financing easily than those with poor or no records.

The findings of this study agrees confirm Limperg's theory of inspired confidence which suggests that the demand for audit services is a direct consequence of the participation of third parties in a firm who demand accountability from the management in return for their investment. These third parties depend on the activities of accountant and auditors for increased confidence in the management and absolute assurance of the reliability of information provided by management. No third party will want to invest in a firm that is not successful and the assurance of this success comes from the report of auditors. Our finding supports the fact that accountability is guaranteed through the issuance of periodic audited financial reports, which ultimately attracts investment, leading to the firm's success.

In relation to the agency theory, where the SME is managed by an agent, the activities of accountants and auditors help to lend credibility to the reports of management, thereby eliminating or diminishing information asymmetry. It gives assurance to the principal that the agent has acted in the principal's best interest. Moral hazard and conflict of interest are also eliminated because the independent auditors have made input in the final report which lends more credibility to the reports and boosts the confidence of the principal and other stakeholders. Indeed, the principal's concern at the possibility of being exploited by the agent is doused by the input of the auditors. The assurance gained through the activities of the auditors enables third parties to invest in the firm, leading to business success.

5. Conclusion

This study sets out to investigate the determinants of demand and supply of accounting and audit services among small and medium scale enterprises (SMEs) in Lagos, Nigeria. The main objective of the study was to empirically ascertain the determinants of demand and supply of accounting and audit services among small and medium scale enterprises (SMEs) in Lagos, Nigeria and to establish whether SME owner-managers know the importance of such services to their business success. Using survey design, views were collected from respondents which, after analysis, revealed that owner-managers' characteristics, legal structure of SMEs, level of education of SME owner-managers, possession of accounting skills by SME owner-managers and capital structure of SMEs determine the demand, while legal structure of SMEs, Accountants' attitude towards marketing, Government policy and owner-managers' characteristics determine the supply of accounting and audit services among SMEs in Lagos, Nigeria. It was also revealed that accounting and audit services significantly contribute to the success of SMEs in Lagos, Nigeria. Finally, the study revealed that SME owner-managers do not know the importance of accounting and audit services to the life of their business.

The finding that services of accountants and auditors significantly contribute to the success of SMEs is consistent with the finding of Samson *et al.* (2012) the role of accounting and audit is crucial to the well-being of small business entities. It also agrees with the findings of Onaolapo and Adegbite (2014) that there is a strong positive relationship between accounting records keeping and performance of small scale enterprises.

This study also revealed that SME owner-managers do not know the importance of accounting and audit services to the life of their business. Again, this agrees with the findings of Ademola *et al.* (2012) that, employing capable hands to keep adequate data of business operations is the concern of the SME business only. Existing works also agree with some of the revealed determinants of demand and supply of accounting and audit services among SMEs in Lagos, Nigeria. For example, the finding of Samson et al., (2012) that the wrong perception and inexperience of small business owners, operators and managers on the audit of a business constitute negative impact on auditors in providing accounting and audit services for small scale businesses in Nigeria agrees with our finding that owner-managers' characteristics determine the demand and supply of accounting and audit services among SMEs in Lagos, Nigeria. Also, the finding of Nelson and Onias (2011) that SMEs do not keep complete accounting records because of lack of accounting knowledge conforms with our findings that level of accounting skills and education of SME owner-managers affect the demand for accounting and audit services in SMEs in Lagos, Nigeria.

Accounting and audit services are essential to the overall success of small and medium enterprises in Lagos, Nigeria. Accounting services help to guarantee the dissemination of vital information about the accountability and stewardship of management to investors and other stakeholders. On its own part, auditing lends credibility to the information contained in the financial statements. However, the owner-managers of SMEs do not recognize this fact. The demand of the services of auditors and accountants is influences by several factors which include, owner-managers' characteristics, legal structure of SMEs, level of education of SME owner-managers, possession of accounting skills by SME owner-managers and capital structure of SMEs. The factors that determine the supply of accounting and audit services among SMEs in Lagos, Nigeria were revealed to include legal structure of SMEs, Accountants' attitude towards marketing, Government policy and owner-managers' characteristics.

Based on the findings of this research work, it is recommended that owner-managers of SMEs should be properly orientated on the importance of accounting and audit services to the life of their business. Also, owner-managers of SMEs should conscientiously correct their perception of the importance of accounting and audit services to the success of their business. Government should make audit of the financial statements of SMEs mandatory, rather than leaving it at the discretion of their owner-managers. Accountants should take their services the SMEs and not sit back, expecting them to voluntarily call for their (Accountants) services. Finally, owner-managers of SMEs should endeavor to acquire necessary education and accounting skills, as this will make them better able to realize the importance of accounting and audit services to their business operations.

Further studies should implement a research design that surveys the views of more SME operators and more accounting firms. The factors that could possibly affect the demand and supply of accounting and audit services should be expanded to include trust, external pressure, percentage of employees that are members of owners' families, willingness of SMEs to settle audit fees, and availability of trained accountants.

In considering the outcome of this study, it is recommended that limitations that are peculiar to research in developing countries, such as ours, should be considered. Such limitations include scarcity of accurate data, reticence on the part of respondents, and unstable personal characteristics of subjects. However, the research design made frantic efforts to control for these limitations.

References

Ademola, G. O., Samuel O. J. & Ifedolapo O. (2012) "The roles of record keeping in the survival and growth of small scale enterprises in Ijumu Local Government Area of Kogi State", *Global Journal of Management and Business Research*, vol. 12(13): 55-66

Association of Chartered Certified Accountants (ACCA) (2011) "Small and medium sized public accounting practices in Singapore- bridging the current to the future", A research project commissioned by the Accounting and Corporate Regulatory Authority, White paper, available online at https://www.acra.gov.sg/uploadedFiles/Content/PublicAccountants /ProfessionalResources/Conference_Materials/2011/SmallandMediumSized PublicAcctPractice.pdf

Banham, H. & He, Y. (2014) "Exploring the relationship between accounting professionals and small and medium enterprises (SMEs)", *Journal of Business & Economics Research,* vol. 12(3): 209-214

Belal, Y. A. S. (2013) "The use of accounting information by small and medium enterprises in south district of Jordan", *Research Journal of Finance and Accounting,* vol. 4(6) 169-175

Blackburn, R.B., Carey, P. & Tanewski, G. A. (2010) "Business advice to SMEs: professional competence, trust and ethics", Certified Accountants Educational Trust (London)

Blackburn, R. & Jarvis, R. (2010) "The role of small and medium practices in providing business support to small and medium-sized enterprises", Information Paper, International Federation of Accountants, April.

Companies and Allied Matters Act (1990) Lagos: Government Press

Courtis, J. K. (1992) "The reliability of perception-based annual report disclosure studies", *Accounting and Business Research,* vol. 23(89): 31-43

Curran, J. & Blackburn, R. (2000) "Panacea or white elephant? A critical examination of the proposed new small business service and response to the DTI consultancy paper", *Regional Studies*, vol. 34(2): 181-206

Devi, S.S. & Samujh, R. H. (2010) "Accountants as providers of support and advice to SMEs in Malysia", ACCA Research Report no. 118, available online at https://www.acca.global.com/content/dam/acca/global/PDF-technical/small-business/rr-118-001.pdf

Dyer, L.M. & Ross, C.A. (2007) "Advising the Small Business Client", *International Small Business Journal*, vol. 25(2): 130-151

Dyer, L.M. & Ross, C.A. (2008) "Seeking advice in a dynamic and complex business environment; impact on the success of small firms", *Journal of Developmental Enterpreneurship*, vol. 13(2): 133-149

Fornell, C. & Larcker, D.F. (1981) "Evaluating structural equation models with unobservable variables and measurement error", *Journal of Marketing Research*, vol. 18 (1): 39-50

Haryani, E. (2012) "Accounting system for Small Business in Indonesia (Case Study of Convection Business Tinkirlor Village)", *Journal of Arts, Science and Commerce,* vol. 3(2):104-111

IASB – IFRS Foundation (2009) IFRS for SMEs, Downloadable from http://www.ifrs.org.

ICAEW (2008) *Comprehensive review of the IFRS for SMEs,* Downloadable at www.icaew.com/~/.../IFRS/icaew-rep-ifrs-for-smes-v11-website.pdf

Institute of Chartered Accountants of Nigeria (2014) *Annual Report and Accounts*, 2013

Ismail, N.A. & King, M. (2007) "Factors influencing the alignment of accounting information systems in small and medium sized Malaysian manufacturing firms", *Journal of Information Systems and Small Business*, vol. 1(1-2): 1-20

Ita, S. L. (2013) "Accounting Practices among Micro, Small and Medium-Sized Enterprises (MSMEs) in Bandung, Indonesia", *The 2nd IBSM, International Conference of Business and Management, Chiang Mai-Bangkok.*

Jayamalathi, J. & Murali, R. (2009) "Outsourcing of accounting functions amongst SME companies in Malaysia: An exploratory study", *Journal of Accounting, Business and Public Interest,* vol. 8(2): 96-114

Jensen, M. C. & Meckling, W.H. (1976) "Theory of the firm: Managerial behavior, agency costs and ownership structure", *Journal of Financial Economics*, vol. 3(4): 305-360

Kamyabi, Y. & Devi, S. (2012) "The impact of advisory services on Iranian SME performance: an empirical investigation of the role of professional accountants", *South African Journal of Business Management*, vol. 43(2): 61-72

Keune, M. & Keune, T. (2015) "The role of small and medium practices in providing business support to small and medium-sized enterprises", IFAC Information Paper, International Federation of Accountants

Libuse, M., Marie, P., Jiri, S., Adela, D., Bohuslava, K. & Dana, D. (2011) "Auditing of SMEs: Issues Caused by International Harmonization of Financial Reporting (From Czech Perspective)", *International Journal of Mathematical Models and Methods in Applied Ssciences*, vol. 5(3): 517-524

Limperg Institute (1932) "The social responsibility of the auditor. A basic theory on the auditor's function", University of Amsterdam, Amsterdam, The Netherlands, Limperg Institute

Mba, O. A. & Cletus, I. E. (2014) "Issues, challenges & prospects of Small and Medium Scale Enterprises (SMEs) in Port Harcourt City, Nigeria", *European Journal of sustainable Development,* vol. 3(1): 101-114

Millichamp, A. & Taylor, J. (2012) *Auditing*, Cengage Learning

Mohammed, A. John, E. & Joshua, A. (2011) "E-Accounting practices among Small and Medium Enterprises in Ghana", *Journal of Management Policy and Practice,* vol. 12(4): 146-155

Nazri, M. (2010) "A standard for SME financial reporting in: SME Toolkit Malaysia", International Finance Corporation

Nelson, M. & Onias, M. (2011) "Accounting practices of SMEs in Zimbabwe: An investigative study of record keeping for performance measurement (a case Study of Bindura)", *Journal of Accounting and Taxation,* vol. 3(8): 171-181

Olatunji, T. E. (2013) "The impact of accounting system on the performance of small and medium scale enterprises in Nigeria – a survey of SMEs in Oyo State – Nigeria", *International Journal of Business and Management Invention,* vol. 2(9): 13-17

Onaolapo, A. A. & Adegbite, T. A. (2014) "The analysis of the impact of accounting records keeping on the performance of Small Scale enterprises", *International Journal of Academic Research in Business and Social Sciences,* vol. 4(1): 1-17

Padachi, K. (2012) "Factors affecting the adoption of formal accounting systems by SMEs", *Business and Economic Journal,* vol.1

Samson, A. A., Mary, J., Clement, E. O. & Sule, U. V. (2012) "Demand and supply of accounting and audit services to Small Scale Business in Nigeria", *Asian Journal of Business Management,* vol. 4(1): 75-80

Shaw, E. (2006) "Small firm networking: An insight into contents and motivating factors", *International Small Business Journal,* vol. 24(1): 5-29

Shehu, A.M., Aminu, I.M., Mat, N.K.N., Nasiru, A., Johnson, P.O.M., Tsagem, M.M. and Jura, K.M. (2013) "The mediating effect between some determinants of SME performance in Nigeria", *Management*, vol. 3(4): 237-242

Statistical Package for Social Sciences Version 20. IBM.

Watson, J. (2003) "The potential impact of accessing advice on SME failure rates", Paper presented at the Small Enterprise Association of Australia and New Zealand 16th Annual Conference, Ballarat, 28 September

Webb, K.J., Hodge, T.G & James, H. & Thompson, J.H. (2012) "Small Business sustainability: What is CPA's Role?", *International Journal of Business and Social science,* vol. 3(12): 1-13

Yahaya, K. A., Osemene, O. F. & Salman, R. T. (2011) "Improving the accounting practice adopted by owners of small and medium-scale enterprises in Kwara State, Nigeria", *British Journal of Economics, Finance and Management Sciences*, vol. 2(1): 21-30

Yomere, G. O. & Agbonifoh, B. A. (1999) *Research methodology in the social sciences*, Benin City: Uniben press

APPENDIX A. Conceptual model for studying determinants of demands and supply for accounting and auditing services by SMEs

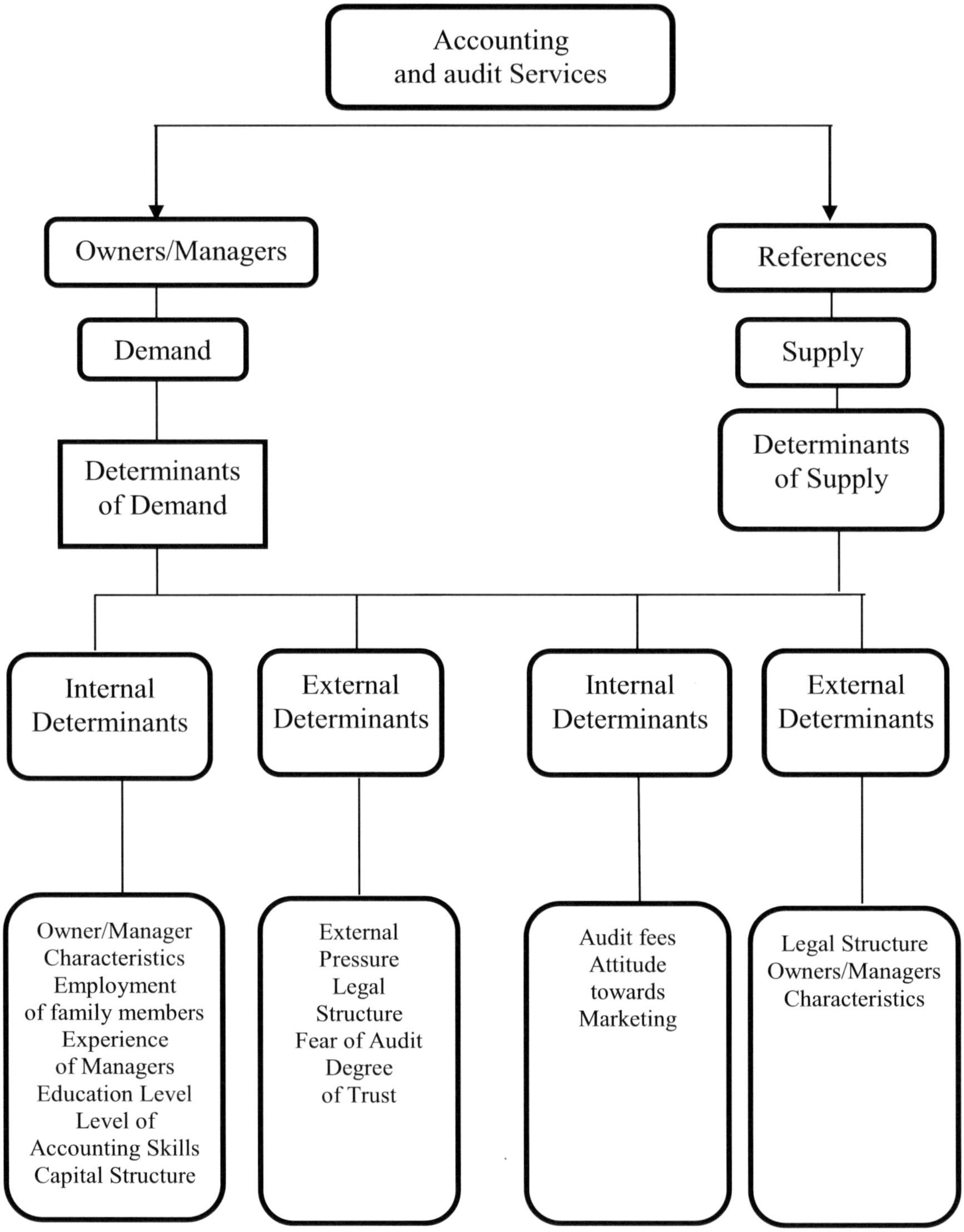

5

Country- specific characteristics influencing Websites based information disclosure practices

Walid Khoufi[a] and Dhouha Khrifech[a, 1]

[a] *University of Sfax, Tunisia*

Abstract: This paper aims to examine and explain the Websites- based financial disclosure practices differences between developed European countries. The development of Internet financial reporting (IFR), as a new corporate reporting practice, was rapidly exploited by large listed companies in the world. A number of accounting research was analyzed the development of online reporting in various countries and they showed that firm specific incentives are the most important factors explaining the IFR practices, however, there was ignored the importance from the politico-socio conditions, as others factors influencing the IFR practices differences (as a accounting practices). As a refinement of Gray (1988)' framework and an extension of Debrency *et al.* (2002) model, this study explore an empirical investigation validating the influence of culture, institutional factors on the financial disclosure level through corporate Websites in France, Germany, Italy, Netherlands, Spain and UK. It reveals the importance of technological and media presentation format as Web- based communication index component. The findings showed that environmental factors were significantly related to Websites technology index and economic development is an important factor determining the Websites financial disclosure practices differences.

Keywords: Financial disclosure practices, corporate Websites, external environment, 2004/109/CE directive.

---

[1] *Corresponding authors*: Governance, Finance and Accounting Laboratory, Faculty of Economic and Management, University of Sfax; Street of the Airport Km 4, 3018, Sfax, Tunisia; *email addresses*: walid.khoufi@yahoo.fr; khrifech.dhouha@gmail.com

1. Introduction

Since 1990's years, traded companies in various countries utilize the *World Wide Web* ("*WWW*") as new support of corporate information publication and they adopt the "Internet financial reporting" (IFR) practices, which refers to "the public reporting of operating and financial data by a business enterprise via the World Wide Web or related Internet-based communications medium" (Lymer *et al.*, 1999: 2). In this sense, IFR was reviewed as a type of voluntary disclosure (Ashbaugh *et al.*, 1999; Oyelere *et al.*, 2003; Poon *et al.*, 2003), implying that the Web content is unregulated and largely discretionary.

IFR was been enabled by the eXtensible Business Reporting Language (*XBRL*), which improves the distribution, the revolution and the security of corporate information on the Internet (Schuster & O'Connell, 2006). Compared with traditional printed report, the Internet "offers many more opportunities to communicate financial and its importance in this regard is rapidly increasing" (Pirchegger & Wagenhofer, 1999: 383), specially, companies can communicate information quickly and directly to investors and stakeholders, exposing an important amount of information available through Web over time and at very lower costs (FASB, 2000). Presentation format modes facilitate the navigation on corporate Websites and help investors and stakeholders to acquire corporate information, insuring more interactivity, flexibility and timeliness of corporate information (Khan, 2015).

The widespread adoption of Websites information dissemination practices has captured the attention of the accounting professional bodies and academics in the world (Debrency *et al.*, 2001). Scholars analyze the managers' motivations to distribute business and financial information through Websites in various countries (Kelton & Yang, 2008; Bekiaris *et al.*, 2014; Aboutera & Hussien, 2017; Arrif *et al.*, 2018), which are principally firm specific characteristics. IFR Empirical investigations were been referring to Asbaugh *et al.* (1999) and Debrency *et al.* (2002) studies. Previously, Debrency *et al.* (2002) were developed a theoretical and empirical framework deriving and determining that IFR practices differences in 22 countries and they showed that these practices are a function of firms and country specific characteristics.

According to international comparative accounting literature, Debrency *et al.* (2002) confirmed that country level characteristics explain also the IFR differences, such as country Internet penetration and the national disclosure environment. This literature highlighted that the international difference accounting development in different countries was been a function of external environment circumstances (Mueller, 1987; Radebaugh, 1975; Nair & Frank, 1980; Nobes, 1983; Choi & Mueller, 1984; Nobes & Parker, 1985). Gray (1988) established a theoretical model, explaining "the importance of Hofstede's dimensions of national culture in accounting is the national culture's influences on the nature of accounting practices" (Kolesnik, 2013: 34), evolving four distinct hypotheses involving the influence of cultural values on accounting values: professionalism, uniformity, conservatism and secrecy.

Numerous comparative accounting studies investigated the influence of culture values and institutional factors on financial transparency, qualifying the national accounting systems (Nobes, 1998) and they were elaborated a cross country analysis, testing the relationship between national culture, institutional factors and financial disclosure (Zarzeski, 1996; Jaggi & Low, 2000; Hopes, 2003, and others). Nevertheless, previous and existing explanatory IFR studies didn't investigate the relationship between countries specific characteristics and IFR practices, as principal explaining factors, simply, it is present some empirical evidence which integrated both firms and countries characteristics in the same empirical model (Debrency *et al.*, 2002; Bollen *et al.*, 2006; Turrent & Ariza, 2012; Zeghal & Moussa, 2015). In their analysis, they haven't valorized the importance of technologies investigating on the Websites, as a principal component of Internet financial disclosure.

Thus, the main objective of this purpose is to examine the impact of environment specific characteristics on online disclosure practices in Europe, appropriated to large companies with a high market capitalization. It aims to explain the web disclosure practices differences between Anglo-Saxon and Continental countries.

Maintaining a high level of investor protection throughout European community, European financial authority harmonizes between national mandatory reporting laws and standards. In 2004, it established 2004/109/EC directive ("Transparency directive"), as a legislative framework which defined and detailed transparency requirements relating the financial publication on European regulated capital market.

This directive was considered that 'electronic mean' (e.g. corporate Website) as a communication support and it authorize traded companies to disseminate periodic and ongoing information electronically to European regulation market.

Therefore, this study wants to contribute in IFR explanatory studies which explore empirical evidence testing the relationship between country characteristics and web financial disclosure. It will demonstrate the importance of Web communication dimensions as a composing the Web disclosure level that dressing empirical models testing the impact of environment specific characteristics on content, timeliness, technology and user support indices.

This paper proceeds as a follows: The second section presents literature review. The third section details main research objectives and hypotheses development. Research methodology is detailed in the fourth section. The fifth section discus and analyzes the results. The conclusion section reviews main finings, gives limitation, contributions and orientation for futures research.

2. Web disclosure practices differences

Accounting professional and scholars delineate characteristics and motivations of IFR practices in various countries.

2.1. Accounting professional pronouncement

Internet financial reporting is a voluntary disclosure practices and unregulated, in this sense, companies are no under obligation to maintain a Web site (Ettredge *et al.*, 2001) and governing regulation, previously, didn't mandate information disclosure on Website (Prentice *et al.*, 1999). Over time, accounting professional and financial markets authorities orientate the "IFR best practices" and others require the creation and the publication of particular information on the Web.

Accounting professionals delivered several studies and projects improving the distribution of business and financial information through Internet: they analyzed the consequence of this new practice in the accounting profession and proposed set of recommendation and guidance recoding the "best practices" of Web financial publication. In (1999), ISAC investigated a study of Web based business reporting by 660 corporations in 22 countries. It established a set of measures helping companies to ensure production of reliable information through Internet, essentially, the establishment of *code of conduct* detailing the corporate information publication via Internet.

CICA piloted study overviewed the use of internet as a financial reporting medium in North America. This research was done by Trites (1999) who selected 370 from 10000 companies traded in the New York exchange, the NASDAQ and the Toronto stock exchange. It reported that 69% of these companies have Website and 35% have some form of financial information on their Websites. This study discussed the implication of electronic information reporting on accounting standards (e.g. the separation between non-audited and audited information).

FASB (2000) report examined the financial information dissemination on the Web in USA and it contained a descriptive study which determined the types of information were communicated electronically. This report developed a comprehensive list of 325 attributes evaluating the corporate 150 fortune web sites. The following results showed that 99% have a Web site and 93 of the 100 fortune corporation presented financial information on their Web sites. Indeed, it fund a set recommendations which indicated that companies should ensure the accessibility and availability of complete financial reports through their websites and publish timely their interim and annual report and notes to financial statements. This project recommended companies to incorporate "investor relation" on the Web site, separated section and easily accessible from its home page.

IFAC (2000) addressed guidance to companies which choose to use Website, as a supplementary medium of financial report. It encouraged to managers elaborate an Internet reporting policy and developed controls and procedures ensuring the Internet financial reporting process.

Again, securities exchange markets authorities monitor the distribution of financial information through Internet in various countries. Some of them created a set of guidance and others required the publication of specific information. COB (1998) recommended that securities laws related to papers reporting are also applied to electronic reporting, ensuring the reliability, credibility and investors' equivalence principals.

TSX (2003) prompted listed companies to maintain a corporate Website and investor relations information available in the site. There should establish a Web reporting polices, according to TSX guidance and there guarantee maximum securities of its sites and E-mail. FSA (2000) authorized companies to distribute their annual report electronically which can forward to third parties an electronic version of annual report, financial statements, and management and auditor reports. SEC (2003) mandated companies to communicate beneficial ownership reports in their Website and they will publish reports forms 3, 4 and 5 in their Websites.

Others financial market commissioners were proposed to harmonize between national financial transparency standards and oriented the use the 'electronic mean' as a communication support: that is the European commission was defined in 2004 a list of norms mandated the financial publication on European regulated capital market.

2.2. European standards harmonization: transparency directive

European Commission proposed a set of recommendations oriented the electronic financial reporting practices in European countries. Fixing information transparency requirements, 2004/109/CE European directive authorized the use of "electronic mean", as a tool of information publication to regulated market. Indeed, European companies can utilize their corporate Web sites and they could communicate regulated information through websites. Transparency directive recommended creating a plat form of electronic network across European member states.

Amending this directive, 2013/50/CE directive simplified transparency obligations applicable to listed small and medium-sized firms and improved the effectiveness of the existing transparency regime and the respect of corporate ownership information disclosure. It indicated that European electronic access point will be established from 1 January 2018 developing by the European Securities and markets Authority (ESMA) and it certified that the preparation of electronic annual financial reports will be mandatory from 1 January 2020.

2.3. Academic research

Producing since (1996), primary studies are descriptive which "give a general overview of the current state of corporate reporting on the Internet" (Marston & Poeli, 2004, p. 287). Some of these studies described Web based reporting in signal country (Gray & Debreceny, 1997; Gowthorpe & Amat, 1999; Turel, 2010; Khan *et al.*, 2013) and others were compared IFR practices in two and more countries (Lymer & Tallberg, 1997; Deller *et al.*, 1999; Allam & Lymer, 2003; Chatterjee & Hawkes, 2008; Al-Sartawi, 2016).

For example, Lymer (1997) described the utilization of the Web as a medium for financial reporting by 50 UK companies. It indicated that 92% have a Website and 52% published financial reports. Gowthorpe & Amat (1999) examined the extent of usage for Internet financial communication by Spanish listed companies. The results showed that 16% have a web site and 34 % presented some kind of financial information on their Web pages. Deller *et al.* (1999) compared the Internet "investor relations" activities on USA, UK and German firms. They found that USA corporations used more Internet "investor relations" activities than UK and German corporations.

Al-Sartawi (2016) illustrated the level of online financial disclosure usage in the Gulf Cooperation Council (GCC) listed companies. They showed that the majority of the GCC companies disclosed a good level of content and format presentation dimension information through their Web site. They indicate that the content dimension differs from one country to other and from industry type to other and that the level of presentation dimension was better in Oman than in Bahrain and on banking companies than insurance and investment companies.

Since (2000), researchers attempted to determined factors explaining IFR practices in various countries. Giving the IFR preliminary empirical evidence, Ashbaugh *et al.* (1999) want to explain "why some firms disseminate financial information on their corporate Websites, while others do not" (Kelton &Yang, 2008: 65). They found that larger and more profitable US firms are more likely to engage on the IFR practices but it did not provide a theoretical rational of IFR determinants.

Extending this paper, Debrency *et al.* (2002) established general model explaining Web financial publication determinants, which are firm and environment specific characteristics. Conformity to these processors, scholars documented empirical evidence explaining the IFR practices in developed and developing countries. They are cases studies (Abdelsalam *et al.*, 2007; Kelton & Yang, 2008; Hindi & Rich, 2010; Boubaker *et al.*, 2012; Alali & Romero, 2012; Dunne *et al.*, 2013; Momany *et al.*, 2013) and comparative studies (Pervan, 2006; Bonson & Escobar, 2006; Henchiri, 2011; Turrent & Ariza, 2012).

Kelton & Yang (2008) analyzed the impact of corporate governance on Internet financial reporting in USA. They demonstrated that shareholders, blockholder ownership, board independence, audit committee expertise and diligence explain the Internet financial reporting. Aboutera & Hussien (2017) examined the Internet financial reporting practices determinants in Egypt. Empirical result showed that firm size, auditor type and firm age are significantly associated with level of electronic information disclosure.

Henchiri (2011) compared the voluntary information publication through websites' companies listed in Moroccan and Tunisian stock exchanges. They demonstrated that firm size, firm performance and foreign ownership determine the extent of online information. Turrent & Ariza (2012) investigated a comparative study of the E-transparency practices in Mexico and Spain, measuring by a disclosure index. They showed significant differences in the disclosure level between listed companies in two countries. The result indicated that ownership concentration, chairman of the board-Chief executive officer (COB-CEO) duality, economic development and inflation are the important factors explaining the E- disclosure practices differences. Mohamed & Baswory (2014) examined the characteristics of voluntary Internet disclosure in three Gulf cooperation Council countries: Qatar, Oman, and Bahrain. They signaled that firm size is a major factor influencing internet financial reporting practices.

Generally, explanatory studies tested the impact of firm specific characteristics on the level and the quality of IFR in various countries. Empirical investigations were demonstrated that organizational and corporate governance mechanisms are determining factors of financial disclosure through Websites in different countries. Nevertheless, comparative accounting studies reveal that country' macro-economic situation can also influence the IFR, as voluntary disclosure.

3. Conceptual framework

International comparative financial accounting research wants to "identify the accounting differences between various countries and to explain why these differences exist" (Ding, 2001: 156), that was identified previously that national culture as an important environment factor explaining cross- national accounting development differences. In (1986), Harrison and McKinnon have proposed a methodological framework incorporating national culture as important element analyzing the change and functioning of national accounting, as a social system.

Complementing Harrison and McKinnon study, Gray (1988) established a theoretical model, explaining how national culture values reinforce the development of accounting systems and practices in various countries. His model developed the causal association between Hofstede (1980)' cultural values (Individualism, power distance, uncertainty avoidance, masculinity) and accounting values, deriving the level of a country's accounting subculture: professionalism versus statutory control; uniformity versus flexibility; conservatism versus optimism and secrecy versus transparency.

Several studies were contributed in the existing literature and they attempted to lengthen the Gray (1988) conceptual framework (Perera, 1989; Frechner &Kilgore, 1994; Baydoun & Willet, 1995; Salter & Niswander, 1995; Chanchani & MacGregor, 1999). In 1995, Doupnik and Salter amplified this theoretical framework and they developed a general model determining country' accounting development: cultural dimensions, external environment and institutional structure can explain accounting development differences (Doupnik & Salter, 1995).

"Secrecy versus transparency[i]" was been extensively studied in prior review because disclosure index "*make it the easiest accounting value to operationalize*" (Tsakumis, 2007: 31). Most of international accounting studies were tested empirically the link between culture, institutional factors and information disclosure (Zarzeski, 1996; Wingate, 1997; Jaggi & Low, 2000; Hopes, 2003; Doupnik & Richter, 2004).

In the 21st century, the corporate reporting processes perceive an important evaluation; it will be more digitally. Listed companies utilize more electronic means as a corporate financial reporting support, essentially, corporate websites will be more privileged and popular use as a communication medium. It offers many advantages, serving as a fantastic mean which deliver corporate information "in a timely fashion to foreign and often sophisticated investors" (Ojaha & Mokoteli, 2012: 71).

Refereeing to the Gray (1988)' conceptual framework and Debrency *et al.* (2002) model, we can predict that environment factors explicate the Internet financial disclosure differences, as a financial transparency practices. We simplified the study' conceptual model by following figure:

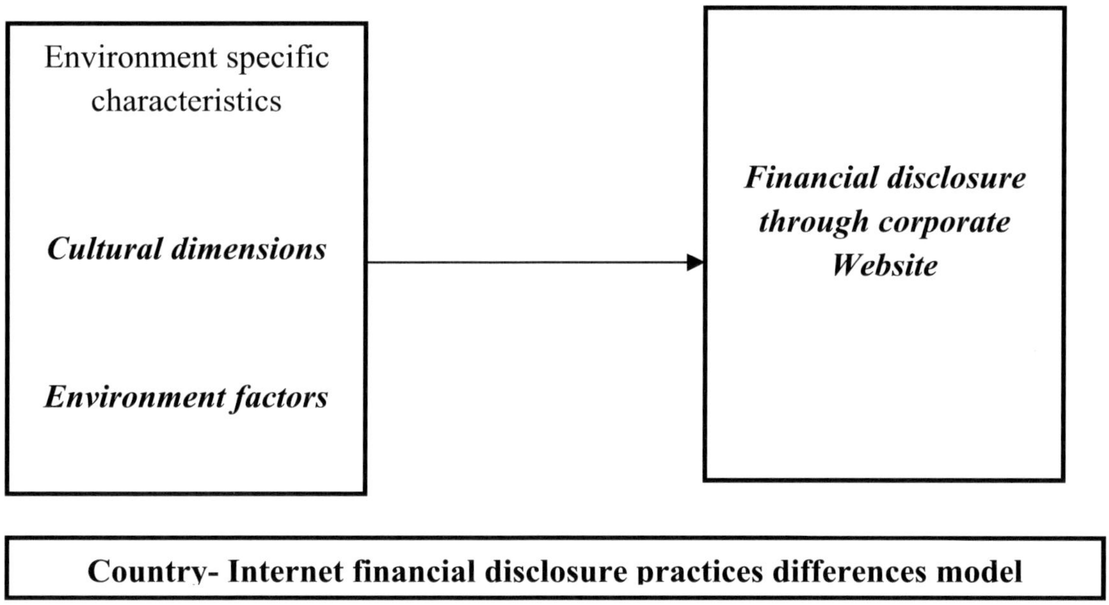

Figure 1: Proposed conceptual framework

4. Hypotheses development

Following to previous review, we explain in the section the incidence of national culture and institutional factors on the financial disclosure via corporate Websites, as an accounting practice, respectively.

4.1. National culture

Culture refers to "the collective programming of the mind that distinguishes the members of one group or category of people from another" (Hofstede, 2001: 9). Culture presents asset of collective beliefs and values that distinguish individuals in the country vary. Investigating a multinational IMB data, Hofstede (1984) identified four culture values:

- ***Individualism versus collectivism***: individualism concerns "a preference for a loosely knit social framework in society wherein individuals are supposed to take care of themselves". It is an opposite; collectivism refers to "a preference for a tightly knit social framework in which individuals can expect their relatives".
- ***Large versus small power distance***: power distance illustrates "the extent to which the members of a society accept that the power in institutions and organizations is unequally distributed".
- ***Strong versus weak uncertainty avoidance***: Uncertainty avoidance defines "the degree to which the members of a society fell uncomfortable with uncertainty and ambiguity".

- ***Masculinity versus femininity***: Masculinity refers to the extent of masculine values on a society such as achievement, heroism, assertiveness and material success and femininity completes the relationship, modesty, caring for the weak and the quality of life.

The relationship between culture and financial "secrecy/ transparency" is described in the following table:

Table 1. Gray framework

	Secrecy	Transparency
Individualism	-	+
Power distance	+	-
Uncertainty avoidance	+	-
Masculinity	-	+

Source: Gray (1988: 11)

Following to Bryan *et al.* (2012), Kanagaretnam *et al.* (2014) and Hooghienstra *et al.* (2015), we focused essentially on individualism and uncertainty avoidance, explaining the implication of manager's choices, behaviors and their relationship to shareholders.

4.1.1. Individualism

Individuals in collectivistic cultures focus on the group interests, implying strong relationship between members. In this sense, companies in these societies apply less control and disclose less information in their annual report (Gray, 1988; Zarzeski, 1996; Hopes, 2003).

In individualistic societies, the environment is more competitive and less secretive, involving a high level of information transparency (Gray, 1988; Jaggi & Low, 2000). Companies are more developed and large state-owned through capital markets, in this situation, managers are more likely to publish information in their annual report to shareholders. It is expected a positive relationship between individualism and information disclosure in annual report (Akman, 2011; Hooghemstra *et al.*, 2015; Maali, 2016).

Individualism level determinates the information technology (IT) adoption by organizations in different countries. In collectivistic countries, individuals comply with standards of the group, maintain collective decisions process and they are more likely to adopt antique innovation (Lee *et al.*, 2007; Ugur, 2017).

In individualistic countries, firms keep personal decisions markers process when employees are more oriented to efficiency, performance, freedom in work and personal achievement (Bagchi *et al.*, 2003). They considered IT as the better mean to acquire available information and to achieve personal goals. Managers in individualistic societies are more likely to utilize the Internet, as a new medium of financial disclosure. We suppose a positive relationship between individualism and Web based disclosure. As extension a Gray (1988)' hypothesis, we hypothesized that:

H_1: Companies in individualistic countries disclose more financial information through their corporate Web sites.

4.1.2. Uncertainty avoidance

In strong uncertainty avoidance cultures, people create laws and rules to avoid ambiguity and uncertain events. Companies attempt the stability and they are less well-off conflict and competition (Bryan *et al.*, 2012), in order to preserve security, managers tend to disclose less information in annual reports, addressing essentially to private users (banks and financial institutions) (Zarzeski, 1996). In weak uncertainty avoidance societies, individuals are more likely to handle ambiguous events and accept competition, conflicts and confrontation, in this situation, corporation are dominated by diffused ownership and complicated business relationship. Market participants need more information to understand the corporate financial situation, thus, managers tend to publish more information in annual report to shareholders and public (Gray, 1988; Zarzeski, 1996). Prior studies was confirmed the negative relationship between uncertainty avoidance and voluntary disclosure (Hopes, 2003; Akram, 2011; Hooghemstra *et al.*, 2015).

Uncertainty avoidance influences the innovation adoption and information technology usage. Companies in strong uncertainty avoidance countries are more resistant to innovations, high formalized management style and constraining of innovations by rules (Hofstede, 2001; Mohammadisadr *et al.*, 2012). Managers create more rigid rules to control the risk and they are less likely to encourage the experimentation and innovation on their firms.

In weak uncertainty avoidance societies, companies have greater tendency to nurture experimentation and they prompt employees to create new ideas and develop emerging innovation, which implicates the rapid development and adoption the new communication technologies in the corporate activities, presuming firm profitability and continuity. Managers, in Weak uncertainty avoidance countries, are more likely to adopt the Web site, as a business financial reporting support.
As an extension to Gray (1988)' hypothesis, we hypothesized that:

H_2: Companies in weak uncertainty avoidance countries disclose more financial information through their corporate Web sites.

4.2. Institutional factors

Comparative studies demonstrated that countries levels institutional factors are important determinants of financial disclosure practices, essentially, legal system[ii], capital market and economic development (Jaggi & Low, 2000; Hopes, 2003).

4.2.1. Capital market size

Larger capital markets present an important number of participants and shareholders, favoring the information demand (Adhikari & Tondkar, 1992). Exercising more pressure, investors require sophisticated information helping to make optimal investment decision (Gray *et al.*, 1984) and order companies to produce more rigorous information and to respect disclosure requirements.
Therefore, companies in countries with larger capital market are more motivated to disclose more regular information in their annual report to public (Adhikari & Tondkar, 1992; Jaggi and Low, 2000; Bushuman *et al.*, 2004).

Larger markets present important activities and voluminous transactions (Salter, 1998), which showed fulfill numerous norms such as reliability, credibility and security. Market participants demand also the quality of financial services and they request the use of new means facilitating the transmission of news and information on the markets. Internet is considered an attractive medium for financial services and transactions at low cost. It "offers unprecedented immediacy, flexibility and interactivity, magnifying the financial services industry's ability to reach into the retail market" (ISOCO, 1998).

Utilizing Internet technologies, investors can access immediately and rapidly to news and actual information available on the market, helping to make optimal choices and conduct investment activity. Consequently, markets participants incite firm to use Internet and create own Web sites, such as a mean corporate information communication.
According to these arguments, we suggest that companies in countries with larger capital markets disclose more electronic financial information. We hypothesized that:

H_3: Companies in countries with larger capital markets disclose more financial information through their corporate Web sites.

4.2.2. National economic development

Developed countries have more resources to devote accounting standard-setting and regulated process (Adhikari & Tondkar, 1992), which involve disclosure requirements. Consequently, companies wanted to communicate more financial information in annual reports (Doupink & Salter, 1995; Salter, 1998; William, 2004).

The level of national income explains the capacity of a country to maintain new innovation (Pohjohe, 2003; Erumbam & Jong, 2005). Countries with high income process more human and technique resources helping individuals to create and adopt new innovations (such as new information technologies).

Internet will generate new opportunities which will translate voluminous national economic activities and domicile managerial companies. Managers will incorporate Web technologies in corporate activities and they develop news activities such as E-Business and E- Voting. However, managers have more incentives to construct their corporate Websites, as a new and important medium of business financial publication and increase the amount of information disclosure. In this study, we predicate a positive relationship between economic growth and Web based financial information. We hypothesized that:

H_4: Companies in developed countries disclose more financial information through their corporate Web sites.

5. Methodology design

5.1. Sample description

The initial sample was included 271 largest groups of companies traded on European securities exchange, in July 2013. The selection criterion of this sample was presumed, as following:

- Internet financial disclosure practices is appropriated to listed firms on international exchanges markets (Ashbaugh *et al.*, 1999; Debrency *et al.*, 2002);
- Firms, with highest market capitalization, are more likely to adopt the Internet financial disclosure practice (Ducassy, 2008);
- European commission fixed appropriated legal framework, identifying transparency norms in the case where listed firms use "electronic mean" as information publication medium.

We eliminated financial sector firms (banks, insurances and others financial services firms) because they have specific and different disclosure requirements (Gul & Leung, 2004), three groups which did not have a Web site or downloadable site (Ezat & El-Masry, 2008) and eight groups which are listed on two or more securities exchanges. The final sample is composed by 205 groups, observed in 2011-2012 accounting exercise.

Table 2. Sample composition

Countries	Accounting systems	Total traded Companies	Financial sector companies	Web inaccessibility	Double listing	Final sample
France	Continental	40	04	0	03	33
Germany	Continental	30	05	0	0	25
Italy	Continental	40	13	01	01	25
Netherlands	Anglo-Saxon	25	03	0	03	19
Spain	Continental	35	08	0	03	24
UK	Anglo-Saxon	101	17	02	03	79
Total		271	50	03	13	205

5.2. Web based disclosure extent

Pirchegger & Wagenhofer (1999) identified four dimensions, evaluating the Web diffusion:

- ***Content***: encompasses financial and corporate information available on the site;
- ***Timeliness***: Web can provide companies and users the possibility to acquire rapid and updating information in real time;
- ***Technology***: it is "the extent to which the companies under investigation make use of some of the more advanced features" (Pirchegger & Wagenhofer, 1999: 365);
- ***User support***: measures the design and layout of the Website.

This framework was reviewed as a "very comprehensive checklist for the evaluation of Web site", Marston & Poeli (2004: 296) and it was been utilized by a great number of IFR studies (Purba *et al.*, 2013; Bekiaris *et al.*, 2014; Pascareno & Hermana, 2015). Consequently, we employed Pirchegger & Wagentofer' instrument and we defined a Web disclosure index measuring the extent of information communicated through corporate European Web site.

In order to develop this index, we were achieved the next steps:

- ***Checklist instrument construction***:

We chose to adopt transparency directive requirements as a "standard", which fixed "regulated information" and we considered others information which communicated through European Web sites, exceeded directive requirements, as "voluntary disclosure". Regulated information includes periodic and ongoing information. Voluntary information, incorporates others financial and non-financial information, concerning business, governance, segment and responsibility information. Completing the voluntary information, timeliness, technology and user support items, we were referred to checklist instruments developed by previous studies dealing the Web based financial disclosure on the European countries (Larran & Giner, 2002; Geernigs & Sinchez, 2008; Boubaker *et al.*, 2012; Sanchez Canadas & Caba perrez, 2013).

The list of items composes 133 items: Web content items (104 items), timeliness items (9 items), technology items (11 items) and user support items (9 items) (Appendix A).

– ***Web sites consultation and analysis***:

We consulted and analyzed financial reports, others documents and pages available and downloadable via sites Web during a short period of three months (as a court period) from 1st July to 31 September 2013.

– ***Web reporting index calculation:***

We performed unweighted dichotomous disclosure index: we noted a score of 1 if a company reported an item figured from the checklist and a score of 0 if the company did not disclose an item. Unweighted scoring procedure reduces the subjectivity and accords equal important to an each disclosure item (Cooke, 1989; Hossain *et al.*, 1995). The Web reporting index of each company is calculated to dividing the total score disclosed by total number of items (n =133), as following:

$$\textbf{Web reporting index (WRI)} = \frac{\textit{total Score obtained by firm}}{\textit{Number total of items}} \quad \textbf{(1)}$$

In addition, the total Web reporting index (TWDI) corresponds to the sum of four indices: content (CONI), timeliness (TIMI), technology (TEHI) and user support (SUPI) indices.

$$TWDI = CONI + TIMI + TEHI + SUPI \qquad (2)$$

5.3. Explanatory variables measurement

We defined measurement of culture dimensions and institutional factors (Appendix B), as a following:

5.3.1. Culture

Following to prior studies (Jaggi & Low, 2000; Williams, 2004; Hooghiemstra *et al.*, 2015), we use the Hofstede's (1984) score represented countries cultural values levels. In this analysis, we focused essentially to individualism (INDV) and avoidance uncertainty (UCER) scores.

5.3.2. Institutional factors

Measurements test and control variable are consistent with the international accounting research, as a following:

- **Stock market size (MCAP)**: measured by the market capitalization, equal to the market capitalization of domestic companies dividing by Gross

Domestic Product (GDP) (Adhikari & Tondher, 1992; Larson & Kenny, 1995).

- **Economic growth (ECGW)**: correspond to the natural logarithm of GDP per capita (Williams, 2004; Turrent & Ariza, 2012; Zeghal & Moussa, 2015).

We identified two control variables can explain the Web based disclosure:

- **National inflation level (INFL)**: Archambault & Archambault (1999) showed that companies operating in countries with high inflation are more likely to use price level accounting and they increase the information publication level, made available to investors. We suggested a positive relationship between inflation and Internet financial reporting and we measured countries inflation level (INFL) by 2012 inflation rate.
- **National education level (EDUC)**: increasing the level of national education involves the importance of financial statements users' numbers (Doupnik & Salter, 1995).
  They acquire more competences, expertise, permitting more capacities to understand and interpret corporate information and helping to make optimal investment decisions, consequently, they will demand a high quality and important amount of financial information (Archambault & Archambault, 2003).
  We suggested that countries- education level (EDUC) affect positively the Web based financial disclosure, measuring by the tertiary education ratios in 2012.

5.4. Research models

We developed a general model testing the influence of country specific characteristics and Web based financial disclosure:

$$WRI = \beta_0 + \beta_1 INDV + \beta_2 UCER + \beta_3 MACP + \beta_4 ECGW + \beta_5 INFL + \beta_6 EDUC + \varepsilon \quad (3)$$

We elaborated five distinct models, detailing the influence of culture, institutional factors on Web reporting dimensions: Web content index, Web timeliness index, Web technology index and Web user support index, respectively:

- Web content index model (WCONI)

$$WCONI = \beta_0 + \beta_1 INDV + \beta_2 UCER + \beta_3 MACP + \beta_4 ECGW + \beta_5 INFL + \beta_6 EDUC + \varepsilon \quad (4)$$

-Web timeliness index model (WTMI)

$$WTMI = \beta_0 + \beta_1 INDV + \beta_2 UCER + \beta_3 MACP + \beta_4 ECGW + \beta_5 INFL + \beta_6 EDUC + \varepsilon \quad (5)$$

- Web technology index model (WTEI)

$$WTEI = \beta_0 + \beta_1 INDV + \beta_2 UCER + \beta_3 MACP + \beta_4 ECGW + \beta_5 INFL + \beta_6 EDUC + \varepsilon \quad (6)$$

- Web user support index Model (WUSI)

$$WSUPI = \beta_0 + \beta_1 INDV + \beta_2 UCER + \beta_3 MACP + \beta_4 ECGW + \beta_5 INFL + \beta_6 EDUC + \varepsilon \quad (7)$$

- Total Web disclosure index model (TWDI):

$$TWDI = \beta_0 + \beta_1 INDV + \beta_2 UCER + \beta_3 MACP + \beta_4 ECGW + \beta_5 INFL + \beta_6 EDUC + \varepsilon \quad (8)$$

Were:
WRI= Web reporting index
WCONI= Web content index
WTIMI= Web timeliness index
WTEHI= Web technology index
WSUPI= Web user support index
TWDI= Total Web disclosure index
INDV= Country individual level
UCER= Country avoidance uncertainty level
MACP= Country stock market capitalization
ECGW= Country economic growth
INFL= Country inflation level
EDUC= Country education level
β_i = coefficients
ε = error

6. Empirical findings

This study aims to explore an appropriated empirical investigation testing the macroeconomics conditions that have a direct and significant impact on web disclosure differences in Europe, as corporate transparency practicing in the 21st century. European countries present a specific characteristics on this issue with imposing listed companies on regulated European market to respect, apply financial transparency standards (transparency directive) and encourage utilizing the 'electronic mean' as a communication support. This section presents the characterization of web disclosure on European context and the linear regression analysis determining the influence of environment specific characteristics on Web disclosure extent.

6.1. Descriptive analysis

We presented a summary statistics, describing the level of information communicated through European corporate Websites and country specific characteristics.

6.1.1. IFR practices tendencies

Appendix C presents descriptive statistics for content, timeliness, technology, user support and total Web disclosure indices, in terms minimum, maximum, means and standards' derivation respectively. The highest mean value of content index in France (58%), Germany (56%), Italy (58%), Netherlands (52%), Spain (53%) and UK (50%) indicated that institutional websites as an important medium of corporate information. European group communicated enormously their annual report, financial accounts and financial information through their sites which facilities the relationship between company and investors. Analyzing the information publication via companies' Websites listed in Eastern Europe countries, Bonson and Escobar (2006) showed that 34.5% of companies published their annual reports, 18.6% communicated their income statements via Internet.

These statistics reveal the importance the Web technology which helps information users' navigation. Timeliness, technologies and user support index values didn't different between companies in European countries. Total Web disclosure indices mean values are ranked in 0.64 to 0.72 which involved that European groups adopt Web sites, new support communication. This result is consistent with results of different studies conducted in European context such as Pirchegger & Wagenhofer (1999), Geerings *et al.* (2003), Marston and Polei (2004), Bonson and Escobar (2006). Geerings *et al.* (2003)'study showed that Euronext listed companies noted a high degree of Web' use as a vehicle for improving investors relations: France (94%), Netherlands (92%) use more Internet' investor relations activities than in Belgium (70%).

Table 3: Web content index mean variation

Country	N	Regulated	%	Voluntary	%	content	%
France	33	0.300	50.37%	0.259	46.3%	0.559	100
Germany	25	0.289	52%	0.267	48%	0.556	100
Italy	24	0.290	52%	0.268	48%	0.558	100
Netherlands	19	0.265	50.5%	0.260	49.5%	0.525	100
Spain	24	0.276	51.8%	0.257	48.2%	0.533	100
UK	79	0.261	51.6%	0.245	48.4%	0.506	100

Table 3 indicated that regulated information constitutes the principal component of informational content of corporate Websites (more of 50 % of content items). Periodic information is the major regulated information categories, composing the Websites content (Appendix D).

European groups developed storage systems through their own Websites cumulating the annual reports, financial statements, and others obligatory information during five years, conformity to the transparency directive requirements. This archive allows investors and websites' visitors the possibility to acquire more regulated information helping to realizing the comparison and more understanding the evolution of corporate financial situation, which favorites the optimal investment decision.

6.1.2. External environment characteristics

Table 4 indicated that Anglo-Saxon countries present a high level of market capitalization, economic development and education then continental countries.

Table 4. Explanatory variables descriptive statistics

	Continental countries		**Anglo-Saxon countries**	
	Mean	**St. derivation**	**Mean**	**St. derivation**
Individualism	66.74	9.05	87.25	3.75
Uncertainty avoidance	78.52	8.724	38.48	7.15
Capital market capitalization	0.55	0.137	1.14	0.14
Economic growth	9.98	0.89	10.66	0.07
Inflation	0.023	0.004	0.027	0.001
Education	0.644	0.104	0.639	0.596
N	107		98	

6.2. Multicollinearity problem analysis

We will realize a linear regression testing the influence of environment factors on web based financial disclosure, as an accounting practice. Before running regression model, we should verify the empirical correlation between different explanatory variables variable and detect the multicollinearity problem between (Field, 2009). Multicollinearity, testing was based on the correlation matrix, which will be detected when the correlation coefficients exceeded 0.6 (Hooghiemstra *et al.*, 2015).

Table 5. Pearson matrix

	INDV	**UCER**	**MCAP**	**ECGW**	**INFL**	**EDUC**
INDV	1					
UCER	-0.863**	1				
MCAP	0.658**	-0.797**	1			
ECGW	0.419**	-0.201**	0.515**	1		
INFL	0.597**	-0.586**	0.410**	0.516**	1	
EDUC	-0.501**	0.248**	-0.040	0.221**	0.132	1

Note: INDV: individualism level; UCER: avoidance uncertainty level; MCAP: capital market capitalization; ECGW: economic growth; INFL: inflation rate; EDUC: territory education level.

Pearson matrix indicated that multicollinearity problem exists between three explanatory variables, describing by a high correlation coefficient: individualism and uncertainty avoidance; individualism and capital market size.
Therefore, individualism was not included on the regression model.

6.3. Linear regression method: Ordinary Least Squares (OLS) transformation

Appling the Ordinary least squares (OLS) regression on financial disclosure studies involves many problems, dealing with disclosure index use (Cooke, 1998). As a solution, major of accounting disclosure studies (Lang & Lundholm, 1993, 1996; Wallace *et al.*, 1994; Wallace & Naser, 1995; Cooke, 1998) legitimated the transformation of both dependent and independents variables before the application of OLS regression, such as full rank transformation and normal scores transformation.

Rank transformation consists to adjust continuous variables with n observations, ranked from the smallest to the highest values. This method is advantageous when the dependent variable is a monotonic and non linear function of the independent variables. Normal scores transformation was obtained by dividing the distribution into the number of observation plus one regression on the basis that each region has equal probability (Cooke, 1998). This method is considered more advantageous than rank scores (Camfferman & Cooke, 2002), that it contributes to exact statistical properties (adjusted R^2 significance levels, meaningful F and t tests).

The OLS regression method application depends to the verification of several assumptions, principally multicollinearity, homoscedasticity, linearity and normality (Cooke & Hannifa, 2002). We performed Q-Q plot testing the linearity of the variable distribution, histograms examining the homoscedasticity residuals analysis and Kolmogorov-Smirnov (K-S Lilliefors) test, capturing the normality problem. The results indicated that OLS assumptions are violated, en consequence, we ruined normal scores regression model, testing the link between institutional factors and Web disclosure index.

6.4. OLS regression findings

In order to validate the research hypotheses and the study' conceptual framework, we performed normal scores OLS regression related to five distinct linear models, programming with SPPS 20. These models predicted respectively the incidence of culture and institutional factors on content, timeliness, technology, user support and total web disclosure indices. OLS regression models results (appendix E) showed that four models are significant at $p<0.001$, except to timeliness model. Content, technology and total disclosure models explain respectively 29.5%, 14.8% and 29.4% of the endogenous variable variation.

In this section, we interpreted and analyzed empirical findings from five models, investigating the incidence of environment specific characteristics on Web disclosure dimensions (content, timeliness, technology and user support indices) and total web disclosure index.

6.4.1. Web disclosure dimensions

Normal scores OLS regression showed that institutional factors are significantly appropriated to content and technology models. Uncertainly avoidance, market capitalization and education level are significantly related to the corporate site content.

Contrary to our expectation, uncertainly avoidance is significantly and positively related to the Web content index, which involved that these companies with high uncertainly avoidance culture have more likely to increase the level of online information. This result can possibly be explained by the composition of sample including in majority continental countries, noted high uncertainly avoidance level. Our findings confirm that companies in countries with high tertiary education have more incentives to use the Web such communication tool and increase the on line information quantity. These countries are dominated by developed accounting profession which demand the respect of auditing and accounting norms favoring the relevance and the comprehensively of information, consequently, companies will communicate more audited annual reports and statements via Internet.

Linear regression demonstrates that uncertainly avoidance, market capital size, economic growth and education are associated significantly with technology index. Conformity to our prevision, findings indicated that uncertainly avoidance affects significantly and negatively the Website technology index, as a communication support. In countries with weak uncertainly avoidance, managers are more likely to incorporate new Internet technology in their corporations facilitating the communication with investors, stakeholders and public. That also, managers encourage the communication responsible to create and diffuse new and sophisticated IT means and applications favoring the Websites pages and assuring the financial information quality.

Websites are important mean on larger capital markets, facilitating financial and listing activities and services: incorporating a higher level and sophisticated technologies improve the transmission of information and news. Companies in countries with larger capital market are more likely to integrate new technologies in their Websites. In these countries, corporate Websites pages constitute a creative privileged support allowing companies to respond to information demand on larger and developed markets. Developing news IT applications, companies can supply more financial information, news and press releases in the time to privileged, foreign investors and others markets' participants. Managers, in developed countries, have more resources to adopt new technologies and they are more likely to incorporate more technologies instruments in corporate Web site.

People in countries with higher education rate were been incited to create new innovation and they accord more attention to new technologies and communication innovations, which have a positive impact to innovations organizational and markers' decisions process. Thus, companies are more likely to integrate and develop new Web technologies though their sites, helping Web navigators.

6.4.2. Total Web disclosure index

Normal scores OLS regression signed that uncertainty avoidance, capital market size, economic growth and level of education are significant related to total IFR index. Our results highlight a significant relationship and to the expectation between uncertainty avoidance and total Web disclosure. Thus, we not support the H2 hypothesis. This result is consistent with Archambault & Archambault (2003) and opposite to Zarzeski (1996), Hope (2003) and Dejong *et al.* (2006)' studies results which analyzing the financial information published on the annual reports.

Maali (2016)' study analysis was demonstrated the similar result which indicated that uncertainty avoidance was positively related to multinational corporation transparency index. Analyzing the multinational governance disclosure policies through websites, Zeghal & Moussa (2015) were demonstrated that uncertainty avoidance is negatively associated to governance disclosure index. They explained this result by the nature of multinational firms which are dominated by "global market culture than a specific country culture".

Linear regression found that capital market size is significantly and negatively (opposite direction to prediction) to the level of online information, therefore we cannot verify our expectation and support H3 hypothesis. Examining the annual reports content, Jaggi & Low (2000), Archambault & Archambault (2003) demonstrated a significant and positive relationship between capital market size and financial disclosure. Zeghal & Moussa (2015) haven't confirmed a significant association related the "capital development" variable and corporate governance disclosure policies through multinational Websites.

In addition, the normal score regression highlight a significant and positive coefficient appropriated to "economic growth" variable, thus, we confirm our expectation, we accept that country's economic development affects significantly and positively the total disclosure index and supported (H4) hypothesis. Companies in developed countries disclose more regulated and voluntary information through their own websites than listed companies in developing countries which they are more likely to adopt this medium. They have more resources to acquire more technologies developing corporate activities, such as financial reporting strategic. Possessing various resources, communication responsible desires to maintain an “efficient communication process”, achieving by the exploitation of news Internet technologies such as corporate websites and social media. Turrent & Aziza (2012) study were confirmed this result, which examine the factors determining the E-transparency in Spain and Mexico and they considered that companies with developed countries disclose more information than companies from others countries.

7. Conclusion

This study analyzes the relationship between environment specific characteristics Websites based disclosure in six developed European countries (France, Germany, Italy, Netherlands, Spain and UK). Our sample was composed in 205 groups of companies traded in selected countries capital markets.

Referring to 2004/109/CE requirements, we defined web content items and we considered that content included regulated and voluntary information. Descriptive analysis underlined the web disclosure practices similarly between European countries.

We performed a normal scores OLS regression testing the incidence of environmental factors on Web based disclosure. Market size, economic growth and education level determinate technologies investigating on corporate Websites. Appropriated regression showed that country economic development (significant and positive) is the determining factor of IFR practices.

Our study contributes to the comparative accounting review through its originality in attempting to examine the influence of external environment to the Web based corporate disclosure, nevertheless, it involves certain limitations related essentially to the sample selection. It was a limited sample, which didn’t present equilibrium between Anglo-Saxon and continental selected countries. This choice is principally justified by a legal/regulatory raison: examining financial disclosure practices differences necessitates the corporate transparency requirements understanding (as a well 2004/109/CE directive). Cross country Web disclosure analysis depends to disclosure requirements and standards. Thus, the accounting professional and regulatory bodies’ position in this subject will help, in future, scholars to explain the influence of external environment to Websites based corporate and financial disclosure internationally.

References

Abdelsalam, O., Bryant, S. & Street, D. (2007) "An examination of comprehensiveness of corporate internet reporting provided by London listed companies", *Journal of International Accounting Research*, 6(2): 1-33

Aboutera, L. & Hussien, A. (2017) "Determining of internet financial reporting in Egyptian companies", *Research Journal of Finance and Accounting*, 8(10): 28-39

Akman, N. (2011) "The effect of IFRS adoption on financial disclosure: does culture still play a role?", *American International Journal of Contemporary Research*, 1(1): 6-17

Alali, F. & Romero, S. (2012) "The use of the internet for corporate reporting in the Mercosur (Southern common market): the case Argentina case", *Advance in Accounting*, 28: 157-167

Allam, A. & Lymer, A. (2003) "Development in internet financial reporting: review and analysis across five developed countries", *The International Journal of Digital Accounting Research*, 3(6): 165-199

Al-Sartawi, A. (2016) "Measuring the level of online financial disclosure in the Gulf cooperation council countries", *Corporate Ownership and Control*, 14: 547-558

Ariff, A.M., Bin-Ghanem, H.O. & Hashim, H.A. (2018) "Corporate ownership, internet penetration and Internet Financial reporting: evidence from the Gulf Cooperation Council countries", *Asian Journal of Business and Accounting*, 11(1):185-227

Ashbaugh, H., Johnstone, K. & Warfield, T. (1999) "Corporate reporting on the Internet", *Accounting Horizons*, 13(3): 241-257

Archanbault, J. & Archambault, M. (1990) "Across national test of determinants of inflation accounting practices", *International Journal of Accounting*, 34(2): 189-207

Bagchi, K., Cerveny, R., Hart, P. & Peterson, M. (2003) "The influence of national culture in information technology product adoption", AMCIS 2003 proceeding 119, https://aisel.aisnet.org/amics2003/119.

Bekiaris, M., Psimada, C. & Sergios, T. (2014), "Internet financial reporting quality and corporate characteristics: the case of construction companies listed in Greek and Cypriot stock exchange", *European Research Studies*, 17(2): 41-57

COB. (1998) "Recommandation n°98-05 relative à la diffusion sur Internet d'informations financières par les sociétés dont les titres sont admis aux négociations sur un marché réglementé ", Bulletin mensuel n°334, avril 1999

Bollen, L., Hassink, H. & Bozic, C. (2006) "Measuring and explaining the quality of internet investor relations activities: a multinational empirical analysis", *International Journal of Accounting Information Systems*, 7(4): 273-298

Bonson, E. & Escobar, T. (2006) "Digital reporting in Eastern European: an empirical study", *International Journal of Accounting Information System,* 7: 299-318

Boubaker, S., Lakhal, F. & Nekhili, M. (2012) "The determinants of Web based corporate reporting in France", *Managerial Auditing Journal*, 27(2): 126-155

Bryan, S., Nash, R. & Patel, A. (2012) "Culture and CEO compensation", Working paper, Http://ssrn.com/absract=2023530.

Bushuman, R., Chan, Q., Engel, E. & Smith, A. (2004) "Financial accounting information, organizational complexity and corporate governance systems", *Journal of Accounting and Economics*, 37: 167-210

Camfferman, K. & Cooke, T. (2002) "An analysis of disclosure in the annual reports of UK and Dutch companies, *Journal of International Accounting Research*, 1(1): 3-30

Chatterjee, B. & Haukes, L. (2008) "Does internet reporting improve the accessibility of financial information in a global world? A comparative study of New Zealand and Indian companies", *Australasian, Accounting, Business and Finance journal*, 2(4): 33-55

Cooke, T. (1989) "Voluntary corporate disclosure by Swedish companies", *Journal of International Financial Management and Accounting*, 1(2): 171-195

Cooke, T. (1998) "Regression analysis in accounting disclosure studies", *Accounting and Business Research*, 28(3): 209-224

Craven, B. & Marston, C. (1999) "Financial reporting on Internet by leading UK companies", *European Accounting Review*, 8(2): 321-333

Deller, D., Stubenrath, M. & Weber, C. (1999) "A survey of the Internet for investor relations in USA, the UK and Germany", *European Accounting Review*, 8(2): 351-364

Doupnik, T. & Salter, S. (1995) "External environment of accounting practice: An preliminary test of a general model of international accounting development", *International Journal of Accounting Education of Research*, 30(2): 189-207

Dunne, T., Helliar, C., Lymer, A. & Moussa, R. (2013) "Stakeholder engagement in internet financial reporting: the diffusion of XBRL in the UK", *British Accounting Review*, 45: 167-182

Ettredge, M., Richardson, V. & Scholz, S. (2001) "The presentation of financial information at corporate web sites", *International Journal of Accounting Information Systems*, 2: 149-168

European Union (EU) (2004), "Directive 2004/109/EC of the European parliament and the council of 15 December 2004 on the harmonization of transparency requirements in relation to information about issuers whose securities are admitted to trading on a regulated market and amending directive 2001/34/EC", Official journal of the European Union, L390/38.

European Union (2013), "directive2013/50/EU of the European parliament and of the council of 22 October 2013 amending directive 2004/109/EC of the European parliament and of the council on the harmonization of transparency requirements in relation to information about issuers whose securities are admitted to trading and commission directive 2007/14/EC laying down detailed rules for the implementation of certain provisions of directive 2004/109/EC", official journal of the European union, L294/13.

FASB (2000) "Business reporting research project: electronic distribution of business reporting information", steering committee report series, Financial Accounting Standards Board

FSA. (2000) "The companies act 1985 (electronic communication) order 2000", Financial Service Autority, London.

Geerings, F., Bolen, L.H.H. & Hessink, H.F.D. (2003) "Investor relations on the Internet: A survey of the Euronext Zone", *The European Accounting Review*, 12(3): 567-579

Gray, S. (1988) "Towards a theory of cultural influence on the development of accounting systems internationally", *Abacus*, 24(1)1: 1-15

Gray, G. & Debrency, R. (1997) "Corporate reporting on the Internet: Opportunities and Challenges", Paper presented at the seventh Asian- Pacific conference

Gowthorpe, C. & Amat, O. (1999) "External reporting of accounting and financial information via the internet in Spain", *European Accounting Review*, 8(2): 365-371

Gul, F. & Leung, S. (2004) "Board leadership, outside directors' expertise and voluntary corporate disclosure", *Journal of Accounting and Public Policy*, 22: 351-379

Henchiri, J. (2011) "Voluntary Web based disclosures by Moroccan and Tunisian companies", *EuroMed Journal of Business*, 6: 55-173

Hindi, N. & Rich, J. (2010) "Financial reporting on the Internet: Evidence from the fortune 100", *Management Accounting Quarterly*, 11(2): 11-21

Hofstede, G. (1984) "Cultural dimensions in management and planning", *Asia Pacific Journal of Management*, 1: 81-99.

Hofstede, G. (2001) "Culture's consequence: comparing values, Behaviors, institutions and organizations across nations", *Sage publications*

Hooghienstra, R., Hermes, N. & Emanuels, J. (2015) "National culture and internal control disclosure: a cross-country analysis", *Corporate Governance: an International Review*, 23(4): 357-377

Hope, O. (2003) "Firm-level disclosures and the relative roles of culture and legal origin", *Journal of International Financial Management of Accounting*, 14: 218-248.

IFAC (2002) "Financial reporting on the Internet", August 2002, New York.

ISOCO (1998) "Report on securities activity on the Internet I", September 1998, www.isoco.org.

Jaggi, B. & Low, P. (2000) "Impact of culture, market forces and legal system on financial disclosure", *the International Journal of Accounting*, 35: 495-519

Kanagaretnam, K. Lim, C. & Lobo, G. (2014) "Influence of national culture on accounting conservatism and risk-taking in the banking industry", *The Accounting Review*, 89: 1115-1149

Kelton, A. & Yang, Y. (2008) "The impact of corporate governance on Internet financial reporting", *Journal of Accounting and Public Policy*, 27(1): 62-87

Kolesnik, K. (2013) "The role of culture in accounting in the light of hofstede's, Gray's and Schwartz's cultural dimensions theories- A literature review", *Financial Internet Quartely, e-finanse*, 9(3): 33-41

Lang, M. & Lundholm, R. (1993) "Cross sectional determinants of analyst ratings of corporate disclosure", *Journal of Accounting Research*, 31(2): 246-671

Lang, M. & Lundholm, R. (1996) "Corporate disclosure policy and analyst behavior", *The Accounting Review*, 7 (4): 467-492

Larran, M. & Giner, B. (2002) "The use of the Internet for corporate reporting by Spanish companies", *The International Journal of Digital Accounting Research*, 2(3): 53-82

Larson, R. & Kenny, S. (1995) "An empirical analysis of international accounting standards equity markets and economic growth in developing countries", *Journal of International Financial Management and Accounting*, 6: 130-157

Lymer, A. (1997) "The use of the Internet in company reporting: A survey and commentary on the use www in corporate reporting in UK", Paper presented at the British accounting association annual conference

Lymer, A., Debrecency, R., Gray, G.L. & Rahman, A. (1999) "Business reporting on the Internet", IASC research report.

Lymer, A. & Tallberg, A. (1997) "Corporate reporting and the Internet – a survey and commentary on the use of the www in corporate reporting in the UK and Finland", Paper presented at the annual congress of the European accounting congress, Graz, Austria

Maali, B. (2016) "Transparency disclosure and cultural values: A test for multinational corporation", *Proceedings of the Academy of Accounting and Financial Studies*, 21(2): 12-16

Marston, C. & Polei, A. (2004) "Corporate reporting on the Internet by German companies", *International Journal of Accounting Information Systems*, 5: 285-311

Mohamed, E.K.A. & Basuony, E.K.A. (2014) "Determinants and characteristics of voluntary Internet disclosure in GCC countries", *International Journal of digital Accounting Research*, 14: 57-91

Mohammadisadr, M., Seyyedali, S. & Azizolloh, A. (2012) "Relationship between managers performance and organizarional health", *International Education Studies*, 5(3): 228-234

Momany, M. & Pillai, R. (2013) "Internet financial reporting in UAE- Analysis and implications", *Global Review of Accounting and Finance,* 4(2): 142-160

Nobes, N. (1998) "Towards a general model of the reasons for international differences in financial reporting", *Abacus*, 34: 162-187

Nurunnabi, M. & Hossain, M. (2012), "The voluntary disclosure of internet financial reporting (IFR) in an emerging economy: a case of digital Bangladesh", *Journal of Asia Business Studies*, 6(1): 17-42

Ojah, K. & Mokoaleli- Mokoteli, T. (2012) "Internet financial reporting, infrastructures and corporate governance: an international analysis", *Review of development finance*, 2(2): 69-83

Oyelere, P., Laswad, F., & Fisher, R. (2003) "Determinants of Internet financial reporting by New Zealand companies", *Journal of International financial Management and Accounting*, 14(1): 26-61

Pascareno, B. & Hermana, B. (2015) "Evaluation internet financial reporting on the website of Indonesian insurance company", *Journal of Internet Banking and Commerce*, 20(1): 1-14

Pirchegger, B. & Wagenhofer, A. (1999) "Financial information on the internet: a survey of the homepage of Austrian companies", *The European Accounting Review*, 8(2): 383-395

Prabowo, R. & Tambotoh, J. (2005) "Internet financial reporting as a voluntary disclosure practice: an empirical analysis on Indonesian manufacturing firms using order Logit regression", *Jurnal Akuntansi and Bismis*, 5(2): 149-160

SEC (2003), "Mandated electronic filing and Website posting for forms 3, 4 and 5", final rule: release n°33-823, http://www.sec.gov/rules/final/33-8230

Schuster, P. & O'Connell, V. (2006) "The trend toward voluntary corporate disclosure", *Management Accounting Quarterly*, 7(2): 1-9

Trites, G.D. (1999) "The impact technology of financial and Business reporting", *Canadian Institute of Chartered Accountants, CICC.*

TSE (2003) "Electronic communications- Disclosure Guidelines", Toronto stock exchange, https://www.tsx.com,

Turel, A. (2010) "The expectation gap in Internet financial reporting evidence from an emerging capital market", *Middle Eastern Finance and Economics*, 8: 94-107

Turrent, G. & Ariza, L. (2012) "Corporate information transparency on the Internet by listed companies in Spain (IBEX 35) and Mexico (IPYC)", *International Journal of Digital Accounting Research*, 12: 1-37

Ugur, N. (2017) "Cultural differences and technology acceptance: a comparative study", *Journal of Media Critiques*, 3(1)1: 123-132

William, S. (2004) "An international investigation of association between societal variables and the amount of disclosure on information technology and communication problems: the case of Y2K", *The International Journal of Accounting*, 39: 71-92

Xiao, J., Yang, H. & Chow, C. (2004) "The determinants and characteristics of voluntary Internet based disclosure by listed Chinese companies", *Journal of Accounting and Public Policy*, 23: 191-225

Zarzeski, M.T (1996) "Spontaneous harmonization effects of culture and market forces on accounting disclosure practices accounting disclosure", *Accounting Horizons*, 10: 18-37

Zeghal, D. & Moussa, M (2015) "An analysis of the determinants of corporate governance disclosure policies in multinational enterprises: a multi-medium study", *Corporate Ownership and Control*, 12(4): 671-694

6

Independent auditing effect on investment decisions of institutional investors

Atila Karkacıer [a,1] and Fatih Coşkun Ertaş [a]

[a] *Gaziosmanpaşa University, Tokat, Turkey*

Abstract: It is very important for investors to get accurate and reliable information so that they can earn large amounts of revenue from decisions they make. However, in recent years, population growth, the expansion of the economy and the complexity of economic life have reduced the credibility of the information presented. The need for accurate and reliable information leads to requests for accounting and auditing activities. The independent audit, which increases the credibility of the information provided by the company and the reports it prepares, is also important in terms of investors, lenders and business owners. The aim of this study is to determine whether institutional investors are influenced by independent audit practices and the results of their investment decisions, and if so, how effective they are. In this study, firstly information about institutional investors is given and the factors affecting investment decisions are mentioned. Later, information on auditing was included. In the last part of the study, a questionnaire was applied to the managers of institutional investors consisting of banks, brokerage houses, investment trusts and portfolio management companies registered in the Turkish Capital Markets Association (TCMA) to investigate whether any independent auditing practices and results had any effect on investment decisions of institutional investors. As a result of the analyzes made, it has been determined that institutional investors consider the independent audit report and its results together with the investment decisions of the independent audit financial tables and have effects on their decisions.

Keywords: Institutional Investor, Investment Decisions, Independent Audit.

---

[1] Correspondence address: Atila Karkacıer, Gaziosmanpaşa University, Research Assistant at GOÜ Faculty of Business/Accounting & Finance Division. E-mail: atila.karkacier@gop.edu.tr

1. Introduction

It is a big deal in terms of the fact that the financial statements prepared by the companies show reliable and timely information. Macroeconomic indicators and the financial position of the investor are the determinants of investors' decisions. Investors, in particular, decide whether to invest in the shares of the enterprises by examining the financial position and results of operations (Coşkun *et al.*, 2013: 11). Instead of small investors, institutional investors are called specialized financial institutions that manage savings in a collective way in terms of the level of risk, return and target of investment.

The presence of new financial instruments in the economy and the feeling of the effects of technological developments on the economy increase the demand for reliable information. In particular, the reliability of the information that they obtain from investing in investments for investors is of utmost importance. Investors should investigate that the information disclosed in the name of the decision will be as reliable as possible. In verifying the reliability of the information disclosed, it is a common practice to check this information by an independent person. Integrity, correctness and impartiality must be audited and verified in order for information to be accepted as reliable information for decision-making (Erdoğan, 2002: 62-63).

At this point, appropriate and sufficient independent audit evidence to provide a reasonable assurance of conformity and accuracy between the financial statements and other financial information formed as a result of the economic activities of an entity and previously established criteria and the application of appropriate independent audit techniques recommended in the independent audit standards, And an independent audit, whose results are linked to the report, has emerged (Kardeş - Selimoğlu *et al.,* 2011: 5).

The main purpose of the research is to demonstrate whether the institutional investor has an independent audit on the investment decisions and the effect of the results. The study also explores the perception differences between independent brokerage firms, portfolio management companies, investment partnerships, and bank, which are among the institutional investor types, to consider independent control when making investment decisions. However, it is important to investigate the contribution of the literature to the measurement and evaluation of the interaction between independent audit results and practices and institutional investors who are making investment decisions.

This study consists of a total of four sections except for the introduction and conclusion section. In the first part of the study, information about institutional investors is given. In the second part, independent audit is examined. In the third chapter, similar studies are introduced in the literature review. In the fourth part, the scope of the research, the method applied in the research, the analysis of the research data, findings and interpretations are given. Finally, in the light of the findings obtained from the survey, the results were evaluated and suggested.

2. Factors affecting institutional investors and investment decisions

Investors are classified as institutional investors and individual investors according to the party to which the funds are directed. Individual investors often do not have the opportunity to follow the market constantly, act according to their developments and manage their portfolios professionally when they do not have the necessary technical equipment and sufficient expertise. Portfolios created with individual savings that do not reach sufficient size are often referred to as risky portfolios. It is also not possible for individual investors to be distracted because they can invest only a few borrowing shares or shares with limited savings they have. As such, institutional investors have been formed in capital markets as collective investment institutions (Akın and Ece, 2011: 12).

Institutional investors who take the role of collecting the fund surplus that individuals make positively between the income they earn and the expenditures they incur and the large amount of these funds being evaluated within the legal boundaries try to operate in order to diversify the funds they collect through individual investors in terms of investor groups and to provide the highest return (Usul and Kocabıyık, 2010: 65). Institutional investors include mutual funds, private pension funds, investment trusts, brokerage houses, portfolio management companies, insurance companies, social security institutions and banks.

Institutional investors are the most important component of the demand trend of capital markets in developed countries because they evaluate the high level funds they obtain from various sources by channeling them to capital market instruments according to expert staff and return expectations and risk expectations (Zor and Aslanoglu, 2005: 185). Institutional investors can play an important role in the development of financial markets as well as contribute to overall domestic economic growth. Institutional investors dynamically influence both financial sector growth and economic growth (Harichandra and Thangavelu, 2004: 7-8).

However, institutional investors are generally considered to have a positive effect on share prices of the companies they invest in. This effect is achieved through different mechanisms. Institutional investors reduce information asymmetry between the firm and other investors. It improves the corporate governance of the companies. It also contributes to the liquidity of companies (Huyghebaert and Hulle, 2004: 690).

Investment decisions are one of the most important tasks and responsibilities of the finance function. In order to be able to make a positive decision about any investment topic in terms of business management, the profit to be provided by this investment should meet the cost that it will cause. However, investment should provide profit for the entrepreneur (Babuşcu and Hazar, 2007: 109). Factors affecting investment decisions can be classified as economic factors, political factors, information sources, socio-cultural factors and psychological factors.

3. Independent audit

In recent years, with the increase of economic activities, the reliability of the information provided by the enterprises due to the more complicated transactions, the surplus of the data and the approaches of the informants have been questioned more and the needs of the information users have become more reliable and widespread (Kardeş-Selimoglu *et al.*, 2011: 2). Relevant and reliable information needs have led to accounting and auditing services. For example; an investor who wants to invest money in stock, a bank that has to give credit to the business, a public institution that is trying to get the right to make a healthy decision definitely needs reliable information (Ataman *et al.*, 2001: 13).

In the business world, it is very difficult for information users to get the information they desire first hand. When knowledge is obtained from others, it is more likely that it is intentionally or otherwise misrepresented. When there is a conflict of interest between the information claimant and the information provider, there is a risk that the information presented is misleading. Here are three things that can be done against the riskier. The first is to obtain and control the desired information on its own; second, to rely on the other side to enter into a risk; and the third is to resort to independent audit opinion (Kardeş-Selimoğlu *et al.*, 2011: 2).

Independent auditing is the audit and compliance and performance audits of the financial statements of the enterprises by an auditor or auditor who, within the scope of an audit agreement, provide the professional audit service to the clients, who work on their behalf as a self-employed person or perform their duties as an auditor. Financial audit is the main objective of independent audit (Uzun, 2007: 4).

An audit is the process of providing assurance about the accuracy of the information taking place in the financial statements prepared in accordance with generally accepted acounting principles or other rules. The responsibility of the financial statements of a company belongs to the management of the company (Soltani, 2007: 4).

Based on these definitions, we can list the main features of the audit as follows (Güçlü, 2008: 1-2):

- Auditing is a process: It covers a certain period.
- Interested in economic activities and other events.
- Auditing has predetermined criteria.
- The audit must be impartial.
- The most basic principle of auditing is to collect evidence and evaluate them.
- Auditing is obliged to report the results to the addressees.

Auditing enhances the reliability of information provided to investors, business owners, lenders and other users. In short, the task of the auditor is to detect mistakes and deceptions. The results of the audit practices appear in the audit report. Today, the primary goal of auditing is to approve the correctness of financial statements. Auditing not only reduces the cost of exchanging information between managers and shareholders as an important part of the capital market framework, but also points to a marketplace where information is trustworthy (Salehi, 2010: 70-82).

4. Literature review

In general, independent audit and its quality with the independent audit report and the internal audit report are found in a number of literature studies examining the effect on investment and lending decisions as well as the effect of investor confidence and stock return. There are studies in the literature that show that auditor opinion is important and should be taken into account when trying to measure the impact of auditor opinions on investment decisions and credit approvals (Gómez-Guillamón, 2003; Holt and DeZoort, 2009; Lai, 2009; Mansi, Maxwell and Miller, 2004; Ruiz-Barbadillo *et al.*, 2004; Salehi, 2010). As a result, it is stated that these studies take into account the auditor's opinion on investment decisions and credit approval. Companies that have significant investment opportunities have been audited by 5 major audit companies; it is also emphasized that the audit report is an important parameter when making investment decisions.

On the other hand, there are also some studies in the literature that are opposite of the results above. Studies in which the audit reports and audit opinions have no effect on the decision makers are also included in the literature (Kabajeh *et al.*,

2012; Martinez *et al.*, 2004; Ogneva & Subramanyam, 2007; Tahinakis *et al.*, 2010; Moradi *et al.*, 2011; Anvarkhatibi *et al.*, 2012). The results of the studies show that both company managers and lenders think that the auditor's report is not completely unbiased, inadequate and inappropriate when making decisions. In addition, lenders declare that these reports do not make a positive contribution to their credit decisions. In addition, the findings of the studies show that conditional audit reports do not have the value of information for investors. They also state that the audit report for investors is not a part of the decision-making process. Lastly, studies show that auditor opinions do not have a significant effect on stock prices and returns. These differences can be caused by the time, country or the methods of the studies.

In general, when the literature is examined, no study was encountered that on how much institutional investors consider independent audit in investment decisions. Than, the views of managers of institutional investors including banks, brokerage houses, investment trusts and portfolio management companies registered with the Turkish Capital Association (TCA) have been consulted in order to determine whether the independent auditing practices and results are influential on the investment decisions of the institutional investor and if so, to determine the degree.

5. A research to determine the effect of independent auditing on investment decisions of institutional investors

In this section, the purpose and the importance of the research, the scope of the research, the method applied in the research, the hypotheses of the research, the analysis and findings of the research data are included.

5.1. The purpose and the importance of the research

The main purpose of the research is to determine whether the results of the independent auditing are effective for the investment decisions of the institutional investor and if so, to determine the degree. The brokerage house, which is one of the institutional investors, is to investigate perception differences related to independent auditing while it decides to invest among the portfolio management company, the investment partnership, and the bank. It is also the purpose of the research to develop recommendations in order to demonstrate the importance of independent auditing.

Institutional investors are required to research the results of independent audits in investment decisions, and to contribute to the literature by measuring and evaluating the effects of their applications.

5.2. The scope of the research

As of October 2015, 228 institutional investors (banks, brokerage houses, investment trusts and portfolio management companies) registered in the Turkish Capital Association (TCA) constitute the scope of the research. 17 of the institutional investors were temporarily suspended. In this case, 211 institutional investors registered with TCA also constitute the main mass of the research at the same time. The data source in the study is the managers in different positions. Questionnaires were sent via e-mail to the 211 institutional investors active in TCA, the main mass of the research. The names of the banks, brokerage houses, investment trusts and portfolio management companies and the telephone numbers, open addresses and / or electronic mail addresses of these companies were obtained from the internet addresses of the CMB and TCA and the internet addresses of the companies. By linking to a web page given in the e-mail, companies are directed to the questionnaire; Answers are recorded in the same database. So they did not have to send e-mails to send their answers. In order to increase the response rate of the questionnaire, necessary correspondences were obtained from TCA. A total of 211 institutional investors registered with TCA were sent a questionnaire and 118 questionnaires were found suitable for analysis. In this case, the return rate is approximately 56%.

5.3. The method of the research

Following the theoretical study in the research, the survey method was used as the method applied to measure the effect of independent auditing of institutional investors on investment decisions. Since there is no scale related to the research topic, the questions on the questionnaire were prepared by taking the literature survey results into consideration, especially by making use of Gomez-Guillamon (2003), Adeyemi and Uadiale (2011), Leung and Chau (2001), Best *et al.* (2001) and Fadzly and Ahmad (2004). The prepared questionnaire was completed in May 2015 after the examination of experts and a pilot study on bank managers in Tokat.

The first section of the two-part questionnaire is a closed-end, 5-point Likert scale for determining how much institutional investors take into account independent control of investment decisions. There are 26 expressions in the first chapter. 1-7 expressions are related to Hypothesis 1, 8-15 expressions are 2. Hypothesis related, 16-21 expressions are related to 3. Hypothesis, and 22-26 expressions are related to the fourth hypothesis. In the second part, there are 9 questionnaires including demographic characteristics of participating institutional investors and participant information. In this case, the questionnaire consists of 26 expressions and 9 questions. Surveys are open on the internet from June 1, 2015 to October 8, 2015.

5.4. Findings of the research

The analysis of the study was first started with reliability analysis and the reliability of the questionnaire was measured. Then frequency analysis was done. To test the research hypotheses, a normality test was performed to determine whether to use parametric or nonparametric tests. Mann-Whitney U test was applied to the hypotheses firstly after Kruskall Wallis test.

Research data were analyzed using SPSS (Statistical Package for the Social Sciences) and Microsoft Office Excel programs. Reliability analysis was done first. It is called reliability that reveals the consistency of all the questions in a measurement (test, questionnaire) with each other and the homogeneity in measuring the problem studied (Akgül & Çevik, 2003: 434). The Cronbach alpha coefficient was used to measure the reliability of the questionnaire. The Cronbach Alpha Coefficient, which investigates whether the whole of the scale in question is homogeneous in order to explain its homogeneity, shows the similarity and closeness of the questions in the cases where the individual scores are collected by the answers given to the questions. The ranges and the reliability of the scale where the Alfa coefficient can be found between 0 and 1 are as follows (Akgül & Çevik, 2003: 435-436):

If $0.00 \leq \alpha < 0.40$, the scale is not reliable.
If $0.40 \leq \alpha < 0.60$, the scale is low reliability.
If $0.60 \leq \alpha < 0.80$, the scale is mostly reliable.
If $0.80 \leq \alpha < 1.00$, the scale is highly reliable.

The Cronbach Alpha coefficient obtained in the study is 0.928. This figure indicates that the survey is highly reliable.

Then frequency distributions were given according to the characteristics of institutional investors who answered the questionnaire. Subsequently, brokerage house managers, investment partnership managers, portfolio management company managers and bank managers are presented with views on statements prepared according to the 5-point Likert scale.

It has been determined whether parametric or nonparametric tests should be applied to the research data by testing normality. The Shapiro Wilks test should be used when the number of subjects is less than 29 in the normality test, and the Kolmogorov-Smirnov test should be used when the number of subjects is more than 29 (Akgül & Çevik, 2003: 99). The results obtained from the normality test for the four hypothesis-related groups (Brokerage House (43), Investment Trust (24), Portfolio Management Company (21), Bank (30)) did not meet the normal distribution ($p < 0,05$). This resulted in the need to use non-parametric tests.

In the test of research hypotheses, Kruskall Wallis test was used to compare nonparametric tests between three or more groups with continuous variables and then to show which group is different from the other group; Mann-Whitney U test was used to test significant differences between two independent groups.

5.4.1. General characteristics of institutional investors participating in the research

73.7% of the managers of institutional investors who responded to the survey were male and 26.3% were females. 73.3% of the institutional investor managers are in the age range of 20-40, 26.7% are in the 40 and above. 36.4% of the institutional investor managers work in the Brokerage House, 25.4% in the Bank, 20.3% in the Investment Trust and 17.8% in the Portfolio Management Company. 25.4% of institutional investor managers are experts, 23.7% are managers, 18.6% are portfolio managers, 9.3% are managers, 8.5% are directors, 5.9% are board members, partners, general managers, Senior manager consisting of assistant general managers, 4.2% assistant manager, and lastly 4.2% senior executive. 49.2% of institutional investor managers have between 1-10 years, 38.1% between 11-20 years and 12.7% more than 21 years. Institutional investor managers account for 60.2% of the bachelor's degree, 35.6% hold a master degree and 4.2% hold a doctorate degree.

5.4.2. Perceptions of institutional investors using independent audit in investment decisions

In this section, for the investment decisions of the institutional investors consisting of brokerage houses, investment partnerships, portfolio management companies and banks participating in the research; *the information contained in the independent audit report of the company to be invested, the audit opinion, whether the audit was carried out by 4 major audit firms, and the perceptions of the extent to which the independent audited financial statements are effective* are presented.

In this part of the study, participants in the survey were asked to indicate whether they participated in the 5-point Likert scale and prepared statements to measure how much they considered independent control of investment decisions. The weighted average for each expression was calculated by giving the weight from 1 to 5, with the answer "I do not Participate Totally" in the direction of the answers obtained and 1 to say "I Participate Totally".

5.4.3. Analysis of the differences among institutional investors' measures of using independent audit in investment decisions

In this part of the study, the existence of the differences in the application of independent auditing in investment decisions of brokerage houses, investment trusts, portfolio management companies and banks was examined. Here, the perception of the brokerage houses, investment partnerships, portfolio management companies and bank managers responding to the questionnaire are examined by matching. The findings of the statistical analyzes were revealed and the findings of the tested hypotheses are explained.

a) Analysis of the differences among institutional investors' perceptions of investment decisions using the information contained in the independent audit report

The perceptions of the brokerage houses participating in the survey, investment trusts, portfolio management companies and banks' perceptions regarding the investment decisions used in the independent audit report are given in Table 1.

Table 1. Average percentage of institutional investors who participated in the research on their use of information in the independent audit report on investment decisions

Information in the Independent Audit Report	Brokerage House (Mean)	Investment Partnership (Mean)	Portfolio Management Firm (Mean)	Bank (Mean)
1. Independent audit reports are considered when making investment decisions for a company.	3.93	4.54	4.71	3.93
2. Independent audit reports are useful for estimating company performance.	3.83	4.41	4.09	3.86
3. Independent audit reports are effective in determining the profitability (efficiency) of a company.	3.81	3.95	3.90	3.80
4. I benefit from the independent audit report, while I assess the future profitability of the new investments of the company that I will invest in.	3.53	3.91	3.80	3.86
5. I make use of the independent audit report when I estimate the future cash flow volume or risk of the company.	3.62	4.04	3.76	3.96
6. An independent audit report may contain important information about a firm's ability to sustain its existence.	3.83	4.29	3.85	3.90
7. The audit report is sufficiently useful and understandable to make informed decisions.	3.51	3.50	3.28	3.66
TOTAL	3.72	4.09	3.91	3.85

Research Hypothesis 1

H0: There is no statistically significant difference among perceptions of institutional investors regarding the effectiveness of the information contained in the independent audit report in investment decisions.

H1: There are statistically significant differences among the perceptions of institutional investors regarding the effectiveness of the information contained in the independent audit report in their investment decisions.

The 1 hypothesis is tested by calculating a dimension of 7 words mentioned. With this dimension, participants' mean scores for 7 expressions are determined. Kruskall Wallis test was applied for the hypothesis and the results are given in Table 2 below.

Table 2. Results of the Kruskall Wallis test on the use of the information contained in the independent audit report in the investment decisions of the institutional investors participating in the survey

	Chi-square	Degree of Freedom	Significance
Information in the Independent Audit Report	0.889	3	0.828

* Statistically significant at 10% significance level.
** Statistically significant at 5% significance level.
*** Statistically significant at the 1% significance level.

According to the results of the Kruskall Wallis test, as shown in Table 2, there is no statistically significant difference among the perceptions of the broker managers, investment trust managers, portfolio managers and managers regarding the information contained in the independent audit report. In other words, the H0 hypothesis has been accepted. Here, although the average of brokerage managers is slightly lower than that of investment trust managers, portfolio management firms and bank managers, it does not make any statistical sense. Here, institutional investors have stated that they use the information contained in the independent audit report on their investment decisions at the same level and use them in investment decisions.

b) Analysis of the differences among institutional investors' perceptions of taking the audit opinion type into consideration in investment decision making

Averages for the perception of brokerage houses participating in the survey, investment trusts, portfolio management companies and banks to consider the audit opinion type in investment decisions are given in Table 3.

Table 3. Average of Institutional Investors' Perceptions of Taking the Audit Opinion Type into Consideration in Investment Decisions

Audit Opinion Type	Brokerage House (Mean)	Investment Partnership (Mean)	Portfolio Management Firm (Mean)	Bank (Mean)
8. The type of audit opinion is influential on investment in a company.	3.53	4.33	3.52	3.86
9. The information obtained by the auditor's opinion is useful when making investment decisions.	3.48	3.91	3.85	3.96
10. The type of audit opinion is influential in deciding the amount of investment.	3.20	3.62	3.38	3.90
11. Auditor's opinion has an impact on the company's share prices.	3.02	3.37	3.19	3.76
12. An independent audit report with a positive opinion is an indication of the investability of the operator.	3.09	3.87	3.09	3.63
13. The conditional audit opinion has a negative effect on the credibility of the investor.	3.34	4.20	3.76	3.33
14. An audit opinion avoided from commenting has an adverse effect on the credibility of the investor.	3.83	4.41	3.80	3.90
15. Negative audit opinion has an effect on my investment decision.	3.88	4.33	4.23	3.93
TOTAL	**3.42**	**4.00**	**3.60**	**3.78**

Research Hypothesis 2

H0: There is no statistically significant difference among institutional investors' perceptions of the impact of audit opinion on investment decisions.

H1: There are statistically significant differences among the perceptions of institutional investors regarding the effectiveness of the audit opinion track in investment decisions.

The second hypothesis is tested by calculating a dimension of 8 words mentioned. With this dimension, participants' averages for 8 expressions between 8-15 are determined. The Kruskall Wallis test was applied for the hypothesis and the results are given in Table 4 below.

Table 4. Results of the Kruskall Wallis test for institutional investors participating in the study to consider the audit opinion type in investment decisions

	Chi-Square	Degree of Freedom	Significance
The Audit Opinion Type	6.977	3	0.073*

* Statistically significant at 10% significance level.
** Statistically significant at 5% significance level.
*** Statistically significant at the 1% significance level.

As seen in Table 4, there is a statistically significant difference in the level of 10% significance among the perceptions of the broker managers, investment trust managers, portfolio managers, and bank managers on the information contained in the independent audit report, according to Kruskall-Wallis test results. In other words, the H0 hypothesis has been rejected.

The Mann Whitney U test was conducted to determine perception differences between the two specific groups. The Mann Whitney U test was conducted between brokerage house managers, investment trust managers, portfolio management company executives and bank managers. The results of the Mann Whitney U test in general are shown in Table 5 below.

Table 5. Mann Whitney U test results concerning the view of the audit opinion in investment decisions of institutional investors participating in the survey

Audit Opinion Type	Investment Partnership with Brokerage House		Portfolio Management Firm with Brokerage House		Bank with Brokerage House		Portfolio Management Firm with Investment		Bank with Investment Partnership		Bank with Porfolio Management Firm	
	Mann-Whitney U	Significance	Mann-Whitney U	Significance	Mann-Whitney U	Significance	Mann-Whitney U	Significance	Mann-Whitney U	Significance	Mann-Whitney U	Significance
Consideration of audit opinion when managers make investment decisions	337.000	0.019 **	441.000	0.880	524.000	0.174	164.500	0.046 **	313.500	0.417	241.500	0.157

* Statistically significant at 10% significance level.
** Statistically significant at 5% significance level.
*** Statistically significant at 1% significance level.

As shown in Table 5, the Mann Whitney U test results for Hypothesis 2 are shown above. According to the Mann Whitney U test results, there is a statistically significant difference in the level of 5% significance between brokerage houses and investment management managers considering the audit opinion type when making investment decisions.

Yet again, according to the Mann Whitney U test results, there is a statistically significant difference in the level of 5% significance between investment partnership and portfolio management company managers' decision on audit review.

In this respect, it was concluded that there was a difference between the opinions of the brokerage house, the investment partnership and the managers of the portfolio management companies regarding the view of the audit opinion when making investment decision. Here are the managers of investment partnerships; Portfolio management company executives, bank managers, and brokerage managers. The brokerage house managers are the ones that are least considered.

c) Analysis of the differences among the perceptions in investment decisions of the institutional investors related to the auditing by the 4 major audit firms

The averages for the perception of the brokerage houses participating in the survey, investment trusts, portfolio management companies and banks to be considered by the 4 major audit firms to audit the investment decisions are given in Table 6.

Table 6. Average Percentage of the perceptions in investment decisions of the institutional investors related to the auditing by the 4 major audit firms

Auditing by the 4 Major Audit Firms	Brokerage House (Mean)	Investment Partnership (Mean)	Portfolio Management Firm (Mean)	Bank (Mean)
16. When the investment decision is made, I check whether the company is audited by the first 4 major audit companies.	2.97	3.95	2.80	3.63
17. The fact that the company was audited by the first 4 major audit companies while receiving an investment decision is influential in the positive direction.	3.30	4.16	2.80	3.83
18. I trust more in the financial statements of the audited firm as the audits conducted by the first 4 major audit firms are of better quality.	3.20	4.00	3.04	3.63
19. Since the auditors of the first 4 major audit firms are better at expertise and competence, they are influential in investing.	3.25	4.00	2.33	3.40

Auditing by the 4 Major Audit Firms	Brokerage House (Mean)	Investment Partnership (Mean)	Portfolio Management Firm (Mean)	Bank (Mean)
20. I only invest in companies audited by the first 4 major audit firms.	2.20	2.79	1.71	2.80
21. I think that the auditors of the first 4 major audit firms are performing audit activities more effectively.	3.06	3.95	3.19	3.33
TOTAL	**3.00**	**3.81**	**2.65**	**3.44**

Research Hypothesis 3

H0: There is no statistically significant difference between perceptions of institutional investors regarding the effectiveness of the audit by the 4 major audit firms.

H1: There are statistically significant differences between the perceptions of institutional investors about the effectiveness of the audit by the 4 major audit firms.

The 3th hypothesis is tested by calculating a dimension of the mentioned 6 expressions. This dimension determines the average of the participants' six expressions, 16-21. Kruskall Wallis test was applied for the hypothesis and the results are given in Table 7 below.

Table 7. Kruskall Wallis test results regarding consideration of the audit by 4 big audit firms by institutional investors participating in the research for investment decisions

	Chi-Square	Degree of Freedom	Significance
Audit by 4 Big Audit Firms	23.436	3	0.000 ***

* Statistically significant at 10% significance level.
** Statistically significant at 5% significance level.
*** Statistically significant at the 1% significance level.

As seen in Table 7, according to Kruskall-Wallis test results, there is a statistically significant difference in the level of significance among the perceptions of the broker managers, investment trust managers, portfolio managers and managers regarding the information contained in the independent audit report. In other words, the H0 hypothesis has been rejected.

The Mann Whitney U test was conducted to determine perception differences between the two specific groups. The Mann Whitney U test was conducted between brokerage house managers, investment trust managers, portfolio management company executives and bank managers. The results of the Mann Whitney U test in general are shown in Table 8 below.

Table 8. Mann Whitney U test results regarding consideration of the audit by 4 big audit firms by institutional investors participating in the research for investment decisions

Audit Opinion Type	Investment Partnership with Brokerage House		Portfolio Management Firm with Brokerage House		Bank with Brokerage House		Portfolio Management Firm with Investment Partnership		Bank with Investment Partnership		Bank with Portfolio Management Firm	
	Mann-Whitney U	Significance	Mann-Whitney U	Significance	Mann-Whitney U	Significance	Mann-Whitney U	Significance	Mann-Whitney U	Significance	Mann-Whitney U	Significance
Consideration of audit opinion when managers make investment decisions	257.500	0.001 ***	341.500	0.115	484.000	0.070 *	51.500	0.000 ***	275.500	0.139	150.000	0.002 ***

* Statistically significant at 10% significance level.
** Statistically significant at 5% significance level.
*** Statistically significant at the 1% significance level.

The Mann Whitney U test results for the 3rd hypothesis are shown above, as shown in Table 8. According to the Mann Whitney U test results, there is a statistically significant difference at the 1% level of significance between brokerage houses and investment partners who consider investment decisions made by 4 major audit firms in charge of investment decisions.

According to the Mann Whitney U test results, there is a statistically significant difference at the 10% level of significance between brokerage firms and bank managers considering that they are made by 4 major supervisory firms that audit the investment decisions.

However, according to the Mann Whitney U test results, there is a statistically significant difference in the level of significance of the investment partnership and portfolio management companies considering that they are being conducted by 4 major audit firms that audit the investment decisions.

Finally, according to the Mann Whitney U test results, there is a statistically significant difference between the portfolio management company and the bank managers at the 1% level of significance, considering that they are being conducted by 4 major audit firms that audit the investment decisions.

In this respect, it was concluded that there were differences between the opinions of the brokerage house, investment partnership, portfolio management company and bank managers regarding the decision of the 4 major audit firms to audit the company to invest while giving investment decision. Here, whereas the investment partnership managers stated that they considered that the investment decisions were made by four major audit firms, the managers of the portfolio management company stated that they have not considered.

d) Analysis of the Differences among the Perceptions of Institutional Investors on the use of Independent Audited Financial Statements in Investment Decisions

Table 9 summarizes the averages of the brokerage houses participating in the survey, investment trusts, portfolio management companies and banks' perception of their investment decisions using their independent audit financial statements.

Table 9. The averages of the institutional investors' perception of their investment decisions using the independent audited financial statements

Independent Audited Financial Statements	Brokerage House (Mean)	Investment Partnership (Mean)	Portfolio Management Firm (Mean)	Bank (Mean)
22. Independent audited financial statements provide an accurate and clear view for my investmentdecision.	3.58	4.25	3.76	3.82
23. I use audited financial statements in monitoring the performance of the company.	3.79	4.16	3.47	3.86
24. I rely on the audited financial statements for the investment decision.	3.74	4.04	3.23	3.83
25. I trust in audited financial statements when evaluating whether the company's assets have been managed well.	3.62	3.95	3.00	3.80
26. I use audited financial statements when I assess whether the assets of the company are well managed.	3.58	3.87	3.47	3.80
TOTAL	**3.66**	**4.05**	**3.39**	**3.82**

Research Hypothesis 4
H0: There is no statistically significant difference between the perceptions of investment decisions of the institutional investors and the effect of the financial statements that were audited by independent auditors.

H1: Institutional investors; There are statistically significant differences between the perceptions of the investment decisions and the effect of the independent audited financial statements.

The 4th hypothesis is tested by calculating a dimension of 5 expressions mentioned here. With this dimension, participants' averages for 5 expressions between 22-26 are determined. Kruskall Wallis test was applied for the hypothesis and the results are given in Table 10 below.

Table 10. Kruskall Wallis test results of the institutional investors' perception of their investment decisions using the independent audited financial statements

	Chi-Square	Degree of Freedom	Significance
Independent Audited Financial Statements	2.707	3	0.439

* Statistically significant at 10% significance level.
** Statistically significant at 5% significance level.
*** Statistically significant at the 1% significance level.

According to the results of Kruskall-Wallis test, as shown in Table 10, there is no statistical difference among the perceptions of brokerage managers, investment trust managers, portfolio management managers and bank managers regarding the use of independent financial statements in their investment decisions. In other words, the H0 hypothesis has been accepted. Here, although the average of portfolio managers is slightly lower than that of investment trust managers, brokerage managers and bank managers, it is not statistically significant. However, institutional investors have stated that they use these statements in their investment decisions at almost the same level as statements about the use of independent financial statements in investment decisions. Only the portfolio management company directors use these tables in a close proximity.

6. Conclusion

The fact that individual investors do not have sufficient knowledge accumulation and that there is a limited number of investment vehicles that they can invest because their savings are at a certain level are an obstacle to the dissemination of risk. Due to these and similar reasons, institutional investors who have the necessary technical equipment and sufficient expertise, follow the bazaars of the markets, take positions according to their developments and manage their portfolios in a professional manner have been formed. Institutional investors fulfill their functions by directing the large amount of funds they collect from individual investors to the capital market instruments through the professionally manageable staff of the portfolio.

It is a very important issue for investors to reach accurate and reliable information in order to make the right decisions. The information they use must be relevant and reliable so that they can benefit significantly from the decisions they make. In recent years, the growth of societies, the increase of economic activities and the increasing complexity of the economic life are decreasing the reliability level of the information presented. The need for relevant and reliable information has revealed the demand for accounting and auditing activities. Independent auditing, the period during which information about the economic activities and events of the company is collected in an unbiased manner to determine and report conformity with previously established and accepted criteria and to be communicated to the information users through a report of the evaluation and conclusion, enhances the reliability of information provided to investors, business owners, lenders and other related users. Independent auditing, which affirms the accuracy of certain financial statements, draws attention to the reliability of information provided by management.

In the direction of our research whose main aim is to determine whether the independent audit applications and results influence on the investment decisions of the institutional investors, according to the findings obtained as a result of the survey conducted to the institutional investors of the Turkish Capital Markets Association, brokerage managers, investment trust managers, portfolio management company managers and bank managers have stated that they have used this information in making investment decision by participating at the same level in the expressions related to the usage of the information in the audit report for investment decisions. Even if the institutional investors use the information contained in the independent audit report in their investment decisions, they were undecided on the positive side that the independent audit report was sufficiently useful and understandable.

According to the analysis results, investment partnership managers are more concerned about the audit opinion on investment decisions than portfolio managers, bank managers and brokerage managers. The managers of the brokerage houses are unstable in this respect. Nevertheless, it was the result that auditor opinions that were negative and refrained from commenting affected the investment decisions of institutional investors more than the positive and conditional audit opinions. In addition, while bank managers participated in the audit opinion that it had an impact on the company's share prices, others were unstable.

According to the analysis results, while the investment partnership managers state that for their investment decisions, they consider the audit by 4 big audit firms for the company that they will invest in, the portfolio management company managers states that they do not consider this. Brokerage house and bank managers have expressed an unstable situation in this regard. Only the investment trust managers are involved in thinking that the first four major audit firms are composed of more competent, more specialized inspectors and that their activities and results are more reliable.

According to the analysis results, the brokerage house managers, investment trust managers, portfolio management company managers and bank managers were attended at almost the same level of the expressions about the use of the independent audited financial statements in the investment decisions and they stated that they use these tables in investment decisions. Only the managers of the portfolio management companies have revealed a near-uncertainty in this matter. The brokerage house, investment partners and bank executives stated that they have confidence in the audited financial statements for the investment decision, while the managers of the portfolio management companies are unstable about trust.

As a result of the findings obtained, institutional investors, including brokerage houses, portfolio management companies, investment partnership and banks, which are included in the research, evaluate the investment decisions taking the information that may be useful for them in the audit report into consideration. When investing in a company, this information affects their attitudes. Although this is not the case at all, it is concluded that the independent audit report is indeed beneficial and useful, as well as affecting investment decisions. This demonstrates the independent and authentic assurance of institutional investors. The fact that the audit is conducted by four major audit firms, which is used as one of the quality criteria of audit in the literature, is not so important for institutional investors when making investment decisions. Finally, we can say that independent audit practices and results provide an information value to the institutional investor.

The result is while showing similarity to the results of the studies performed by Gomez-Guillamon (2003) and Salehi (2010); on the other hand differs with the results of the studies conducted by Anvarkhatibi *et al.* (2012) and Martinez *et al.* (2004). These differences can be caused by the time of the studies, countries or the methods applied.

This study has been analyzed in terms of the opinions of brokerage houses, investment trusts, portfolio management companies and bank managers registered in the Turkish Capital Association in Turkey. In future studies, researchers can create a larger sample, or can include other institutional investors in the sample. It is also possible to examine the extent to which individual investors use independent audit practices and results in their investment decisions.

References

Adeyemi, S. B. & Uadiale, O. M. (2011) "An empirical investigation of the audit expectation gap in Nigeria", *African Journal of Business Management,* vol. 5(19): 7964-7971

Akgül, A. & Çevik, O. (2003) *İstatistiksel Analiz Teknikleri: SPSS'te İşletme Yönetimi Uygulamaları [Statistical Analysis Techniques: Management Applications in SPSS]*, Emek Ofset Ltd. Şti.,Ankara.

Akın, F. ve Ece, N. (2011) "Kurumsal yatırımcılar ve Türk sermaye piyasasında kurumsal yatırımcıların gelişimi üzerine bir değerlendirme [Institutional investors and an evaluation on the development of institutional investors in the Turkish capital market]", *ABMYO Dergisi*, vol. 22: 11-26

Anvarkhatibi, S., Safashur, M. & Mohammadi, J. (2012) "The effect of auditors opinions on shares prices and returns in Tehran stock exchange", *Research Journal of Management Science*, vol. 1(1): 23-27

Ataman, Ü., Hacırüstemoğlu, R. ve Bozkurt, N. (2001) *Muhasebe Denetimi Uygulamaları [Audit Practices]*, İstanbul: Alfa Yayınları.

Azibi, J., Tondeur, H. & Rajhi, M. T. (2011) "Auditor choice and institutional investor characteristics after the enron scandal in the French context", *International Journal of Economics and Accounting*, vol. *2*(1): 32-52

Babuşcu, Ş. & Hazar, A. (2007) *Finansal Yönetim [Financial Management],* SPK Lisanslama Serisi 16. Ankara: Akademi Consultin & Training.

Best, P. J., Buckby, S. & Tan, C. (2001) "Evidence of the audit expectation gap in Singapore", *Managerial Auditing Journal,* vol. 16(3)134-144

Coşkun, A., Güner, M. F. & Okudan, F. (2013) *Denetim [Auditing]*, Kamu Gözetimi Muhasebe ve Denetim Standartları Kurumu Geçiş Dönemi Eğitimi Notları. İstanbul: Fatih Üniversitesi Sürekli Eğitim Merkezi.

Erdoğan, M. (2002) "Muhasebe, denetim ve bağımsız denetimin gerekliliği [Accouinting, auditing and the necessity of independent auditing]", *Doğuş Üniversitesi Dergisi,* vol. 5: 51-63

Fadzly, M. N. & Ahmad, Z. (2004) "Audit expectation gap", *Managerial Auditing Journal*, vol. 19(7): 897 – 915

Gomez-Guillamon, A. D. (2003) "The usefulness of the audit report in ınvestment and financing decisions", *Managerial Auditing Journa*l, vol. 18(6): 549-559

Güçlü, F. (2008) *Muhasebe Denetimi: İlkeler ve Teknikler* [Auditing: Principles and Techniques], Ankara: Detay Yayıncılık

Harichandra, K. & Thangavelu, S. M. (2004) "Institutional Investors, Financial Sector Development and Economic Growth in OECD Countries", *National University of Singapore Department of Economics Working Paper*, 0405.

Holt, T. P., & DeZoort, T. (2009) "The effects of internal audit report disclosure on investor confidence and investment decisions", *International Journal of Auditing,* vol. 13(1): 61-77

Huyghebaert, N. & Hulle, V. C. (2004) "The role of institutional investors in corporate finance", *Tijdschrift voor Economie en Management*, 49 (4): 689-726

Ittonen, K. (2012) "Market reactions to qualified audit reports: Research approaches", *Accounting Research Journal*, vol. 25(1), 8-24

Kabajeh, M. A. M., Al Shanti, A. M., Dahmash, F. N. & Hardan, A. S. (2012) "Informational content of auditor's report and its impact on making decisions from lenders and management's view in the jordanian industrial public firms", *International Journal of Humanities and Social Science,* vol. 2(14): 93-103

Kaplan, S. E., Mowchan, M. & Weisbrod, E. (2014) "Does Institutional Investor Behavior Influence the Market Reaction to Going Concern Audit Reports?", *working paper*

Kardeş-Selimoğlu, S., Özbirecikli, M., Uzay, Ş. Kurt, G., Alagöz, A. ve Yanık, S. (2011) *Muhasebe Denetimi [Auditing],* Ankara: Gazi Kitabevi

Lai, K. W. (2009) "Does audit quality matter more for firms with high investment opportunities?", *Journal of Accounting and Public Policy*, vol. *28*(1): 33-50

Leung, P. & Chau, G. (2001) "The problematic relationship between audit reporting and audit expectations: Some evidence from Hong Kong", *Advances in International Accounting*, vol. 14: 181-200

Mansi, S. A., Maxwell, W. F. & Miller, D. P. (2004) "Does auditor quality and tenure matter to investors? Evidence from the bond market", *Journal of Accounting Research*, vol. *42*(4): 755-793

Martínez, M. C. P., Martínez, A. V. & Benau, M. A. G. (2004) "Reactions of the Spanish capital market to qualified audit reports", *European Accounting Review,* vol. *13*(4): 689-711

Moradi, M. Salehi, M. Rigi, M., & Moeinizade, M. (2011) "The effect of qualified audit report on share prices and returns: Evidence of Iran", *African Journal of Business Management*, vol. *5*(8): 3354-3360

Ogneva, M. & Subramanyam, K. R. (2007) "Does the stock market underreact to going concern opinions? Evidence from the US and Australia", *Journal of Accounting and Economics*, vol. *43*(2): 439-452

Ruiz-Barbadillo, E., Gómez-Aguilar, N., De Fuentes-Barberá, C. & García-Benau, M. A. (2004) "Audit quality and the going-concern decision-making process: Spanish evidence", *European Accounting Review*, vol. *13*(4): 597-620

Salehi, M. (2010) "Evaluating effectiveness of external auditors' report: empirical evidence from Iran", *Pakistan Journal of Commerce and Social Sciences*, vol. 4(1): 69-83

Soltani, B. (2007) *Auditing. An International Approach*, Harlow: Prentice Hall-Pearson Education.

Tahinakis, P. Mylonakis, J. & Daskalopoulou, E. (2010) "An appraisal of the impact of audit qualifications on firms' stock exchange price fluctuations", *Enterprise Risk Management*, vol. *2*(1): 86-99

Usul, H. & Kocabıyık, T. (2010) "Kurumsal yatırımcıların hisse senedi seçiminde göz önünde bulundurduğu etmenlerin faktör analiziyle incelenmesi: Türkiye örneği [Investigation by factor analysis of factors considered in the selection of stocks by instutional investors: The case of Turkey]", *Süleyman Demirel Üniversitesi İktisadi ve İdari Bilimler Fakültesi Dergisi*, vol. 15(3): 63-78

Uzun, F. (2007) "İç denetim ve Fransa uygulaması [Internal auditing and France implementation]", *Yerel Yönetim ve Denetim Dergisi*, vo. 12(9), 1-11

Zor, İ. & Aslanoğlu, S. (2005) "Kurumsal yatırımcı olarak özel emeklilik fonları: Türkiye'de oluşturulan sisteme yönelik değerlendirme ve geleceğe yönelik bir tahmin [Private pension funds as institutional investors: Evaluation of a system created in Turkey and a forecast for the future]", *Muhasebe ve Finansman Dergisi*, vol. 26: 184-197

7

Financial auditing and financial reporting for Romanian state-owned companies – modified opinions and observations

Costel Istrate[a1]

[a]*Alexandru Ioan Cuza University of Iași, Romania*

Abstract: Starting with 2016, the Romanian authorities decided that 17 state-owned companies should use IFRS in their individual financial statements. The objective of this paper is to analyse how these companies have applied the accounting standards – before the transition to IFRS (2010-2017) – through the observations included in the reports delivered by the financial auditors. The main findings are: the presence of Big 4 auditors is quite limited, but in line with the situation of others categories of Romanian companies (especially the listed companies); the modified opinion are, by far, the most frequent (more than 78%). The main justifications of the modified opinions are the non-observance of the accounting rules on the provisions, followed by problems in the measurement of the assets/liabilities, and the consequences of the prudence principle. Emphasis of matters paragraph is also very present in the audit reports: the main observations in these paragraphs is about the going concern matters ant about the dependence of the state owned companies on the decisions of some public authorities.

Keywords: state-owned companies, audit reports, modified opinions, emphasis of matter paragraph, financial reporting

1. Introduction

An important consequence of the state's presence in the economy is the existence of state-owned companies, either wholly-owned enterprises or companies of which the

[1] *Corresponding author*: Department of Accounting, Management Information Systems and Statistics, Alexandru Ioan Cuza University of Iași; Carol 1 Bd., email address: istrate@uaic.ro

state it is the main shareholder. The extent of this presence depends on several variables, including economic policy promoted at some point by the public authorities (at all levels: national, regional and local). These policies are, in most cases, the result of electoral confrontation between programs and politicians. The latter often take into account political ideologies that may give the State a more or less important place in the control of certain areas of activity. In Romania (but also in the other countries of Central and Eastern Europe), after a few decades of almost total control of the state over the economy, the 1990s brought massive privatizations (especially after 1996 - for political reasons) which led to a sharp decline in the state's position as a shareholder. This trend towards the privatization of former state-owned companies has been accompanied by the creation of many new private entities. But the Romanian state has never completely renounced on its position as a major economic player. Moreover, all over the world, the state is more or less involved in business: Kowalski *et al.* (2013) found that the presence of the state in the economic sectors of many countries (including in developed countries) is significant and that, for example, state-owned firms hold an important place in the trade and in business takeovers in other countries (Karolyi & Liao, 2017). Burkard (2009) finds that the state, even if it has waived participation, remains very important as a regulator.

The reputation of the state, as an economic actor, is not always a very good one. Shleifer and Vishny (1997: 768, cited by Guedhami *et al.*, 2009), argue that, despite the fact that in theory these firms are subject to public control, in reality *de facto* control belongs to the bureaucrats, and the goals of the latter are not always to ensure the general well-being, but rather to satisfy their political, individual and/or group interests. In respect to the performances reported by companies, Wang and Shailer (2018) found that government ownership is associated with inferior performance.

The literature (Profiroiu & Profiroiu, 2007; Kowalski *et al.*, 2013) distinguishes, on the one hand, between state-owned enterprises that produce goods and public services of a collective nature and whose functioning does not rest necessarily on principles of financial profitability and, on the other hand, state-owned enterprises comparable to private entities, because it produces and sells goods and services in accordance with market principles.

All entities are subject to the general accounting and financial reporting requirements. There are even more binding obligations for these state-owned firms, because of the fact that they manage public money. Thus, in accordance with Romanian Law 544/2001 on free access to information of public interest, state-owned enterprises are assimilated to public authorities and institutions, and therefore obliged to respect a fairly strict regime of transparency. Among the information considered of public interest and which must be published by these companies are the *financial resources, the budget and the balance sheet*. As a result, in principle, the financial statements of these companies are available *ex officio*. The easiest way to meet this legal obligation is to put these documents on the Internet Sites. I do not propose to make an exhaustive analysis of these firms - it is impossible for us to identify them and to obtain the necessary information for all firms whose public authorities (central and/or local) are the sole or majority shareholders. The main selection criterion is to retain large state companies that appear in an order of the Minister of Public Finance (OMFP 666/2015) which impose the application of IFRS in their separate and consolidate (if applicable) financial statements. There are, in an appendix to this order[i] 17 national companies. For comparability reasons, I add to this very limited sample the state-owned firms listed on the Bucharest Stock Exchange (BSE): there are 9 companies who apply IFRS since 2012 (on the regulated market) and another 14 who apply the Romanian Accounting Standards (RAS – on the alternative market AeRO). What interests us in the financial reports of these state firms are the audit reports that accompany the financial statements.

In this descriptive study, I try to highlight, through the opinions of financial auditors, how state-owned companies apply accounting standards. Since the opinions of the auditors of the 17 state firms are (very) mostly modified, the explanations of these modified opinions and the other observations included in the audit reports allow us to have a certain image of the most important difficulties encountered by these companies in the implementation of the accounting regulations. An important premise to be aware of is that these 17 companies are very large, have complex activities and therefore the organization of accounting and financial reporting are, themselves, very complex and require significant logistical and human resources[ii]. The financial reporting system for state-owned firms is considered very important by the OECD, which (according to Kowalski & Perepechay, 2015) recommends for this category of companies the same obligations as for listed entities. Wang and Shailer (2018) propose that studies on the state owned companies listed on the financial market are more relevant, due to the availability of data and to the quality of the financial reporting.

To our knowledge, the analysis on the Romanian state-owned companies particularly focuses on the economic aspects or performance, and there are not so far to study the content of audit reports of these firms. In the international literature on this type of company, the most discussed themes concern the effects of privatizations on performance, the choice of auditors, financing, the presence on the financial markets, the evolution of the level of corruption, the earnings management etc. This study complements part of the research in this area and I am sure that it can be useful for a better understanding of the functioning of state-owned enterprises and that it can be used for specific decision-making factors and also for accounting standard setters.

The reminder of the study includes a literature review (section 2), a description of the methodology and sample (section 3) results and discussions (section 4), before concluding and presenting the references.

2. Literature review

In OECD countries, the presence of state-owned companies, although significant[iii] is less important than in emerging countries and is particularly evident in sectors such as energy, telecoms, transport and banks (Kowalski *et al.*, 2013). Using data from Forbes Global 2000 (the largest 2,000 companies in 66 countries, including OECD countries), Kowalski *et al.* (2013) identify more than 10% of state-owned companies, firms with subsidiaries and own interests in 330,000 other companies. The figures differ from one country to another, with the top places being held by China, India and Russia. The overall sales of these state-owned companies are about 10% of the total sales of the top 2,000 Forbes companies. The dimensions of state-owned firms are analysed by Cuervo-Cazurra *et al.* (2014) who find that, in 2010, among the 100 largest multinationals, 19 belonged to the states. In Romania, according to a report published by an organization of the managers and of the investors (PIAROM & ZF, 2017), the state-owned firms are (in 2015) in number of 1,095, compared to the active private firms, about 470,000. Thus, with less than 0.2% of the total number of Romanian firms, state-owned companies generate 4% (in 2014 and 2015) of the overall sales of Romanian firms, employ 7% of the workforce, have average wages as high as in the multinationals and achieve a productivity twice as low as private companies (and even three times lower than firms whose shareholders are mainly foreign).

The specific governance of state-owned firms presents important particularities compared to private firms (Kloviene & Gimžauskiene, 2014). These particularities derive from the fact that the successive responsibilities in obtaining and monitoring the performance of these firms are more complex and involve actors such as: the executive direction, the board of directors, various state authorities, the government, the parliament. Under these conditions, it is not always easy to establish the precise users of the financial information provided by these companies, let alone the beneficiaries of their performance.

The financial presentation requirements of state-owned enterprises are often the same as for other firms operating in the same jurisdiction and under the same conditions. I have already shown that these state-owned firms have specific obligations of financial transparency because they manage public money. On the other hand, Havrylyshyn & McGettigan (1999) found that the discipline of managerial labour markets may be weaker or absent under government ownership if managers are usually chosen for ideological or political reasons rather than their managerial ability.

The auditing standards state that the financial auditor must express an opinion on the financial statements of the audited firms. These opinions are modified or unmodified. The proportion of modified opinions differs from one country to another, from one period to another, from one category of firms to other categories (listed vs. unlisted, state vs. private, large vs smaller etc.), from one business sector to another. In the case of listed firms, the type of audit opinion depends on the auditor's observations during the engagement, but also on the position of the regulatory authorities. For example, in the United States, the SEC considers that a modified opinion means a failure of the firm in the application of the specific rules and, consequently, the modified opinions received by listed firms are rare[iv] (Cipriano *et al.*, 2017).

The literature on audit opinions is rich, but most studies analyse listed firms, among which a minority belong to the state. The fact that large state-owned companies may have characteristics in common with listed private firms of similar size means that, at the level of audit reports, there are common elements regarding the justification of opinion and the determinants of modified opinions. Paananen (2016) warns us that the specificity of state-owned firms must be taken into account and comparisons with private firms should be made with caution. Paananen (2016) proposes to test the case of state firms (more precisely, municipal) the influence of certain determinants on the audit opinions: the level of profitability, solvency, liquidity indicators, the auditor's type (none of these determinants are confirmed), the length of the audit report, the size of the audit firm, the size of the firm audited (confirmed). In Romania, Bunget and Dumitrescu (2012) analyse the justifications for modified opinions, by accounting principle not respected, but their sample is limited to the clients of an audit firm.

3. Methodology and sample

OMFP 666/2015 establishes the list of Romanian state firms subject to the obligation to apply IFRS (see Appendix 1). I have already pointed out that, in my opinion, the main reason for this application is the influence of international financial organizations (WB and IMF). At the same time, there are recommendations in this regard in the OECD documents. Unlike Romanian companies listed on the regulated BSE market – which had very little time to prepare for transitions to IFRS - OMFP 666/2015 sets a more generous timetable for the transition of the 17 state firms. Thus, for the 2016 and 2017 fiscal years (all of these firms close at December 31), companies keep their current accounts in RAS, prepare financial statements in RAS and restate these financial statements in order to obtain an IFRS set of financial statements. However, as of 2018, these companies are fully transitioning to IFRS, both in their current accounting and in the presentation of financial statements.

To achieve this objective, there was identified on the websites of these 17 companies, the accompanying financial statements and audit reports. The selected period is 2010 - 2017: there is very little information available from before this year: even for 2010, only 3 available audit reports could be found. Gradually, as we approach 2017, the number of available reporting increases (Table 1).

The areas of activity of the companies studied are fairly well in the international average: Kowalski *et al.* (2013) finds that economic sectors where the state and most present in OECD countries are: support activities for the mining sector, civil engineering, land and air transport, coal mining, oil and gas. These findings are confirmed by Kwiatkowski and Augustynowicz (2015), for state-owned firms that appear in Fortune Global 500.

The data of interest in the audit reports identified for the 17 Romanian firms are as follows:

1. the auditor category: Big 4 vs. Non Big 4, but with the identification of auditors belonging to the latter category who are affiliated with international firms;
2. the type of opinion: unmodified vs. modified (qualified, disclaimer of opinion, adverse opinion);
3. the explanations proposed by the auditor to justify the modified opinion;
4. the existence, in the report, of an emphasis of matter paragraph and the justifications presented in this paragraph.

Based on these data, I propose to describe the way Romanian state-owned firms comply with accounting and financial reporting standards and to highlight the main findings that financial auditors made after their audit work. In the almost complete absence of other similar research (to our knowledge), I has chosen to compare the main results with data specific to state-owned companies listed on the BSE, both in the regulatory market and on a secondary market (AeRo). There will be no statistical treatment in this study, to establish relations between the various variables characteristic of Romanian state-owned companies.

4. Results

Audit reports are an important source of information for the users of financial statements. When the opinion is unmodified, users find in the reports the ready-made paragraphs that confirm the financial statements' compliance with applicable standards. On the other hand, in the case of a modified opinion, users (especially those with sufficient accounting knowledge) can quickly see what are the situations in which the application of the standards is not completely correct and/or the significant risks that may affect the performance of the entity. In all cases, the audit reports are supposed to contribute to a better appreciation of the financial and managerial performances of the firms analysed.

4.1 Big 4 versus not Big 4

To begin, there will be presented data on the categories of auditors who give opinions for the 17 state firms analysed in this study. As often in the literature, I separate the big auditors (Big 4) from the others (Non Big 4). This distinction is justified by the very common idea in the audit literature that the Big 4 ensure a better quality of the audit. This hypothesis is confirmed in some studies, but there are some authors who consider that Big 4 vs. Non Big 4 differences are not significant[v]. The approach is simple – counting the reports from the Big 4; in more sophisticated studies, the presence of the Big 4 is calculated by weighting the type of auditors to take into account the dimensions of the firms audited and arriving at values much higher compared to simple percentages. But in this study, the important dimensions of all the firms involved allow us to appreciate that the weighting would not lead to significantly different figures.

For the sample (see Table 1), the overall weight of 46.39% of Big 4 is not very suggestive, given the small number of observations for the first three years analysed. We can consider that the figures of the last years (29.42% in 2017 and 37.50% in 2016) are more representative to describe the presence of Big 4 in the case of the Romanian companies in the sample. This situation is comparable to that presented by Guedhami *et al.* (2009) who find 34% of Big 4 in a sample of 176 privatized state firms (in 32 countries, including 21 emerging); at the same time, Guedhami *et al.* (2009) find that the presence of the state as majority owner decreases the likelihood of using a Big 4 auditor.

Comparing the figures reported in Table 1 with the situation on the Romanian financial market leads to the following findings:

1. for the regulated market and for the period 2007-2017 (962 observations available, including firms whose activities are financial), the weight of Big 4 is 37% (it drops to 30% after the elimination of financial activities);
2. for the same regulated market and for the period analysed in this study (2010 - 2017: 698 observations), the weight of Big 4 is about 39%;
3. by retaining only state-owned firms listed on the regulated market (9 companies), the weight of Big 4 is more than 60% (61% for the period 2007 - 2017; 63% for the period 2010-2017);
4. in the alternative market (AeRo), for the period 2010-2017 (1,978 observations), there is only 7% of Big 4 and no auditor of this category is found for the state-owned firms listed on this segment (14 companies for the period).

In all cases, the weight of the Big 4 is (much) lower than the situations that we could find in the literature, for other countries, especially developed. Still in Romania, Berinde and Groşanu (2013) found only 18% of Big 4 for a sample of firms in the North West region. I can comment on the specific situation of Romania in the sense that the exposure on a large financial market (such as the regulated segment of the BVB), the public exhibition by the dimensions and/or the obtaining of the financing from some international organizations (the case of large state-owned companies) can be decisive factors in choosing a Big 4, although the weight of this category of auditors is not yet very important.

Table 1. Categories of auditors for Romanian state-owned firms in OMFP 666/2015

Year	Total audit reports available	From which							
		Big 4		No Big 4					
						Whose			
		N	%	N	%	Affiliated to an international network		Local	
						N	%	*N*	%
2017	17	5	29.42	12	70.58	6	35.29	6	35.29
2016	16	6	37.50	10	62.50	5	31.25	5	31.25
2015	17	6	35.29	11	64.71	5	29.42	6	35.29
2014	15	6	40,00	9	60,00	3	20.00	6	40,00
2013	14	9	64.29	5	35.71	3	21.43	2	14.28
2012	9	6	66.67	3	33.33	1	11.11	2	22.22
2011	6	4	66.67	2	33.33	0	0.00	2	33.33
2010	3	3	100.00	0	0.00	0	0.00	0	0.00
Total	**97**	**45**	**46.39**	**52**	**53,61**	**23**	**23.71**	**29**	**29.90**

Francis *et al.* (2012) calculate the concentration of the audit market in 42 countries and, from more than 115,000 observations (for the period 1999-2007), identify around 43,000 reports issued by non-Big 4 auditors; that's over 63% of Big 4. In the case of state-owned companies, the Chinese setting is particular, in the sense that the Big 4 presence is very limited (Su & Wu, 2017); the explanation is that the state ownership being associated with a weaker demand for high-quality audits (Wang & Shailer, 2018).

All the calculations presented take into account only two categories of auditors (Big 4 and non-Big 4). But, there are authors (notably in Romania) who suggest the classification of the auditors in several categories: Păunescu (2015) proposes 4 categories: Big 4, not Big 4 affiliated with international firms, other non-Big 4 and individual auditors. For the sample, we can add to the Big 4, the auditors internationally affiliated (BDO and PKF, more precisely) and we obtain 46.39% + 23.71% = 70.00% for the whole sample (more than 60% for the last years). This shows that the access of local audit firms to contracts offered by large state-owned firms (more than 30% in recent years) seems rather difficult.

4.2 Types of opinions in the audit reports of the analysed state firms

In the case of state-owned firms, users must have access to financial information by virtue of the public nature of these activities. It is interesting to see how public money is spent, how goods and services are produced. The peculiarities of these firms, the individual and collective interests of the managers of these firms and the bureaucracy that makes them work are all reasons for the introduction of an independent intermediary – the financial auditor – between the producer and the users of specific financial information. The role of the auditor is to verify the extent to which the financial statements are prepared in accordance with accounting standards and to express an opinion on how the financial statements fairly reflect the financial position and the performance of the audited entity. A report that contains an unmodified opinion and contains no comments allows the user to be confident that the financial statements represent what they are meant to represent. In Table 2, I have centralized the various opinions expressed by the auditors of the firms analysed.

Table 2. Types of opinions in the audit reports of Romanian state-owned companies appearing in the OMFP 666/2015

Year	Number of observations	Unmodified opinions		Qualified opinions		Disclaimer of opinion	
		N	%	N	%	N	%
2017	17	4	23.53	12	70.59	1	5.88
2016	16	3	18.75	12	75.00	1	6.25
2015	17	4	23.53	12	70.59	1	5.88
2014	15	3	20.00	11	73.33	1	6.67
2013	14	3	21.43	9	64.29	2	14.28
2012	9	2	22.22	6	66.67	1	11.11
2011	6	2	33.33	4	66.67	0	0.00
2010	3	0	0.00	3	100.00	0	0.00
Total	**97**	**21**	**21.64**	**69**	**71.14**	**7**	**7.22**

The weight of the modified opinions is extremely high – about 78% (71.14 + 7.22) – even taking into account only the last years. This allows us to appreciate that, in the opinion of the auditors, there are significant risks that the financial statements contain significant information that is not fully compliant with the accounting framework applicable by the Romanian state-owned companies. For other firms whose audit reports are available, we found the following figures:

1. for companies listed on the regulated market of the BVB, for the period 2007-2017 (962 observations available), we have 27.03% of modified opinions; of these firms, the state-owned ones (85 observations) show 35.29% of modified opinions;
2. on the second segment of the BVB (AeRo), where are listed small firms, for the period 2010-2017 (1,978 observations), I found only 23,31% of modified opinions (17.85% for the state owned firms - 112 observations).

The data shows us that the 17 state-owned firms that should apply IFRS face significant difficulties in complying with Romanian accounting standards, which are reflected in the majority of their auditors' opinions.

For a comparison with state firms from another country, I found the analysis of Paananen (2016) who finds that 31% of Finnish municipal firms receive modified

opinions. Wang et al (2008) found about 12% of modified opinion in the case of some state-owned companies from China, whit a smaller probability to issue a modified opinion for the small local auditors.
Modified opinions (in all their forms) are often presented in the literature as proof of the auditor's independence and, therefore, of the quality of the audit. In the table 3, I presented the types of opinions by category of auditors (Big 4 vs. others). There too, we can consider that the last years are the most representative.

Table 3. Type of opinion by categories of auditors

Year	Modified opinions (qualified and disclaimer of opinion)	From which			
		Big 4		non Big 4	
		N	%	N	%
2017	12 + 1 = 13	4	30.74	9	69.23
2016	12 + 1 = 13	6	46.15	7	53.85
2015	12 + 1 = 13	6	46.15	7	53.85
2014	11 + 1 = 12	6	50.00	6	50.00
2013	9 + 2 = 11	8	72.73	3	27.27
2012	6 + 1 = 7	6	85.71	1	14.29
2011	4 + 0 = 4	4	100.00	0	0.00
2010	3 + 0 = 3	3	100.00	0	0.00
Total	**69 + 7 = 76**	**43**	**56.58**	**33**	**43.42**

As we could expect, the weight of the modified opinions issued by Big 4 (more than 56%) is greater than their weight in the total number of auditors. This confirms, in a way, that Big 4 prove more independent than others. But, these data must be completed with an important detail: among the non-Big 4, there are those affiliated with international firms (23 observations) and, put together, the modified opinions of these two categories of auditors represent 86.84% of all modified opinions. As a result, local auditors (29 observations) are much less likely to give modified opinions: 10, or 13.16% from the total number of the modified opinions. Or, perhaps, local auditors have come across state-owned firms that ensure more compliance with standards. Păunescu (2015) comments on a similar situation and explains the unmodified opinions of local (Romanian) auditors through pressure from the management of the audited firms and the interest of these auditors in keeping their clients.

4.3 Justifications of the modified opinions for the analysed state firms

The auditor issuing a modified opinion must justify this qualification specifying the aspects that it considers that the presentation is wrong or where it has not obtained sufficient audit evidence. ISA 705 (2012) states that modified opinions are issued in the following situations:

1. qualified opinion: the auditor determines that the financial statements as a whole contained misstatements, which are material, but not pervasive or the auditors is unable to obtain sufficient appropriate audit evidence to conclude that the financial statements as a whole do not contain any misstatements significant;
2. adverse opinion: the auditor concludes, after obtaining sufficient and appropriate evidence, that misstatements, individually or in aggregate, have both a material and pervasive character in the financial statements;
3. disclaimer of opinion: the auditor is unable to obtain sufficient appropriate audit evidence on which to formulate his opinion and concludes that the potential impact on the financial statements of undetected misstatements could be both material and pervasive.

In the reports analysed, 69 of the modified opinions are qualified opinions, while in 7 cases it is disclaimer of opinion. The paragraphs in which the auditors justify the modified opinions include one or more explanations, which were grouped into a few major themes (Table 4, in descending order of the frequency of appearance, for the items with more than five appearances). It is obvious that by this codification I have lost some of the auditors' message, but this has allowed us to do minimal quantitative processing. In each individual report, we could find between one and 16 different explanations for the modified opinion.

I have not found in the literature any study on this type of justification; therefore, I will compare the results with what has already been noted for listed companies. Istrate (2017) shows that, for Romanian firms listed on the BSE regulated market, the main explanations of the modified opinions refer to revaluations of fixed assets, provisions and items relating to measurement and to other assets/liabilities in the closing works. Bunget and Dumitrescu (2012) analyses the justifications for modified opinions by grouping them by accounting principle; they observe that most explanations concern (in descending order) the principle of prudence, the comparability, the accrual accounting and the going concern assumption.

For the firms analysed in this study, unlike for the listed Romanian companies, the revaluation of the fixed assets does not represent the first explanation which justifies the modified opinions. In fact, it is the application of the prudence principle (which joins the results of Bunget & Dumitrescu, 2012) that is at issue in the judgments made by the auditors: six of the first ten explanations concern the non-consideration of certain risks, impairments and depreciations. To this is added the doubtful accounting of certain assets/liabilities and/or revenues and expenses, as well as the classification of these items for presentation in the financial statements.

Table 4. Explanations of the modified opinions in the audit reports of Romanian state-owned firms in OMFP 666/2015

Explanation[vi]	*Frequency of the appearance*
1. Insufficient provisions or other difficulties in estimating provisions	36
2. Recognition of certain assets and/or liabilities	30
3. Insufficient attention paid to depreciation of fixed assets	28
4. Existence of litigation that may have adverse effects on the entity	26
5. Insufficient consideration of future obligations towards employees	22
6. Accounting for certain revenues and expenses	19
7. Revaluation of fixed assets	18
8. Inventory impairment	16
9. Receivables impairments	14
10. Non-participation of the auditor on the closing works	14
11. Incorrect estimate of some other depreciation	10
12. Approximate application of accounting rules for error correction	10
13. Problems in the levels of certain indicators imposed by the banks so that the credits remain in the long term	9
14. Incorrect presentation of certain assets/liabilities	9
15. Deficiencies in the confirmation of the balances of receivables and liabilities at closing date	9
16. Existence of legal problems (other than litigation) for the entity and/or for members of management	8
17. Insufficient provisions for the restauration of some land	6
18. Other elements concerning the organization and the progress of closing work	6
...	

The auditor's opinion may have some influence on users, although in the case of state-owned firms, user decisions often take into account other criteria than the performance displayed or compliance with accounting standards. Thus, the management of the audited entity would have an interest in the opinion being unmodified. Managers can arrive at this result by correcting the aspects observed by the auditors, but also by applying the technique that the literature calls *opinion shopping*, that is to say the change of the auditor having expressed a modified opinion. I counted the auditor changes in the sample and the impact of these changes is reported in Table 5 (it's not about the rotation of the partner, but about the audit firm). Among the 17 firms analysed, 12 had two or more changes in auditors during the analysed period: 6 firms changed once the auditor, 6 firms changed twice and 1 firm changed the auditor 3 times.

From the data in Table 5, we observe that, despite a significant rotation of the auditors, the effects on the audit opinion are not significant – only 4 cases of change of opinion, and only one form a modified to an unmodified opinion. We can conclude, with all the risks that derive from a limited sample – that the possible hypothesis of *opinion shopping* is not confirmed in the case of Romanian state-owned companies – Păunescu (2015) comes to a similar conclusion for firms listed on the BSE).

Table 5. Rotation of auditors by the analysed state-owned firms

Sense of the rotation	Number of observations	Change of opinion following the auditor's change: From a modified opinion to an unmodified opinion	Change of opinion following the auditor's change: From an unmodified opinion to a modified opinion
From Big 4 to Big 4	5	-	1
From Big 4 to non-Big 4	8	1	-
From non-Big 4 to Big 4	1	-	2
From non-Big 4 to non-Big 4	7	-	-
Total changes of auditors	**21**	**1**	**3**

4.4 Explanations in the emphasis of matters paragraphs from the audit reports of the analysed state-owned companies

The international standard ISA 706 *Emphasis of matter paragraphs and other matter paragraphs in the independent auditor's report* states that if the auditor considers it necessary to draw the attention of the users to a matter presented or mentioned in the financial statements which, according to its own judgment, is of such importance that it is essential for their understanding of the financial statements or it considers that users' attention should be drawn to aspects that do not appear in the financial statements that may be important in terms of understanding the audit process and the audit report, the auditor shall include in his audit report a paragraph provided that he has obtained sufficient and appropriate evidence that the item presented or referred to in the financial statements does not include significant anomalies.

This type of paragraph is very common in audit reports issued for Romanian firms. In the Table 6, I centralized the information on the presence of such a paragraph, by category of auditor and type of opinion. For reasons of comparability, I have chosen to continue the presentation in parallel of the specific situation to the Romanian listed companies. Istrate (2017) finds for the BSE regulated market that the main explanations included in this paragraph concern: going concern matters (the most important, by far), items related to tax obligations and litigation, (non) consideration of certain other risks, other litigation, transactions with related parties, exposure to a single customer or a single business, provisions, revaluation and depreciation of fixed assets and other assets.

Table 6. Presence of emphasis of matter paragraphs in audit reports

Elements		State- Owned firms (OMFP 666/2015)	Companies listed on the BSE – the market regulated	Companies listed on the BSE – the AeRo segment
Period		2010 – 2017	2007 – 2017	2010 - 2017
Observations available (audit reports)		98	962	1,978
Reports that contain an emphasis of matter paragraph	**Total, from which**	**72 (73.47%)**	**287 (29.83%)**	**669 (33.82%)**
	associated with unmodified opinions	16 (22.22%)	159 (55.40%)	458 (68.56%)
	associated with modified opinions	56 (77.78%)	128 (44.60%)	211 (31.54%)

Like the firms listed on the regulated market (Istrate, 2017), the first explanation presented by the auditors in this paragraph section are related to the going concern issues, but unlike the listed firms, this explanation is joined by a specific aspect to state-owned firms: the dependence of public policies and decisions made by various state authorities that establish, for example, tariffs or other matter related to the environment, investments etc. (Table 7). Another common explanation is for provisions, whether related to employee profits or litigation.

Verifying the management's assertions of going concern is an important task for the auditor. It should be noted that going concern does not appear in any of the reports studied as a justification for the modified opinion and is only highlighted in the emphasis of matter paragraph. This situation is due, probably (and here I join Paananen, 2016), to the fact that the companies analysed are state-owned and that the State will not let them go bankrupt, because they carry out business activities of public interest, it employs a lot of people and, often, are *big to fail*. Moreover, Romania has a recent rich history of rescue of some state-owned firms, considered strategic and without any consideration for financial indicators that are largely negative. For example, on the regulated market, there is a state-controlled entity whose equity has been highly negative (with a few exceptions) since 2000 and which is still operating and which is still listed on the financial market.

Table 7. Justifications of observation paragraphs

Explanation	Frequency of appearance
Going concern matters	30
Dependence on public policies, decisions of public authorities	30
Provisions	14
Restructuring of the firm	14
Litigations	12
Problems of a legal nature for the firm or for the members of the management	10
Difficulties in the relationship with the tax authorities	9
Existence of environmental problems	7
Impairment of fixed assets	6
Revaluation	6
Approximate accounting recognition for certain assets and/or liabilities	5
Not enough attention in calculating and accounting for benefits granted to employees	3
The company depends on commercial relations with a single partner	2
Related parties	1
Impairment of receivables	1
The auditor did not participate in the inventory work	1

5. Conclusions

The state is present as a shareholder of some companies in many countries, including in developed countries. State-owned companies must fulfil the general accounting and financial reporting requirements and, in addition, because they are public-interest entities, must transmit this information to users, in the interests of financial transparency (otherwise imposed by law). At the same time, the financial statements of these firms need to be audited, so that users can see how firms comply with specific accounting standards. An order from the Romanian Minister of Public Finance (OMFP 666/2015) requires 17 large state-owned companies to apply IFRS from 2016 (by restatement of information obtained applying RAS for 2016 and 2017 and effective application of IFRS in accounting current from 2018). I selected these firms and, before analysing the impact of the transition to IFRS, I studied the audit reports for the 2010-2017 period, in order to identify the main explanations offered by the auditors to justify their opinion and the main observations included in the specific paragraph.

The first results relate to the presence of Big 4 in the list of auditors of state firms (97 observations). The average is 46%, but because the observations for the last part of the analysed period are more complete, we consider that a figure of about 30-35% would be more credible. This weight of Big 4 is not far from the results for Romanian firms listed on the regulated market. To complete these results, it should be said that, among non-Big 4, there are some who belong to international audit firms, which means that the weight of local auditors is 29.90%.

The audit opinions expressed by the auditors of the 17 state firms are mostly modified (78.36%), which means that the auditors have detected significant risks regarding the information provided in the financial statements and that compliance with the accounting framework is not fully acquired. This proportion of modified opinions is very important compared to the other studies I have had access to. For example, for firms listed on the Romanian financial market (BSE), the modified opinions represent about 27% (for the regulated market) and about 23% for the AeRo segment. The main justifications for these modified opinions concern: provisions, recognition of certain assets/liabilities, impairment of fixed assets, litigation, recognition of employee benefits, recognition of other income and expenses, revaluation of fixed assets etc. Overall, most explanations refer to aspects related to closing works. I have found that the possible hypothesis of *opinion shopping* is not confirmed in the case of the firms in the sample.

In analysing the audit reports of the state-owned firms, I also identified the emphasis of matters paragraphs - also very numerous (73.47%). The most frequent elements that appear in these paragraphs are the going concern and the exposure of the state firms to the decisions of the public authorities. Other topics are: provisions, the effects of restructuring, involvement in litigation, the existence of legal and tax problems, etc.

The main limitations of this study are the limited number of observations in the sample, the exclusively descriptive nature of the analysis and the fact that I did not correlate the variables extracted from the audit reports and other variables that characterize the firms considered.

The most appropriate future research directions are precisely the identification of correlations between variables specific to audit reports and other variables, the introduction of indicators of audit quality in correlations with the quality of the financial reporting. Another direction of research may concern the explanations given by the auditors of the firms selected in the sample in the paragraph of justification of appreciations (KAM - *key audit matters*), like in some other studies (Barbe & Rimbault, 2015 or Moreau, 2017). The transition of state firms analysed to IFRS also opens up a new field of research on this type of firm.

References

Barbe, O. & Raimbault, S. (2015) "La justification des appréciations améliore-t-elle la valeur du rapport d'audit?", Available on-line at https://documents.bsb-education.com/pdf/cig2014/ACTESDUCOLLOQUE/BARBE_RAIMBAULT.pdf (accessed at 15 December 2017)

Berinde, S. & Groşanu, A. (2013) "Particularities concerning the beneficiaries of audit services provided by Big 4 companies: evidence from Romania", *Annales Universitatis Apulensis Series Oeconomica*, vol. 15, no. 2: 483-492

Bunget, O. C. & Dumitrescu, A. C. (2012) "A Study on the Relationship between Audit Opinion and Accounting Principles", *Audit Financiar*, vol. X, no. 1: 6-11

Cameran, M., Prencipe, A. & Trombetta, M. (2016) "Mandatoory audit firm rotation an audit quality", *European Accounting Review*, vol. 25, no. 1: 35-58

Cipriano, M. Hamilton, E. L. & Vandervelde, S. D. (2017) "Has the lack of use of the qualified audit opinion turned it into the "Rotten Kid" threat?", *Critical Perspectives on Accounting*, vol 47: 26–38

Cuervo-Cazurra, A., Inkpen, A., Musacchio, A. & Ramaswamy, K. (2014) "Governments as owners: State-owned multinational companies", *Journal of International Business Studies*, vol. 45, no. 8: 919-942

DeAngelo, L. E. (1981) "Auditor size and audit quality", *Journal of Accounting and Economics*, vol. 3, no. 3: 183-199

Francis, J. R., Michas, P. N. & Seavey, S. E. (2012) "Does audit market concentration harm the quality of audited earnings? Evidence from audit markets in 42 countries", *Contemporary Accounting Research*, vol. XX, no. X: 1-31

Guedhami, O., Pittman, J. A. & Saffar, W. (2009) "Auditor choice in privatized firms: Empirical evidence on the role of state and foreign owners", *Journal of Accounting and Economics*, vol. 48, no. 2-3: 151-171

Havrylyshyn, O., D. & McGettigan (1999) "Privatization in transition countries: A sampling of the literature", IMF Working Paper No. 99/6 (available on-line at https://www.imf.org/en/Publications/WP/Issues/2016/12/30/ Privatization-in-Transition-Countries-A-Sampling-of-the-Literature-2879, accessed at 12 aprilie 2018

Istrate, C. (2017) "Justifications for the modified opinions and for other observations in the audit reports of Romanian listed companies", paper presented on the 12th AMIS Conference, Bucharest, 7-9 June 2017 (available on-line at https://amis.ase.ro/2017/docs/AMIS2017Proceedings.pdf, accessed at 12 April 2018)

Karolyi, G. A. & Liao, R. C (2017) "State capitalism's global reach: Evidence from foreign acquisitions by state-owned companies", *Journal of Corporate Finance*, vol. 42: 367-391

Kloviene, R. & Gimžauskiene, E. (2014) "Performance measurement model formation in state-owned enterprises", *Procedia - Social and Behavioral Sciences*, vol. 156: 594-598

Kowalski, P., Buge, M., Sztajerowska, M. & Egeland, M. (2013) "State-Owned Enterprises - trade effects and policy implications", *OECD Trade Policy Papers*, no. 147, OECD Publishing, Paris (http://dx.doi.org/10.1787/5k4869ckqk7l-en)

Kowalski, P. & Perepechay, K. (2015) "International Trade and Investment by State Enterprises", *OECD Trade Policy Papers*, no. 184, OECD Publishing, Paris. (http://dx.doi.org/10.1787/5jrtcr9x6c48-en)

Kwiatkowski, G. & Augustynowicz, P. (2015) "State-owned enterprises in the global economy – analysis based on Fortune Global 500 list", *TIIM Joint International Conference 2015* (available on-lilne at http://www.toknowpress.net/ISBN/978-961-6914-13-0/papers/ ML15-353.pdf, accessed at 25 August 2017)

Lobo, G., Paugam, L., Zhang, D. & Casta, J. F. (2017) "The effect of joint auditor pair composition on audit quality: evidence from impairment tests", *Contemporary Accounting Research*, vol. 34, no. 1: 118-153

Ministerul Finanțelor (2015) "Ordinul ministrului finanțelor publice nr. 666 din 9 iunie 2015 privind aplicarea Reglementărilor contabile conforme cu Standardele internaționale de raportare financiară de către unele entități cu capital de stat" [Order of the Ministry of Public Finance no. 666 from 9 June 2015 concerning the application of accounting regulations conforming with international fianncial reporting standards by some companies with state participation], *Monitorul Oficial*, no. 442/ 22 June 2015

Moreau, J. (2017) "Les justifications d'appréciation du commissaire aux comptes (et les pratiques internationales assimilées): revue de littérature, analyse des pratiques et perspectives de recherché", *38ème Congrès annuel de l'Association Francophone de Comptabilité*, Poitiers

Paananen, M. (2016) "Modified audit reports in the case of joint municipal authorities: Empirical evidence from Finland", *International Journal of Auditing*, vol. 20, no. 2: 149–157

PIAROM & ZF (Patronatul Investitorilor Autohtoni și Ziarul Financiar) (2017) "Capitalul privat românesc [The Romanian Private Capital]", available on-line at https://www.piarom.ro/wp-content/uploads/2017/02/brosura-PIAROM-ianuarie-2017.pdf?x76754 (accessed at 13 novembre 2017)

Păunescu, M. (2015) "The Romanian audit market structure in case of listed companies and the impact of adopting IFRS", *Procedia Economics and Finance*, vol. 32: 686-693

Profiroiu, A. & Profiroiu, M. (2007) "Cadrul de analiză a performanțelor sectorului public" [Framework for the performance analysis in the public sector], *Economie Teoretică și Aplicată*, no. 1 (506): 41-50

Sirois, L. P., Marmousez, S. & Simunic, D. A. (2016) "Proposition d'une nouvelle approche de la relation entre la taille de l'auditeur et la qualité de l'audit : l'importance de la technologie d'audit", *Comptabilité – Contrôle – Audit*, tome 22, vol. 3: 111-144

Su, X. & Wu, X. (2017) "Public discolsure of audit fees and bargaining power between the client and the auditor: evidence for China", *The International Journal of Accounting*, vol. 52, no. 1: 64-76

Wang, K. T. & Shailer, G. (2018) "Does ownership identity matter? A meta-analysis of research on firm financial performance in relation to Government versus private ownership", *Abacus*, vol. 54, no. 1: 1-35

[i] In 2015, the Romanian Minister of Public Finance issued order 666/2015, which requires some state-owned companies (the largest) to convert to IFRS in their individual accounts. The rationale for this decision is the need for more transparency and comparability in the financial reporting of these companies. Another explicit explanation lies in the recommendations of the international financial organizations (World Bank and International Monetary Fund) and here I find, in fact, the main motivation for the mandatory application of IFRS in Romania, in the individual accounts of companies (European regulations limit the mandatory application of IFRS to the consolidated financial statements of listed groups).

[ii] Kowalski *et al.* (2013) find that the accounting and auditing standards applicable to state-owned enterprises are the same as for other companies, but that state-owned firms have to undergo other controls, from specific authorities. In Romania, these additional controls may come from the Romanian Court of Accounts, from the government control bodies and/or the different ministries.

[iii] Kwiatkowski and Augustynowicz (2015), based on the top Fortune Global 500, found 5% of state-owned firms in developed countries, with France and Germany very well represented. The trend is on the rise.

[iv] The cited authors identify 11 modified opinions, for the period 2000-2015, for all firms registered with the SEC!

[v] The first explanations of the better quality of the audits carried out by the Big 4 consist in their greater independence and competence (the characteristics proposed by DeAngelo, 1981). Thus, it is argued that the Big 4 provide quality audits to avoid risks that are more significant for them, arising from the loss of reputation and from financial losses (Sirois *et al.*, 2016, Cameran *et al.*, 2016, Lobo *et al.*, 2017). Other explanations relate to the resources available to the Big 4, both human and logistical and training. Francis *et al.* (2012) establish, on a statistical basis, that the audit is of a better quality in countries where at least two of the Big 4 dominate the market relatively equally, and this quality is manifested both in the reports issued by the Big 4, only for those issued by non-Big 4.

[vi] The explanations appearing 5 times or less than 5 times are: The absence of a written statement from the management of the firm, difficulties in the comparability of the information provided in the financial reports, use of grants outside the framework of contracts, other difficulties in the valuation at closing of certain assets and/or liabilities, difficulties in evaluating revenue and expenses, incorrect classification of certain revenues/charges, elements relating to the calculation and declaration of certain tax obligations and other problems in the relationship with the tax authorities, difficulties in valuing assets/liabilities other than at the date losing, overly optimistic estimation of securities held in subsidiaries, existence of transactions that the auditor qualifies as abnormal, problems in establishing and controlling the tariffs charged to customers, calculation and granting of discounts under conditions not provided for in the documents provided by the entities, difficulties in calculating the costs of certain products and services, problems with funding from European bodies, the entity is in insolvency.

The effects of IFRS adoption and Big 4 audit firms on audit and non-audit fees

Alhassan Musah[a,1], Fred Kwasi Anokye[b] and Erasmus Dodzi Gakpetor [a,1]

[a] *Dominion University College, Ghana*
[b] *University of Ghana, Legon*

Abstract: The study was conducted to examine the effect of IFRS adoption on audit and non-audit fee and also the relationship between the big4 audit firm and audit and non-audit fees. Using a sample of financial and non-financial firms in Ghana, the results show that IFRS adoption has a positive and significant relationship with audit and non-audit fees post IFRS adoption. The results further revealed that there is positive association between the year of IFRS adoption (transition period) and audit and non-audit fees. On the big4 audit firms, the results show that the big4 charge higher audit and non-audit fees than non-big4 as there was a positive and significant relationship between Big4 and audit and non-audit fees. The results support the argument that the adoption of IFRS increased the complexities of financial reporting and audit risk resulting in a higher audit and non-audit fees charged during the transition period and post IFRS adoption. The paper extends previous studies on the subject matter by including the year of IFRS adoption and non-audit fees within the context of a developing economy with weak financial regulatory regime.

Keywords: International Financial Reporting Standards, Audit fees, Non-audit fees, Big4, Ghana National Accounting Standards

---

[1] *Corresponding author*: School of Business, Dominion University College; PMB CT69, Accra. email address: a.musah@duc.edu.gh

1. Introduction

Prior to the adoption of IFRS for financial reporting by public entities in Ghana, companies were using the Ghana National Accounting Standards which was issued by the Institute of Chartered Accountants – Ghana (ICAG). Osei-Afoakwa and Asare (2013) the institute was expected to ensure that Ghana's Accounting Standards were in harmony with International Accounting Standards (IAS). Unfortunately, the ICAG did not have the legal mandate to enforce compliance with its directives as there was no legal basis for its operations (Osei-Afoakwa & Asare, 2013). Rahman (2004) noted that even though these standards were supposed to be in harmony with IAS, they were never reviewed and this compelled most practitioners who got confused by the inconsistencies in the standards and the lack of guidelines to abandon them. In 2004, a report by the World Bank and the International Monetary Fund (IMF) titled Report on the Observance of Standards and Codes (ROSC) listed a number of weaknesses in the financial reporting framework of Ghana and stated that the ICAG lacked the capacity to function properly as an effective professional accounting body. A number of recommendations were made which included legal reforms as well as regulatory and structural reforms including adopting or converging with IFRS/IAS.

Ghana adopted IFRS for listed firms, government businesses, banks, insurance companies, security brokerage firms, pension funds and public utility companies in 2007 based on the recommendations of the ROSC report in 2004. The date for full compliance was set a year later even though some companies had complied by the end of 2007. The ROSC report (2004) revealed that the GNAS had significant weaknesses in regulation, compliance and enforcement of standards. This placed doubts on the quality of accounting information prepared in accordance with the GNAS. Assenso-Okofo *et al.* (2011) reviewed the development of accounting and reporting in Ghana and reported that IFRS adoption improved earnings quality and analyst forecast. Most importantly, previous studies on disclosure requirements under the GNAS standards reported that disclosure was generally low (Aboagye-Otchere *et al.*, 2012; Assenso-Okofo *et al.*, 2011; Bokpin, 2013; Tsamenyi *et al.*, 2007). The ROSC report argued that the country must improve on its financial reporting regulatory systems and framework and to that effect recommended that the country should fully adopt IFRS and the IFRS for SMEs when they are available without any attempt to modify them. Osei-Afoakwa and Asare (2013) argue that there was a significant gap between the GNAS and the IFRS/IAS which compelled the country to fully adopt IFRS instead of issuing its own standards in harmony with IFRS/IAS.

Researchers have argued that the adoption of IFRS for listed and non-listed firms globally is the most significant regulatory change in the history of the accounting profession in most countries (Klibi & Klibi, 2016; Camaran & Perrotti, 2014;

Nulla, 2013; Daske *et al.*, 2008). The results of this major regulatory change on audit and its related cost such as audit and non-audit fees has gained the attention of researchers, practitioners and other stakeholders (Loyeung *et al.*, 2016; Choi & Yoon, 2014; Kim *et al.* 2013; Mudawaki, 2012; Choi *et al.*, 2010). The perceived benefits of instituting a single set of global accounting standards are: potential improvements in the quality of reported information to stakeholders as well as convergence benefits such as greater ease of comparing financial statements of companies across countries; increased ability to secure cross-border listing, better management of global operations and decreased cost of capital (De George *et al.*, 2013; Naoum *et al.* 2011). However, these benefits must be contrasted with the potential cost of mandatory adoption of IFRS. Vieru and Schadewitz (2010) argue that auditors view the complexity of the IFRS transition and the client's potential insufficient preparations as issues that increase the uncertainties and risks in their audit assignments. For example, Hoogendoorn (2006) further notes that companies have underestimated the complexities, effects and costs of IFRS (see also Jermakowicz & Gornik-Tomaszewski, 2006).

Auditing activity is a critical aspect of switching to the application of new accounting standards, and audit fees represent a part of the related implementation costs (Loukil, 2016; Cameran & Perroti, 2014). The mandatory adoption of IFRS has two opposing effects on audit fees: on the one hand, greater effort is required from auditors, which is likely to be reflected by higher fees; on the other hand, if IFRS improve the quality of financial reporting, expected liability costs could decrease, and lower fees may be demanded (de Feuntes & Sierra-Grau, 2015; Choi *et al.* 2010; Cameran & Perroti, 2014).

The effect of the adoption of IFRS on fees paid to auditors is at the Centre of a debate among practitioners. Cameran and Perroti (2014) documents that only a few academic works are concerned with the change in audit fees after IFRS adoption. Griffin *et al.* (2009) find an audit fee increase associated with the adoption of IFRS and the concurrent introduction of new corporate governance rules in New Zealand. Loukil (2016) found evidence of increased audit fees in the year of adoption using French companies but found no significant increase in audit fees post-adoption period. Vieru and Schadewitz (2010) examined fee determination in the transition year to the IFRS for small and medium-sized Finnish companies. Lin and Yen (2016) study on Chinese firms found that auditors with IFRS experience charged significantly higher fees in the initial years of adoption. The results of the study generally revealed an increase in fees after IFRS adoption. The sample of all the analyses is limited to developed and emerging economies even though countries like Kenya adopted IAS/IFRS in 1998. The studies in Africa on IFRS has focused on adoption and implementation and compliance with IFRS (Osei-Afoakwa & Asare, 2013; Madawaki, 2012; Atsunyo *et al.* 2017) and the impact of IFRS adoption on reporting quality (Ames, 2013; Assenso-Okofo *et al.* 2011; Klibi & Klibi, 2016). Majority of these studies have also focused on only audit fees but it is argued that the cost of the transition should also be looked at within the context of consultancy fees companies will have to incur in order to change from the local GAAP to IFRS. Moreover, a lot of work is expected to be done by way of consultancy and audit in the year of adoption like reinstatement of previous years' financial statement in compliance with IFRS which could translate into higher audit and non-audit fees

It is obvious from the forgoing arguments that evidence of the impact of IFRS adoption on audit and non-audit fees has focused on western economies particularly the developed countries with little on Africa and for that matter Ghana. Ghana was the first country in West Africa to adopt IFRS after other Africa countries in Eastern and Southern Africa had adopted it. It is argued, that the institutional environment in which a firm operates to a large extent influence the impact of the mandatory IFRS adoption on audit and non-audit fees (Wang *et al.*, 2008; Taylor and Simon, 1999). Ghana is said to have a weak financial regulatory regime (World Bank & IMF, 2004). Thus, in order to better understand audit and non-audit fee formation during IFRS transition, more insight is needed to assess whether the complexity of the transition coincides with audit and non-audit fees in the African context. Furthermore, the magnitude of the impact of IFRS adoption on audit and non-audit fees will depend largely on the difference between the local GAAP and IFRS. This study therefore addresses the knowledge gap in the literature and explores the effect of the mandatory IFRS adoption in Ghana and its association with audit and non-audit fees.

The study makes significant contribution to literature and policy. The study goes beyond current research on IFRS and audit fees by introducing variables such as the year of IFRS year of adoption, and non-audit fees into the research. These variables have received little attention in literature even in developed economies. The study is relevant because it responds to the limited literature on IFRS and audit and non-audit fees and its implication in Sub-Saharan Africa especially for countries who are considering adopting IFRS. The results have significant implications for other African countries that have not adopted IFRS yet but have plans to adopt it in the near future.

2. Literature review

2.1 Adoption of IFRS in Ghana and Africa

Adoption of IFRS in Africa started in the late 1990s with countries such as Uganda and Kenya adopting it in 1998 and 1999 respectively (Atsunyo *et al.*, 2017). This was followed by Malawi and Mauritius in 2001, Botswana in 2003, Tanzania in 2004, South Africa in 2005, Ghana in 2007, Rwanda and Zambia in 2008, Sierra Leone in 2009, Algeria and Mozambique in 2010, and finally Swaziland and

Nigeria in 2012. What is common among the African countries that have adopted IFRS is that 10 out of the 16 countries are in Southern Africa with only Ghana, Sierra Leone and Nigeria in West Africa. Algeria and Mozambique adopted IFRS with modifications to suit local content but the rest of the African countries including Ghana fully adopted IFRS as published by the International Accounting Standard Board (IASB). Nigeria delayed in adopting IFRS because the Nigerian Accounting Standards Board unlike Ghana had the legal authority, the financial support and the structural integrity to issue accounting standards and enforce same (Osei-Afoakwa & Asare, 2013).

Ghana's adoption of IFRS in 2007 was spearheaded by weaknesses in the local GAAP (ROSC, 2004) and lack of confidence by practitioners in Ghana (Rahman, 2004). Atsunyo *et al.* (2017) posited that the Institute of Chartered Accountants Ghana realised that there was a significant gap between the GNAS and International Accounting Standards and therefore decided to migrate to IFRS. The study further argued that the adoption of IFRS by Ghana in 2007 was also informed by the unprecedented inflow of Foreign Direct Investment (FDI) into West Africa and the increasing need for companies to raise foreign capital through the Stock Exchange. Ghana subsequently adopted IFRS for Small and Medium Scale Enterprises (SMEs) in 2009 even though effective implementation was delayed till 2012 (Aboagye-Otchere & Agbeibor, 2012). Osei-Afoakwa and Asare (2013) argues that Ghana's decision to adopt IFRS was a hasty decision born out of desperation as a result of the inability of the ICAG to provide credible reporting standards for use in Ghana.

It is important to add that despites the adoption of IFRS by some African countries, studies have not examined the effect on audit and non-audit fees which can guide other countries yet to adopt.

Ghana plays a critical role in the West African Sub-region in terms of financial accounting practices through the Association of Accountancy Bodies in West African (ABWA) where it is a founding member. Ghana has been assisting and continues to assist Anglophone countries in the sub-region on Accounting practice and regulations. Currently, ICAG professional Exams are written in Liberia. Other countries such as The Gambia and parts of Cameroun get assistance from the ICAG to develop and enhance financial reporting practices. The Anglophone countries in West Africa follow France domestic guideline in financial reporting and as such have not adopted IFRS yet.

2.2 Empirical review

Several studies have examined the impact of IFRS adoption on audit fees and to some extent on non-audit fees in different jurisdictions. Majority of the results shows a positive relationship between IFRS adoption and audit fees even in developed economies where there exist an efficient Professional Accounting regulatory body. The results are usually attributed to differences in the gap between local GAAP and IFRS in these jurisdictions as well as weaknesses in financial reporting regulations which require more effort during adoption and post-adoption of IFRS. For instance, Houque (2017) examined the effect of IFRS adoption on New Zealand firms. The study based on a sample of 141 firms found evidence to support the hypothesis that IFRS adoption has a positive effect on audit fees.

Chen and Khurana (2017) examined the impact of IFRS versus US GAAP on audit fees and going concern opinion using a sample of US foreign firms. The results of the study revealed that on average foreign IFRS firms pay more audit fees than foreign US GAAP firms. The study argues that the rigidities in IFRS as well as the judgments that preparers of financial statements exercise increase audit risk, hence higher audit fees is charged. Higgins *et al.* (2016) extended previous studies on the impact of IFRS adoption to include increases in audit fees during IFRS adoption and post-IFRS adoption and whether the increases are consistent in the post-adoption period. The results of the study revealed that post-IFRS adoption increase in audit fees is consistent and not driven by short term transitional cost. The results also showed that PwC and Deloitte experienced lower (higher) marginal pricing post- IFRS adoption meaning that they have relatively higher (lower) fixed cost and higher (lower) variable cost structure. Shan and Troshani (2016) examined the impact of mandatory eXtensible Business Reporting Language (XBRL) and IFRS adoption on audit fees using listed firms on the Shanghai Stock Exchange. The results showed that IFRS increased audit fees for all the companies sampled while XBRL was negatively associated with audit fees.

Loukil (2016) studied the impact of IFRS adoption on audit fees using a sample of large French listed companies. The results of the study showed that audit fees increased during the transition period but were not significant during the post-adoption period contrary to the findings of Higgins *et al.* (2016). De Fuentes and Sierra-Grau (2015) examined the impact of IFRS adoption on audit and non-audit fees using a sample of listed firms in Spain. The study revealed an unexpected higher audit fees associated with group accounts for the firms three consecutive years of adoption. The study revealed that the behaviour of non-audit fees was more erratic compared to the audit fees during the same period. Camaran and Perotti (2014) examined the effect of IFRS adoption on audit fees using a sample of Italian banks. The results show that the real audit cost of these banks increased by 19.29% after the adoption of IFRS. The study also revealed that the increase in audit fees is associated with the presence of financial derivatives held for hedging purposes. The study however did not find any effect of IFRS on financial reporting quality.

Choi and Yoon (2014) studied the effect of IFRS adoption, the big N factor, and IFRS-related consultancy services on auditors and audit fees using firms from Korea. The results of the study showed that for Korean firms that are audited by the big N, there is a positive relationship between IFRS adoption and audit fees. The results also showed that IFRS-related consultancy service provided by auditors have a negative association with IFRS adoption. The study concluded that provision of consultancy service by auditor increase auditors' knowledge of the client which mitigates audit costs. De George *et al.* (2012) examined the cost of IFRS in the transition period using sampled firms from Australia. The study reported that the mean cost of IFRS adoption in the transition period increased by 23% beyond the normal yearly increase. The study also showed that firms that have a higher exposure to audit complexity have a greater cost of compliance in the transition period.

Yaacob and Che-Ahmad (2012) examined the impact of IFRS on audit fees after the adoption by Malaysian listed companies. The results of the study showed that there is a significant positive association between IFRS adoption and audit fees. Griffen *et al.* (2009) examined the relationship between overseas and New Zealand governance regulatory reforms on audit and non-audit fees. The study used IFRS indicator variables to relate the timing of the fee changes to the incidence of the overseas and New Zealand reforms. The results of the study showed an increase in audit fees after the adoption of IFRS by New Zealand firms. The study also reported a decrease in non-audit fees which could not be linked with the adoption of IFRS.

Kim *et al.* (2012) examined the effect of mandatory IFRS adoption on audit fees using a sample of firms within the European Union. The results of the study showed that the mandatory adoption of IFRS within the European Union increased audit fees. The result also showed that audit premium increased with increase in audit complexities as a result of IFRS adoption and reduces the quality of financial reporting. The results further showed that IFRS related premium fees are lower in countries with strong legal regimes. Risheh *et al.* (2014) studied the effect of IFRS adoption on audit fees using listed Jordanian firms. The results from a sample of 1274 Jordanian listed firms revealed a positive and significant association between IFRS adoption and audit fees. The study also reported a positive association between international audit firms and audit fees.

Redmayne and Laswad (2013) examined the impact of IFRS adoption on public sector audit fees and audit effort using sample firms from New Zealand. The results of the study showed a significant increase in audit fees and audit effort in the first year of IFRS adoption. With regards to sectors with the most increase in audit fees and audit effort, the study revealed that local authorities and energy sector had the most significant increase. Schadewitz and Vieru (2009) examine the fees paid to statutory auditors of the small and medium sized companies that are in the stage of using IFRS for the first time in Finland. They used the magnitude of IFRS adjustments on income before tax, net income, equity and total liabilities as the proxy of the complexity of IFRS transition. They find a positive relation between the complexity proxy and the pricing of auditing services which suggest that audit fees are related to the degree of IFRS adjustments. Hart *et al.* (2009) found that prior to the adoption of IFRS in New Zealand and in the year of the adoption, audit fees increased by 48%. Lim *et al.* (2009) examined the practical challenges in the adoption of IFRS through a survey of auditors, auditees and other important users of accounting information and found a 30% increase in audit time, audit risk and audit fees after the adoption of IFRS.

The overall conclusion from previous studies in different jurisdiction is that IFRS adoption increases audit fees. However, very few studies examined the effect of IFRS adoption on non-audit fees. Also, these studies have not examined the subject matter within an African context even though some African countries adopted IFRS even before the compulsory adoption by the European Union in 2004/2005. This study is conducted to address these discrepancies in literature by examining the effect of IFRS adoption of both audit and non-audit fees within an African context and a developing country for that matter.

3. Hypothesis development

3.1 IFRS adoption and audit fees

Prior studies document that the most important factors that affect audit premium and hence audit costs are litigation risk, audit risk and the complexity of audit assignment (Chen & Khurana, 2017; Musah, 2017; Khaled *et al.* 2014; Redmayne & Laswad, 2013; Schelleman & Knechel, 2010; Diehl, 2010; Hay *et al.* 2006). Extant literature document that the adoption of IFRS will increase the additional effort to become knowledgeable about the new standards to allow them evaluate if the firms have duly complied with the reporting standards which will add up to the audit cost (De George *et al.* 2013; Kim *et al.* 2012). Previous studies have even found evidence that IFRS financial statement prepared after first time adoption is about 60% longer than the financial statements in the pre-adoption period (Webb, 2006; Ernst and Young, 2005). Johnson (2009) reports that IFRS adoption and its transition costs ranges between 0.1 to 0.7 percent of annual revenue. Other studies have reports that the mandatory shift from local GAAP to IFRS increases audit risk at the time of the mandatory shift (Charles *et al.* 2010; Ghosh & Pawlewicz, 2009). Several other studies in Europe reports that IFRS adoption by the European Union increased the burden on private companies and the complexities in financial reporting and auditing leading to a higher audit cost (Hung & Subramanyam, 2007; Hoogendoorn, 2006; Jermakowicz & Gornik-Tomaszewski, 2006).

Based on the above review, the study posits that auditing firms will charge higher audit fees to compensate the increased litigation risk, efforts and audit cost after the adoption of IFRS in Ghana especially as it was established that the GNAS was of low quality and suffered various weaknesses. As a result, the study expect that more audit fees are required to compensate the higher level of litigation risk and the more auditing complexities after the IFRS adoption in Ghana. The study therefore hypothesis that:

H1: IFRS adoption is positively and significantly associated with audit fees in Ghana.

3.2 IFRS adoption and non-audit fees

According to Choi and Yoon (2014) audit firms the world over provide both audit and other non-audit or consultancy services to companies and their clients. The study argues that non-audit services include such themes as accounting assistance, accounting compilation, ad hoc accounting advice, due diligence, and tax consulting. The decision to engage the service of audit firms in non-audit roles is a decision that rest with management of the respective organizations. Some researchers have argued that the provision of non-audit services by auditors will affect their independence as there could be some potential self-review threats (Hay *et al.* 2006; Levitt, 2000).

As auditors are likely to prefer non-audit duties that could generate higher profitability than audit duties could, the loss leader phenomenon can occur in the audit services (Choi & Yoon, 2014; Shin & Kim, 2010). Sharma and Sidhu (2001), however, concluded that large non-audit fees to total fees undermine auditor independence when auditors have a tendency to not issue a going concern qualification to clients. Prior research has usually found a positive relationship between IFRS adoption and audit and non-audit fees whiles others did find significant association between IFRS adoption and non-audit fees. For instance, Choi and Yoon (2014) and Naoum *et al.* (2011) have all documented a positive relation between audit and non-audit fees, while no relationship is found by Griffen *et al.* (2009) and O'Keefe, *et al.* (1994). Whisenant *et al.* (2003) and Geiger and Rama (2003) also provide evidence of a positive relationship between IFRS adoption and audit and non-audit fees in a single-equation estimates. However, the relationship between the variables is not evident when simultaneous-equation analysis is employed, suggesting that audit fees and non-audit fees are jointly determined. Antle *et al.* (2006) extended the analysis to include abnormal accruals as suggested by Frankel *et al.* (2002) since the strength of the economic bond between auditors and their clients is believed to be positively associated abnormal accruals.

In practice, auditors are usually the most natural IFRS advisors and consultants for a company (Jermakowicz & Gornik-Tomaszewski, 2006). Indeed, in many annual reports it is explicitly written, among other things that part of the non-audit fees is related to IFRS transition consultation (Choi and Yoon, 2014). Research has shown that a lower audit qualification or modification incidence is associated with non-audit fees (Firth, 2002). Also, the lack of competition in the IFRS transition market for non-audit services can result in a positive relationship between audit and non-audit fees (Solomon, 1990). If there are only few IFRS specialists available, and the common understanding within companies about the IFRS transition requirements is poor (Jermakowitz & Gornik-Tomaszewski, 2006), it is tempting to charge extra fees from the clients. Accordingly, the following hypothesis is developed.

H2: IFRS adoption is positively and significantly associated with non-audit fees in Ghana

3.3 Auditor type and audit fees

Previous studies have argued that auditing firms charge differently for same or similar jobs depending on the level of audit quality (Choi & Yoon, 2014; Redmayne & Laswad, 2013). Lin and Yin (2009) argued that audit quality is enhanced by externally-connected audit firms as they get to share experiences and skills acquired in other jurisdictions. Based on the expectation that members of international accounting firms are capable of providing better auditing service than other local Ghanaian audit firms, the study expect higher incremental audit fees will be charged by member firms during the implementation. Previous studies in other jurisdiction have found a positive relationship between externally-connected audit firms (herein referred as Big4) (Campa, 2013; Choi & Yoon, 2014; Redmayne & Laswad, 2013; Choi *et al.*, 2008). Positive effect of auditor type on audit fees was reported for firms that have not adopted IFRS in Ghana based on a study of Microfinance companies in Ghana (Yalley *et al.*, 2013). Also Musah (2017) study on determinants of audit fees in Ghana using a sample of listed non-financial firms in Ghana reported a positive relationship between auditor type and audit fees. Very few studies have examined auditor type and non-audit fees. Choi and Yoon (2014) study reported a positive association between internationally-connected audit firms and non-audit fees. Based on these findings the following hypothesis can be deduced.

H3: Big four audit firms are associated with higher audit fees and non-audit fees.

4. Methodology

The study is based on firms sampled in Ghana. The study used sample firms in Ghana because Ghana was the first West African country to adopt IFRS in 2007 before Sierra Leone and Nigeria did same in 2012. Ghana is the second largest economy in West Africa and has a lot of influence in the sub-region because of its history as the first independent country and the beacon of democracy in Africa. Also, previous reviews by the World Bank and IMF as well as previous studies all agree that Ghana had a very weak accounting standards and regulatory environment and structures prior to the adoption of IFRS (Osei-Afoakwa & Asare, 2013; Atsunyo *et al.*, 2017; Assenso-Okofo *et al.*, 2011). Ghana joined the International Federation of Accountants (IFAC) in 2005 and was advised to adopt IFRS as its local standards were not up to international standards.

The study did not include Nigeria and Sierra Leon who are the other two countries to adopt IFRS and are Anglophone countries in the sub-region because of currency differences which makes it impossible to convert at a common currency. Previous studies on IFRS adoption and audit fees have focused on only audit fees to the neglect of non-audit fees. In developing countries like Ghana where accounting practice were low at the time of adoption, more effort is needed in terms of preparing and even transition costs. To perfectly capture the full effect of transition costs of IFRS adoption, the study include non-audit fees as well as the year of adoption (IFRSYR) into the model.

Also, in an attempt to increase sample size as the number of listed non-financial firms in Ghana are few, the study extended the sample to included banks and insurance companies who were all mandated to adopt IFRS. This resulted in the dropping of control variables that are unique to manufacturing and trading firms like inventory and receivable which previous studies argue influence audit fees.

The study adopted a quantitative approach relying on panel data regression analysis to achieve the objectives of the study. Previous literature indicate that several variable that influence audit fees include clients size, operational risk and complexities, the type of auditor, profitability of the clients etc. (Houqe, 2017; Camaran & Perotti , 2014; Choi & Yoon, 2014; Griffin *et al.*, 2009; Kim *et al.*, 2012; De George *et al.*, 2013; Vieru & Schadewitz, 2010). The study examined the effect of these variables including IFRS adoption on both audit and non-audit fees. Based on the above, the study developed a cross-sectional regression model as follows:

$$AF_{it} = \beta_0 + \beta_1 IFRS_{it} + \beta_2 IFRSYR_{it} + \beta_3 BIG4_{it} + \beta_4 SIZE_{it} + \beta_5 LEV_{it} + \beta_6 ROA_{it} + \beta_7 LOSS_{it} + \varepsilon_{it}$$

$$NAF_{it} = \beta_0 + \beta_1 IFRS_{it} + \beta_2 IFRSYR_{it} + \beta_3 BIG4_{it} + \beta_4 SIZE_{it} + \beta_5 LEV_{it} + \beta_6 ROA_{it} + \beta_7 LOSS_{it} + \varepsilon_{it}$$

Table 1. Variable definition and their measurement

Variable	Measurement
LogAF	Natural log of the audit fees
IFRSYR	Dummy, IFRS-adoption year coded 1 for First time IFRS financial statements
IFRS	Dummy variable, coded 1 if firm adopt IFRS, 0 Otherwise
SIZE	Natural log of total assets at end of financial year to measure size
LEV	Ratio of total debts (total liabilities - deferred tax) to total assets
LogNAF	Natural log of non-audit fee
LOSS	Net loss (or negative income) reported by a company in the current year coded as 1 if company suffers loss and 0 otherwise.
ROA	Ratio of earnings before interest and tax to ending total assets.
BIG4	Auditor type=1 if the current auditor were a BIG 4 or 0 otherwise

4.1 Control variable

Previous studies have found that firm characteristics such as leverage, loss in a particular year, complexity of operations, company size, riskiness of operations, and profitability of the audited firm affect audit fees (Choi & Yoon, 2014; Shan & Troshini, 2016; Yalley, 2013). In the Ghanaian context Yalley *et al.* (2013) found that the size of rural banks was positively associated with audit fees whiles Musah (2017) fond a positive relationship between audit fees and firm size. The study included some of these variables as control variables.

4.2 Data

The study is based on publicly available data obtained from financial statement of the sampled firms. All public companies including banks and insurance are required to publish their financial statement online and with the relevant regulatory bodies. The data was hand-collected from the annual report of these companies. The sample consist of 530 financial statement for the audit fee model equivalent to 53 firms and 350 financial statement for the non-audit fees model representing 35 firms because some companies did not disclose non-audit fees in the note to their accounts. The sample comprise of 20 non-financial firms, 24 banks and 5 insurance companies. The sample period covers 2003 to 2013 but based on an unbalanced panel data. The effective year of IFRS adoption for all these firms is 2007 even though some complied with the directive in 2008 because of technical difficulties in complying and the need to train staff to be familiar with the new standard.

5. Analysis and discussion

Table 2 presents the descriptive analysis of the study.

Table 2. Descriptive statistics

Variable	Mean	St. Deviation	Minimum	Maximum
AF	4.811	0.466	3.398	6.799
NAF	3.526	0.341	2.664	4.558
IFRS	0.614	0.488	0.000	1.000
SIZE	8.604	0.543	7.234	9.754
LEV	0.870	0.075	0.092	0.997
IFRSYR	0.154	0.414	0.000	1.000
ROA	0.059	0.031	-0.053	0.085
LOSS	0.065	0.247	0.000	1.000
BIG4	0.622	0.487	0.000	1.000

On the adoption of IFRS, the results show that 61% of the firms' sampled financial statements have been prepared in compliance with IFRS. The results from the descriptive statistics also shows that firm in the financial sector are highly leveraged with 87% of capital being debt. The results of the Big4 suggest that majority of the firms are audited by internationally-linked audit firms.

5.1 Effect of IFRS adoption on audit fees

To examine the impact IFRS adoption have on audit and non-audit fees, a panel regression model was used to establish the relationship between the two variables. Various tests were undertaken to determine the reliability of the estimate and to decide which model (fixed effect or random effect) was best for the model. For instance the Breusch- Pagan test was conducted to test for heteroscedasticity. The results for the two models were significant at 5% suggesting that null hypothesis is rejected and that there is heteroscedasticity. The robust estimates in STATA were applied to both models to resolve issues of autocorrelation and heteroscedasticity. The study also used the variance inflation factor (VIF) to test for multicollinearity. The results show that the overall VIF for the first and second model were 1.85 and 1.35 respectively which are less than 2 and as such there is little or no problem for multicollinearity. Finally, the Haussmann test was conducted to decide which model to use. After conducting the Haussmann test, the study settled on the random effect model for the first model and fixed effect for the second model because it's provided more consistent results using the R^2 values and the outcome of the Haussmann test in line with previous studies.

The overall Adjusted R-square is 0.818 for the first model and 0.627 for the second model which suggest that the independent variables have higher explanatory power. The Wild Chi^2 which is a measure of the fitness of the model in the case of a random effect model in a Stata program also had a significant probability for both models which suggest that the model is well fit. The regression results for the first model that examined the effect of IFRS adoption on audit fees is presented in Table 3 below.

Table 3. Regression results on IFRS adoption and audit fees

Variables	Coefficient	Standard Deviation
IFRS	0.091**	1.970
IFRSYR	0.028***	4.289
BIG4	0.096***	2.845
SIZE	0.577***	13.621
LEV	0.004	0.210
ROA	0.011	0.129
LOSS	0.081**	1.966
CONST	0.120	0.314
Number of observations	530	
Wald Chi^2	39.299	
Prob > Chi^2	0.000	
Adjusted R	0.818	

(***significant at 1%, ** significant at 5%, * significant at 10% level)

The results show that IFRS adoption is positive and significantly associated with audit fees at 1% significance level. This suggests that the adoption of IFRS has increased audit fee. This result confirms the results of previous studies (Camaran & Perotti, 2014; Choi & Yoon, 2014; De George *et al.* 2012; Kim *et al.* 2012; Redmayne & Laswad, 2013; Kim *et al.* 2012; Griffin *et al.* 2009; Shan & Troshani, 2016) as well as the first hypothesis of the study which states that IFRS adoption has significant effect on audit fees in Ghana. The year of adoption (IFRSYR) however also showed a positive association with audit fees which also suggest IFRS adoption increased during the transitional period. The results is consistent with previous studies (Camaran & Perotti, 2014; Choi & Yoon, 2014).

The variable Big4 was positively associated with audit fees at a 1% significance level. The result confirms previous studies such as Hongerdoorn (2006) as well as Schadewitz and Vieru (2010) and suggests that big4 audit firms charge higher audit fees than non-big4.

On the control variables; size of the firm and loss which is a measure of risk is significantly associated with audit fees. Size was significant at 1% significance level and had a positive relationship with audit fees as expected. Firm reporting loss was also positively associated with audit fees as expected because of additional risk loss reporting brings.

Other control variables were found not to have any significant association with audit fees. Some of these control variables include; leverage and return on asset which is a measure of profitability and leverage which is a measure of risk. The expectation of these variables as per literature is that they influence audit fees positively.

5.2 Discussion of findings on IFRS and audit fees

The results of the first model as discussed above show that IFRS adoption has resulted in an increase in audit fees consistent with literature and the first hypothesis of the study. The results imply that additional effort was brought to bear on auditors with the mandatory adoption of IFRS by listed firms in Ghana. The results show that auditors in Ghana consider IFRS adoption as causing significant changes to the components which determines audit fees.

The results can be interpreted from three different perspective based on literature. First, the risk that financial statement prepared in compliance with IFRS could be materially misstated is high. Second, the fact that auditors in Ghana provided non-audit and consultancy services which could increase their knowledge of the client financial statement and result in a spill over effect from non-audit service to auditing may not exist. Third, there is less competition for audit firms in Ghana resulting in these firms translating IFRS compliance financial statements auditing into audit costs. This result is not consistent with the finding of Vieru and Schadewitz (2010) that conducted a similar study in Finland and had a positive but statistically insignificant relationship with audit fees.

The results are however consistent with most studies across the globe especially from Europe, Australia and New Zealand. From the auditor's point of view there was an increase in accounting regulation as a result of mandatory IFRS adoption, therefore, increases client related risk and potentially results in more time-consuming work for the auditor to collect evidence in support of the audit opinion (Choi & Yoon, 2014; Kim *et al.*, 2012). The results confirm the assertion in literature that IFRS adoption increases the complexities in the client's financial statements and its associated risk which auditors compensate that additional responsibility with a higher audit fees.

5.3 Big 4 audit firms and audit fees

The results from the regression also confirms the third hypothesis which is to the effect that the Big4 audit firms charge higher audit fees as compared to non-big 4. The significant positive coefficient on BIG4 suggests that a member of the Big 4 firms charge a much higher level of auditing fees than the domestic auditing firms in Ghana. The significant positive effect is not explained by the adoption of IFRS but the fact that the big4 provide high quality audit hence charge higher fees. This finding is consistent with the results of Campa (2013) and Lin and Yen (2016) but different from the findings of Jianfang *et al.* (2012). The higher audit fees charged by the Big4 is as a results of the perceived audit quality and richer expertise and experience to assist them to deal with the higher level of demand for the auditing quality under the new accounting standards.

Table 4. Effect of IFRS adoption on non-audit fees

Variables	Coefficient	Standard Deviation
IFRS	0.141***	2.988
IFRSYR	0.027***	4.336
BIG4	0.106***	2.872
SIZE	0.500***	11.411
LEV	0.002	0.010
ROA	0.080	0.869
LOSS	0.209**	2.348
CONST	0.274	0.699
Number of observations	350	
Wald Chi2	96.150	
Prob > F	0.000	
Adjusted R	0.627	

(***significant at 1%, ** significant at 5%, * significant at 10% level)

The results of the regression analysis show that IFRS adoption has a positive effect on non-audit fees just like audit fees. Also, the relationship is statistically significant at 1% significance level suggesting that IFRS adoption have significant impact on non-audit fees as it did in audit fees. The year of adoption also have significant positive relationship with non-audit fees.

The Big 4 audit firm as expected had also a positive and significant relationship with non-audit fees. The results imply that the big4 audit firms charge higher amount as non-audit fees just like audit fees in the first model.

Almost all the control variables in the model were statistically insignificant with the exception of firm size and Loss which had a positive significant relationship with non-audit fees at a 1% and 5% significance level respectively.

5.4 Discussion of findings on IFRS and non-audit fees

The results of the study revealed that IFRS adoption have a significant impact on non-audit and accounting consultancy services cost. This result is consistent with the second hypothesis which states that IFRS adoption has significant effect on non-audit fees in Ghana. The reason for this result could be attributed to the fact that there was a significant gap between the Local GAAP which is the Ghana National Accounting Standards and IFRS which required that auditors assist companies to comply with the new standards by proving consultancy services. The results suggest that IFRS adoption required technical skills which most of the listed firms did not have and had to engage these audit firms who have the expertise as a result of working in other jurisdictions where IFRS was adopted before Ghana. The result was not just significant for the post-adoption period but was significant during the transition period as IFRSYR was also positively associated with non-audit fees.

The result of the study is consistent with prior studies as more research has usually found a positive relationship between IFRS adoption and non-audit fees. Prior research (Choi & Yoon, 2014; Shin & Kim, 2010; Whisenant *et al.*, 2003; Geiger & Rama, 2003 and Naoum *et al.*, 2011) has documented a positive relation between IFRS adoption and non-audit fees the result is however inconsistent with the findings of O'Keefe *et al.* (1994) which found no significant relationship between IFRS adoption and non-audit fees.

Overall, it can be said that IFRS adoption did not require companies adopting IFRS for the first time to engage the services of professional accounting bodies in the transition period as the year of adoption was also negatively associated with non-audit fees. The overall impact was felt on the post adoption period and not the year of adoption.

5.5 Big 4 Audit firm and non-audit fees

The results of the second regression analysis in table 4 shows that firms that are audited by the big 4 audit firms or the internationally-linked audit firms charge higher audit fees than non-big 4. This result has nothing to do with IFRS adoption but simply suggest that the internationally-linked audit firms have the expertise and produce high audit quality hence they charge premium for their service. The result is consistent with the expectations of the third hypothesis and consistent with the results of Choi and Yoon (2014).

6. Conclusions

IFRS is a principled-based accounting standard that requires preparers of financial statements to establish logic and reason within the context of the framework of accounting and apply those principles consistently. The complexities that mandatory IFRS brings as well as the related audit risk requires that auditors exercise high levels of professional scepticism, more effort both as consultants to their clients and auditors. The increased burden as a result of mandatory IFRS adoption has translated into increased audit and non-audit fees in even developed economies which are supported by the findings of this study. The results of the study showed that there was a positive and significant association between mandatory IFRS adoption by firms in Ghana and audit and non-audit fees. The results emphasize the complexities of IFRS and the professional judgement needed to be exercised by preparers of financial statements required more effort and technical skills from audit firms in the form of consultancy services and audit fees. Also both the audit fees model and the non-audit fee model had a positive association with the year of adoption suggesting that IFRS cost increased in the transition period consistent with the finding of some studies in other jurisdictions.

The results also show that big 4 audit firms charge higher audit fees than non-big4. This finding means that Ghanaian affiliated Big 4 firms can offer high-quality audit services because they have invested heavily in gaining experience and in improving expertise and as such charge higher fees for their expertise.

This study has implications for African countries that are yet to adopt IFRS especially companies in Liberia and other Anglophone African countries and even the Francophone countries. Companies in those countries should anticipate the cost associated with the mandatory adoption of IFRS and compare it with the anticipated benefits. Also, future studies could expand the scope of the study to include specific IFRS requirements that increases the complexities and audit risk which results in higher audit fees. A related research question could involve the nature of the longer-term trend of fees after IFRS adoption.

References

Aboagye-Otchere, F., & Agbeibor, J. (2012) "The International Financial Reporting Standard for Small and Medium-sized Entities (IFRS for SMES) Suitability for small businesses in Ghana", *Journal of Financial Reporting and Accounting*, vol. 10, no. 2: 190-214

Aboagye-Otchere, F., Bedi, I. & Ossei Kwakye, T. (2012) "Corporate governance and disclosure practices of Ghanaian listed companies", *Journal of Accounting in Emerging Economies*, vol. 2, no. 2: 140-161

Adeyemi, S.B., Okpala, O. & Dabor, E.L., (2012). "Factors affecting audit quality in Nigeria", *International Journal of Business and Social Science*, vol. 3, no. 20:

Ames, D. (2013) "IFRS adoption and accounting quality: The case of South Africa", *Journal of Applied Economics and Business Research*, vol. 3, no. 3: 154-165

Antle, R., Griffin, P.A., Teece, D. & Williamson, O.E. (1997) "An economic analysis of auditor independence for a multi-client, multi-service public accounting firm"

Assenso-Okofo, O., Ali, M. J., & Ahmed, K. (2011) "The development of accounting and reporting in Ghana", *The International Journal of Accounting*, vol. 46, no. 4: 459-480

Atsunyo, W., Gatsi, J. G. & Frimpong-Manson, E. (2017) "The success of IFRS in Africa: Comparative evidence between Ghana and Kenya", *European Journal of Business, Economics and Accountancy,* vol. 5, no. 1: 46-56

Ball, R. (2006) "International Financial Reporting Standards (IFRS): pros and cons for investors", *Accounting and business research*, vol. 36, no. 1: 5-27

Basioudis, I.G., Geiger, M.A. & Papanastasiou, V. (2006) "Audit fees, non-audit fees, and auditor reporting on UK stressed companies", In *National Auditing Conference*, 1-24

Bokpin, G.A. (2013) "Determinants and value relevance of corporate disclosure: Evidence from the emerging capital market of Ghana", *Journal of Applied Accounting Research*, vol. 14, no. 2: 127-146

Cameran, M. & Perotti, P. (2014) "Audit fees and IAS/IFRS adoption: evidence from the banking industry", *International Journal of Auditing*, vol. 18, no. 2: 155-169

Campa, D. (2013) "Big 4 fee premium and audit quality: latest evidence from UK listed companies", *Managerial Auditing Journal*, vol. 28, no. 8: 680-707

Charles, S.L., Glover, S.M. & Sharp, N.Y. (2010) "The association between financial reporting risk and audit fees before and after the historic events surrounding SOX", *Auditing: A Journal of Practice & Theory*, vol. 29, no. 1: 15-39

Chen, L. H., & Khurana, I. K. (2017) "The Impact of IFRS versus US GAAP on Audit Fees and Going Concern Opinions: Evidence from US-Listed Foreign Firms". Unpublished paper. Accessed from m.xmu.edu.cn/uploadfile/2017/0401/20170401090320734.pd.

Choi, J.H., Kim, C., Kim, J.B. & Zang, Y. (2010) "Audit office size, audit quality, and audit pricing", *Auditing: A Journal of practice & theory*, vol. 29, no. 1: 73-97

Choi, W. & Yoon, S. (2014) "Effects of IFRS adoption, Big N factor, and the IFRS-related consulting services of auditors on audit fees: the case of Korea", *Asian Journal of Business and Accounting*, vol. 7, no. 1

Daske, H. & Gebhardt, G. (2006) "International financial reporting standards and experts' perceptions of disclosure quality", *Abacus*, vol. 42, no. 3-4: 461-498

Daske, H., Hail, L., Leuz, C. & Verdi, R., (2008) "Mandatory IFRS reporting around the world: Early evidence on the economic consequences", *Journal of accounting research*, vol. 46, no. 5: 1085-1142

de Fuentes, C., & Sierra-Grau, E. (2015) "IFRS adoption and audit and non-audit fees: empirical evidence from Spanish listed companies", *Spanish Journal of Finance and Accounting/Revista Española de Financiación y Contabilidad*, ol. 44, no. 4: 387-426

De George, E.T., Ferguson, C.B. & Spear, N.A. (2012) "How much does IFRS cost? IFRS adoption and audit fees", *The Accounting Review*, vol. 88, no. 2: 429-462

Diehl, K.A. (2010) "The real cost of IFRS: The relationship between IFRS implementation and audit, tax, and other auditor fees", *International Research Journal of Finance & Economics*, vol. 37: 96-101

Ernst & Young (2005) "The impacts of IFRS on Australian companies: A study of the financial statement disclosures by Australia's top 100 listed companies" Available at: http://www.ey.com

Firth, M. (2002) "Auditor–provided consultancy services and their associations with audit fees and audit opinions", *Journal of Business Finance & Accounting*, vol. 29, no. 5-6: 661-693

Ghosh, A. & Pawlewicz, R. (2009) "The impact of regulation on auditor fees: Evidence from the Sarbanes-Oxley Act", *Auditing: a journal of practice & theory*, vol. 28, no. 2: 171-197

Griffin, P. A., Lont, D. H., & Sun, Y. (2009) "Governance regulatory changes, International Financial Reporting Standards adoption, and New Zealand audit and non-audit fees: empirical evidence", *Accounting & Finance*, vol. 49, no. 4: 697-724

Hail, L., Leuz, C. & Wysocki, P. (2010), "Global accounting convergence and the potential adoption of IFRS by the US (Part I): Conceptual underpinnings and economic analysis", *Accounting Horizons*, vol. 24, no. 3: 355-394

Hart, C., Rainsbury, E.A. & Sharp, J. (2009) "NZ IFRS–the impact on fees paid to auditors", *Chartered Accountants Journal*, vol. 88, no. 6: 42-43

Hay, D.C., Knechel, W.R. & Wong, N. (2006) "Audit fees: A Meta-analysis of the effect of supply and demand attributes", *Contemporary accounting research*, vol. 23, no. 1: 141-191

Higgins, S., Lont, D., & Scott, T. (2016) "Longer term audit costs of IFRS and the differential impact of implied auditor cost structures", *Accounting & Finance*, vol. 56, no. 1: 165-203

Hoogendoorn, M. (2006) "International accounting regulation and IFRS implementation in Europe and beyond–experiences with first-time adoption in Europe", *Accounting in Europe*, vol. 3, no. 1: 23-26

Houqe, M. N. (2017) "IFRS adoption and audit fees-evidence from New Zealand", *International Journal of Business and Economics*, vol. 16: 1-75.

Hung, M. & Subramanyam, K.R. (2007) "Financial statement effects of adopting international accounting standards: the case of Germany", *Review of accounting studies*, vol. 12, no. 4: 623-657

Jermakowicz, E.K. & Gornik-Tomaszewski, S. (2006) "Implementing IFRS from the perspective of EU publicly traded companies", *Journal of International Accounting, Auditing and Taxation*, vol. 15, no. 2: 170-196

Johnson, M.F., Nelson, K.K. & Frankel, R.M. (2002) "The Relation Between Auditor's Fees for Non-audit Services and Earnings Quality" (No. 1696r).

Johnson, S. (2009) "Guessing the costs of IFRS conversion", *CFO Magazine*.

Kim, J.B., Chung, R. & Firth, M. (2003) "Auditor conservatism, asymmetric monitoring, and earnings management", *Contemporary Accounting Research*, vol. 20, no. 2: 323-359

Kim, J.B., Liu, X. & Zheng, L. (2010) "Does Mandatory IFRS Adoption Impact Audit Fees?: Theory and Evidence", In *Annual Conference of the Canadian Academic Accounting Association, CAAA 2010*. Canadian Academic Accounting Association Inc...

Kim, J.B., Liu, X. & Zheng, L. (2012) "The impact of mandatory IFRS adoption on audit fees: Theory and evidence", *The Accounting Review*, vol. 87, no. 6: 2061-2094

Klibi, M. F., & Klibi, M. F. (2016) "Using international standards as a complement to overcome the unachieved nature of local GAAPs: The case of a developing country", *Journal of Applied Accounting Research*, vol. 17, no. 3: 356-376

Lin, H.L. & Yen, A.R. (2016) "The effects of IFRS experience on audit fees for listed companies in China", *Asian Review of Accounting*, vol. 24, no. 1: 43-68.

Loukil, L. (2016) "The impact of IFRS on the amount of audit fees: the case of the large French listed companies", *Quarterly Journal of Finance and Accounting*, vol. 54, no. 1/2: 41

Loyeung, A., Matolcsy, Z., Weber, J., & Wells, P. (2016) "The cost of implementing new accounting standards: The case of IFRS adoption in Australia", *Australian Journal of Management*, vol. 41, no. 4: 611-632

Madawaki, A. (2012) "Adoption of international financial reporting standards in developing countries: The case of Nigeria", *International Journal of Business and management*, vol. 7, no. 3: 152.

Musah, A. (2017) "Determinants of audit fees in a developing economy: evidence from Ghana", *International Journal of Academic Research in Business and Social Sciences*, vol. 7, no. 11: 716-730

Naoum, V.C., Sykianakis, N. & Tzovas, C. (2011) "The perceptions of managers of Greek firms regarding the Costs and Benefits ensuing from the adoption of International Financial Reporting Standards in Greece", *International Journal of Economic Sciences & Applied Research*, vol. 4, no. 3:

Nulla, Y.M. (2013) "IFRS adoption in research and development companies", *Journal of Administrative Sciences and Policy Studies*, vol. 1, no. 1: 34-48

O'Keefe, T.B., Simunic, D.A. & Stein, M.T. (1994) "The production of audit services: Evidence from a major public accounting firm", *Journal of Accounting Research*, 241-261

Osei-Afoakwa, K., & Asare, M. (2013) "From accounting standard-setters to standard-takers: The Nigerian and Ghanaian standard-setting experiences in retrospect", *International Journal of Social Science Tomorrow,* vol. 2, no. 4: 1-12

Previts, G.J., Walton, P. & Wolnizer, P.W. (2010) *A Global History of Accounting, Financial Reporting and Public Policy: Europe*, Emerald Group Publishing.

Rahman, M.Z., Linde, G. & Yankey, F. (2004) "Report on the Observance of Standards and Codes (ROSC): Ghana-Accounting and Auditing. *ROSC", Under the initiative of the World Bank and IMF.[Online]. Available: http://www. worldbank. org/ifa/rosc-aa. html. Accessed on*, *27*(12), p.12.

Redmayne, N.B. & Laswad, F. (2013) "An assessment of the impact of IFRS adoption on public sector audit fees and audit effort–some evidence of the transition costs on changes in reporting regimes", *Australian Accounting Review*, vol. 23, no. 1: 88-99

Risheh, K.E.A. (2014) "The impact of IFRS adoption on audit fees: evidence from Jordan", *Accounting and Management Information Systems*, vol. 13, no. 3: 520

Schelleman, C. & Knechel, W.R. (2010) "Short-term accruals and the pricing and production of audit services", *Auditing: A Journal of Practice & Theory*, vol. 29, no. 1: 221-250

Shan, Y.G. & Troshani, I. (2016) "The effect of mandatory XBRL and IFRS adoption on audit fees: Evidence from the Shanghai Stock Exchange", *International Journal of Managerial Finance*, vol. 12, no. 2: 109-135

Sharma, D.S. & Sidhu, J. (2001) "Professionalism vs commercialism: The association between non-audit services (NAS) and audit independence", *Journal of Business Finance & Accounting*, vol. 28, no. 5-6: 563-594

Simunic, D.A. (1980) "The pricing of audit services: Theory and evidence", *Journal of accounting research*, 161-190

Sun, Y., Lont, D.H. & Griffin, P.A. (2008) "Governance regulatory changes, IFRS adoption, and New Zealand audit and non-audit fees: Empirical evidence", working paper

Taylor, M.H. & Simon, D.T. (1999) "Determinants of audit fees: the importance of litigation, disclosure, and regulatory burdens in audit engagements in 20 countries", *The International Journal of Accounting*, vol. 34, no. 3: 375-388

Tsamenyi, M., Enninful-Adu, E. & Onumah, J. (2007) "Disclosure and corporate governance in developing countries: Evidence from Ghana", *Managerial Auditing Journal*, vol. 22, no. 3: 319-334

Vieru, M. & Schadewitz, H. (2010) "Impact of IFRS transition on audit and non-audit fees: evidence from small and medium-sized listed companies in Finland", working paper

Walker, A., & Hay, D. (2013) "Non-audit services and knowledge spillovers: An investigation of the audit report lag, *Meditari Accountancy Research*, vol. 21, no. 1: 32-51

Wang, X., Young, D. & Zhuang, Z. (2008) "The effects of mandatory adoption of International Financial Reporting Standards on information environments", *Unpublished paper, The Chinese University of Hong Kong*

Webb, R. (2006) "Brace yourselves: IFRS will be bumpy", *Financial Review*, vol. 25, no. 1: 26-34

Whisenant, S., Sankaraguruswamy, S. & Raghunandan, K. (2003) "Evidence on the joint determination of audit and non-audit fees", *Journal of Accounting Research*, vol. 41, no. 4: 721-744

World Bank & International Monetary Fund (2004) Report on the observance of Standards and Codes (ROSC), Corporate Governance Country Assessment: Ghana, Washington, DC: World Bank and IMF.

Yaacob, N.M. & Che-Ahmad, A. (2012) "Audit fees after IFRS adoption: Evidence from Malaysia", *Eurasian Business Review*, vol. 2, no. 1: 31-46

Yalley, P.M., Henry, A.A., Zhongming, T.A.N. & Yaw, N.E. (2013) "The Determinants of Audit Fees in Rural and Community Banks in Ghana: An Empirical Analysis", *International Journal of Business and Social Research*, vol. 3, no. 5: 212-218

9

Introduction to the Special issue on Corporate Social Reporting in Central and Eastern Europe

Cătălin Nicolae Albu[a1], Cagnur Balsari[b2] and Joanna Krasodomska[c3]

[a] *Bucharest University of Economic Studies, Romania*
[b] *Dokuz Eylul University, Turkey*
[c] *Cracow University of Economics, Poland*

Abstract: Corporate Social Responsibility (CSR) regulations, frameworks and practices have increasingly preoccupied accounting researchers over the last decades. The countries in Central and Eastern Europe (CEE) have significantly evolved after the fall or the decline of their non-democratic regimes, and improved reporting by companies in such countries is called for and supported by international and regional organizations, as well as driven more or less successfully by local bodies. In the midst of such evolutions, CSR-related matters are an important concept materializing in the accounting academic and practitioner literature in the CEE region, as well as in the practices of local companies. We then devote this special issue of the Journal of Accounting and Management Information Systems to studying the state of CSR reporting in the CEE region. We include in this special issue six papers that treat the respective cases of Poland, Romania and Turkey as exponents of the CEE region. Results of the papers published attest to the increased interest showed by accounting researchers in the CEE region to CSR-related matters. However, a number of issues still require further investigation, such as the determinants and consequences of good CSR practices, the process of change in integrating the CSR thinking in organizations,

---

[1] Corresponding author: Cătălin Albu, Bucharest University of Economic Studies, 6 Piata Romana, Bucharest, Romania. E-mail: catalin.albu@cig.ase.ro

[2] Author 2: Cagnur Balsari, Dokuz Eylul University, Tinaztepe Yerleskesi, Buca, Izmir, Turkey. E-mail: cagnur.kaytmaz@deu.edu.tr

[3] Author 3: Joanna Krasodomska, Department of Financial Accounting, Cracow University of Economics; Rakowicka Str. 27, 31-510 Cracow; E-mail: joanna.krasodomska@uek.krakow.pl

CSR disclosures and the impact of the institutional context, the role of regional and national regulators in establishing adequate CSR regulations and frameworks that promote sound CSR practices in the region, the perception of CSR-related matters by the millennials, or the impact of Information Technology advancements on CSR practices.

Keywords: Corporate Social Responsibility, Central and Eastern Europe, CSR reporting

1. Introduction

We currently witness increasing efforts of regulators, professional associations, international organizations and companies to strengthen the relevance of organizational reporting. Some milestones include value added accounting practiced in the United Kingdom in the 1970s (Burchell *et al.*, 1985), voluntary environmental and social reporting (mainly referred to as CSR reporting) later on (Cohen *et al.*, 2012; KPMG, 2013), and recently integrated reporting (IR). IR is considered as a superior stage in approaching and reporting sustainability (Deloitte, 2011). While IR is recently of interest for market regulators, accounting firms, preparers and professional bodies, most of the existing studies, especially in the CEE region, concern CSR practices.

The focus of this special issue is on CSR developments in three countries in the CEE region, i.e. Poland, Romania and Turkey. Therefore, the aim of this special issue is twofold: (1) to collect significant findings regarding the CSR practices in the three countries, and to summarize the main initiatives in this area; and (2) to disseminate to an international audience the results of research published in other languages than English, to provide a solid background for conducting future research in these countries and in the region in the CSR area. Moreover, the papers included in the special issue have policy-relevant implications, and suggest research opportunities in this area.

Besides JAMIS' commitment to increase the visibility of accounting research conducted in the CEE region, publishing such studies is also backed by their economic importance. The countries selected for this special issue represent the two biggest former communist countries members of the European Union (EU), i.e. Poland and Romania, and a strong candidate country, i.e. Turkey. Poland and Romania share some similarities in their communist past and reforms undertaken, but they are different in their economic and institutional development (as reflected for example by their different accession year to the EU – 2004 for Poland and 2007 for Romania, or by the development of their respective capital markets). On the other hand, Turkey had many institutional initiatives designed to improve the country's economic landscape and to attract foreign investors, with a general view to join the EU and other Western organizations. Focusing on CEE countries thus gives us a chance to observe, investigate and explore the similarities and differences across countries situated in close geographical proximity and of comparative degree of economic development, as well as to identify and exploit the consequences of such comparisons. The global CSR movement can only be successful if the external incentives in each country can be aligned.

The remainder of this article is thus organized: in part 2 we briefly motivate the need to investigate CSR developments in CEE countries; in part 3 we outline the main such developments in Poland, Romania and Turkey as exponents of the CEE region; while in part 4 we conclude and provide opportunities for future research in the areas investigated.

2. Why is it important to conduct CSR research in CEE countries?

CSR has been the buzzword used in international agenda of the corporate world and the regulators in the recent years. However, this does not preclude the existence of definitional confusion about it in the world. Literature analyzing the different definitions of CSR begins with Carroll (1999) and continues with Moir (2001), Carter and Jennings (2004) among others. In a recent study, Dahlsrud (2008) analyzed 37 definitions of CSR from five dimensions, i.e. environmental, social, economic, stakeholder and voluntariness. The study concludes that each dimension is an important part of CSR but the most important problem is not how to define CSR but how to incorporate it as a part of business strategy by balancing these dimensions.

With such confusion regarding the definition and application, CSR has evolved differently depending on the social, economic and legal condition of each country. Studies discussed in literature outline significant cross-national differences in how companies approach stakeholders' prioritization, managerial processes, communication, and other CSR-related problems (Paliwoda-Matiolańska, 2015). Recently, efforts have been put forward in the international arena to reach a better and more comparable CSR practice and reporting. At this point, it is important to document where each country stands on the CSR issue in terms of demand, supply, culture and enforcement. This special issue is a good starting point in understanding the differences in CSR application, effects and improvements and why these differences exist in certain countries. Moreover, responsible persons and organizations in CEE countries should investigate their institutional environment that influences socially responsible activities in order to create an adequate CSR framework that would take account of the limitations of their economies in transition and their backgrounds (Paliwoda-Matiolańska, 2015).

While the international CSR research grew significantly over the last decade, there is a shortage of research investigating the nature and extent of CSR in CEE countries, as compared to more developed countries. Well-designed, performed and presented studies on the CSR concept will reveal the importance of its implementation not only for particular enterprises but also for states in general. A comparison of the results of research studies carried out in various countries will make it possible to identify the areas for improvement, as well as to determine a set of good practices which could be followed by the countries where the CSR development processes are less advanced. Finally, different streams of CSR empirical research should lead to more conceptually-relevant work on the CSR notions, frameworks, or models that are more applicable to CEE countries. Alongside these efforts, there seems to be a specific need for research with a greater focus on CSR practices, including those in the field of accounting. It appears that the relation between CSR and company value, as well as the usefulness of CSR disclosures for the users still count among the most important research topics in this area.

3. The main advancements in CSR practices and research in Poland, Romania and Turkey

3.1 Poland

The research results compiled and presented by Dyczkowska *et al.* (2016) indicate an increasing CSR awareness in Poland. The studies reviewed were expectedly conducted mostly among large, international companies, so caution must be exercised when interpreting their results. There are several CSR leaders, and at the same time plenty of smaller companies that do not get involved in the CSR practices. CSR is still perceived by many as an activity focused on promotion, increases expenses and legal responsibility. Nevertheless, the following initiatives related to CSR deserve special attention and seem to distinguish Poland from other CEE countries.

The first one is the RESPECT Index covering a portfolio of listed companies that adopted CSR standards, established in 2009 for the first time in the CEE region. The Index currently comprises 23 companies. It is worth mentioning that, in the last three years, the cumulative return rates of RESPECT index outperformed the WIG indices (which are indexes comprising the largest companies listed on

Warsaw Stock Exchange). According to the results of Deloitte research (Dyczkowska *et al.*, 2016), most professional participants of the Polish capital market are aware of the RESPECT Index. However, they are not aware of the companies that are included in it, and they do not use this information while making investment decisions.

The second is the activity of the Responsible Business Forum (RBF) and its contribution to the evolution of the CSR concept. RBF is the largest and longest-operating (15 years) non-governmental organization in Poland. It is involved in national and international cooperation, and supports the operations of the Ministry of Economy. Many initiatives referred to in the paper by Dyczkowska *et al.* (2016) were realized in cooperation with this institution. RBF is a co-author of the sustainable development vision for Polish business organizations (The new "2050 Vision"), which fosters the publication of the General Ranking of Responsible Firms and is a collaborator of audit companies (such as Deloitte or KPMG) on several research studies.

The third issue is Deloitte's active involvement in CSR projects and initiatives in Poland. Deloitte is the partner of the RESPECT Index Project, co-author (in collaboration with the WSE) of two research studies concerning the use of CSR-related information by institutional investors, and a study of Polish managers' opinion as to the main CSR achievements. Irena Pichola (who is Polish) was appointed the team leader of The Sustainability Consulting Central Europe Team which operates within Deloitte's organizational structure, conducts projects and provides training for customers in CEE.

The Polish literature review conducted by Waniak-Michalak *et al.* (2016) reveals an increasing number of publications by Polish authors related to the CSR issues over the last 15 years. According to BazEkon (i.e., the most popular Polish economic research database) 136 papers on CSR were published in 2015, and 14 of them referred to accounting and reporting issues. Topics investigated representing the accounting discipline included, for example, social accounting, communication of the CSR activity, the quality and content of CSR reports, legitimization theory, and factors influencing CSR reporting development. For the last few years, IR also seems to have gained significant attention from Polish academia. 8 such papers were indexed in the BazEkon Database for the period 2012-2015, and the Google scholar web search engine identifies 41 publications. Authors studied the usefulness of integrated reports and Polish companies' practices in this respect.

The research method used in most such studies was the literature review, which is traditionally the most common method within the Polish academia. Other methods, less frequently applied, included content analysis, case study, survey, cluster or regression analysis. Despite the fact that Polish journals also offer the possibility to publish in English, few papers have been written in this language. The largest number of the identified papers were published in Theoretical Journal of Accounting, which is perceived as the most important and noticeable journal by the Polish accounting scholars. International publications of Polish authors appeared in such journals as *Quality & Quantity, Social Responsibility Journal, Engineering Economics,* and *Social Sciences*.

The inclusion of CSR matters within the scope of the accounting domain has many supporters among the academia representatives, but at the same time, not much backing from the Ministry of Economy and Polish accounting organizations, such as the Accounting Association in Poland or National Chamber of Statutory Auditors. Their reluctance towards can be justified by the Polish accounting traditions. The centrally planned economy period from the late 1950s was the time when accounting was reduced to book-keeping, much similarly to other CEE former communist countries. In practice, it implied the lack of experience and expertise and unwillingness to make decisions on one's own. That is why Polish accounting still relies more on detailed law regulations than on accountants' professional judgment. The strong legal enforcement of accounting issues in Poland stems from the legal traditions and cultural heritage whereby people's freedom and their right to use it in their professional life for making independent decisions are constrained by the limits set by the law (Surdykowska, 1999). So far CSR has not been included in the accounting law and has not been perceived as subject of accountants' interest. This situation might change in the nearest future because of the introduction of the Directive 2014/95/EU on non-financial information into the Polish legal framework.

3.2. Romania

The Lungu *et al.* (2016) paper included in this special issue employs literature review and archival research to establish, respectively, the characteristics of CSR research and the contribution of Romanian authors to such literature. CSR-related literature is reviewed in the first part of the paper, in an attempt to synthesize it. 186 papers published between 2011 and 2015 and written by Romanian authors (some in international teams) are reviewed in the second part of the paper, with respect to the paper's content, research methods, citations and references, and document an increased interest of such authors to CSR matters.

The literature review part of the Lungu *et al.* (2016) paper addresses first the evolution of corporate responsibility-related concepts, and attests for the wide array of characteristics and meanings that emerged over time. Terms such as corporate social performance, corporate social responsiveness, triple bottom line, corporate citizenship, or corporate sustainability or application of sustainability at the corporate level emerged and were used in literature over time. Additionally, the lack of a mandatory framework and guidelines for CSR reporting and the various perspectives of disclosing companies' responsibilities related to other than financial aspects of their activity stand as resilient arguments for the diversity of CSR research. Research reviewed in Lungu *et al.* (2016) identified significant gaps emphasizing that research is almost entirely quantitative, conceptualization is limited, and the effects of corporate philanthropy on society are currently under-researched, thus calling for a multilevel analysis.

The main part of the Lungu *et al.* (2016) paper analyzes 186 papers published between 2011 and 2015 by Romanian and international economics journals indexed by Thomson Reuters database and by other international databases, namely EBSCO, Emerald, ProQuest, Science Direct and SpringerLink. The sampled papers differentiated in 155 articles published by Romanian authors in journals indexed in international databases, and 31 articles published by Romanian authors in journals indexed by Thomson Reuters. 78% of the papers reviewed are published in Romanian journals, with the remaining of 22% being published in international publishing houses. About 83% of the papers reviewed in Lungu *et al.* (2016) apply qualitative research methodologies, based mostly on literature review and content analysis. In terms of themes commonly investigated in the papers reviewed in the same paper, the most popular one refers to CSR in action, followed by meaning, definitions, and models of CSR and the impact of CSR on stakeholders and financial performance, or the relationship between CSR and financial performance. Additionally, on average, each paper has two authors, most of the authors being affiliated with Romanian universities. Nevertheless, the 11 papers with at least one international author support the fact that Romanian researchers expanded their national working team and seek collaboration with international researchers in CSR topic.

The second Romanian paper included in this special issue is Guşe *et al.* (2016). They focus on the forces that drive the institutionalization of CSR reporting in Romania. They outline the important role played in this process by the government and the European institutions, as well as by the other stakeholders (such as academia, Big 4 firms and companies), calling for a coordination effort. The authors use institutional theory to build their theoretical framework, and they document the importance of both coercive and mimetic isomorphic mechanisms. As an important contribution of the paper, the authors do not limit their analyses to the company-level, by expanding them to the macroeconomic level as well.

Guşe *et al.* (2016) first identifies the extensive role played by governmental and the European bodies in the institutionalization of CSR reporting in Romania. They find however that CSR policies and actions seem to attract more interest from Romanian legislators than CSR reporting. Another limitation highlighted in the paper is that the current CSR reporting requirements target listed companies, which are not necessarily the most socially responsible, while non-listed companies are not subject to non-financial reporting requirements.

Secondly, Guşe *et al.* (2016) find coercive and mimetic behaviors displayed in Romania, while normative behavior seems to be still lagging. They evidence both the case of those companies that are mandated to make CSR-related disclosures, but that only focus on checking the list of requirements without significantly improving their CSR practices, and the contrasting case of companies that are actually evolving their CSR practices without being under the scope of such regulations. Such efforts are accompanied by similar efforts by academic institutions who included CSR-related courses in their curricula, contributing to increasing students' awareness regarding these matters. Actions taken by international professional bodies and accounting firms promote as well CSR related practices, and the authors also encourage the Romanian professional bodies to involve in similar actions, as a means to furthering the development of the country's accounting profession. Another stakeholder that the authors identify as needing intensifying its efforts are the local non-governmental organizations. While such organizations are, at the declarative level, focused on CSR or sustainability matters, their practices seem to lag behind their good intentions, as least based on the information that is publicly available. Greater coordination efforts are therefore called for by the authors, so as to significantly institutionalize such practices in Romania.

3.3 Turkey

Demir *et al.* (2016) included in this special issue focuses on the CSR practices employed in Turkey, the institutional context, national and international related regulation, and good practices. The study points out that CSR practices in Turkey can mostly be seen as corporate philanthropy rather than strategically focused CSR. Philanthropy has been an important part of Turkish culture since the very early ages. In the time of the Ottoman Empire, charitable foundations and Ahi-order organizations[1] had been important vehicles leading institutional philanthropy. This tradition and historic foundation is thus one of the factors explaining the current state of CSR understanding focusing on the voluntariness dimension in the Turkish corporate world. The study also looks at the current state of CSR practice in Turkey by providing profiles of companies reporting under the Global Reporting Initiative (GRI) framework. The authors find that large private companies are the mostly involved in CSR practices, and some evidence of industry clustering. Although the analysis is mostly descriptive in nature, it gives an idea about the companies that are assuming a role in the CSR movement.

Another important contribution of the paper is to put together different national and international regulations relating to CSR in Turkey. Thus, the authors outline that different dimensions of CSR are covered under different laws. Since these are dispersed and the overall governance of regulation has not been assured, the effectiveness of regulation is limited. It is expected that regulatory framework for

CSR movement will be accelerated by the efforts of EU-Turkey legislation harmonization.

Aslan and Sigalı (2016) provide an extensive literature review on CSR research in Turkey under the accounting discipline. The study shows that early stages of CSR research in Turkey are more of a normative nature, focusing on creating and developing CSR awareness. In recent years research the focus shifted to investigating the determinants and consequences of CSR activities and reporting. Research shows that CSR awareness is increasing. However, currently the corporate CSR reporting is not at desired level. Additionally, the reporting extent and substance vary considerably among firms, usually resulting in focusing on one or two dimensions of CSR. The opinion studies point out to the lack of demand for CSR practice and reporting in the business world and calls for regulation to support the CSR movement.

When determinants and consequences of CSR practices are analyzed at the firm-level, it can be concluded that sound corporate governance structures are the driving force behind good CSR practices. This is not surprising when related regulation for listed companies keeps the board of directors responsible in reporting CSR activities in the annual reports of the company. Additionally, the board of directors is responsible for acting sensitively towards the firm's stakeholders concerning various social responsibilities, ethical rules and complying with the regulations with respect to environment, consumers and public health. More empirical research on this area is needed to reach sound conclusions since sample sizes and research methodology problems exist in these studies.

The understanding of the Turkish context, as resulting from the two studies, can be summarized in three main parts, namely the demand for CSR information, the supply of CSR information, and enforcement.

The demand side for CSR information is fairly limited in Turkey. It can be seen in opinion studies that economic decision makers in Turkey do not consider CSR as an integral part of their business analysis. Since the public does not pay attention to CSR activities of firms either, the lack of CSR or CSR-related information is not included in the mostly financial based performance evaluation models. Additionally, the lack of influential non-governmental organizations pressuring Turkish companies to increase their CSR activities creates an important obstacle on the improvement in this area. The demand issue was thus summarized by Ararat *et al.* (2011):

> "Without the demand for sustainability and sustainable investments, the emerging interest in Environmental, Social, and Corporate Governance (ESG) disclosure in Turkey will not be materially instrumental in improving the ESG performance of Turkish firms; and the current upsurge in voluntary disclosure may remain an inefficient practice."

The supply side of CSR in Turkey consists of large private firms, having stronger corporate governance. Since CSR activities are seen as part of long term reputation building efforts, larger and more established companies seem to be better suited to get involved in CSR activities. Additionally most of the largest companies in Turkey are family owned and CSR activities are well-matched with the philanthropy culture of the owners. In terms of CSR practices of SMEs, it has to be noted that eighty percent of Turkish SMEs do not survive beyond five years. In this situation, it is hard for SME managers to focus on long term impact of CSR.

When the market conditions of demand and supply do not support CSR activities and reporting, regulation and enforcement is called for. This holds for the Turkish case, as well for as other developing and transition economies. Effective and complete regulation would help improve the situation but it should be noted that the future of CSR depends on the establishment of sound market mechanisms. This is why a better defined and understandable CSR concept, highlighting the gains to the society, has to be promoted by academics, opinion leaders and regulators. The demand from both society and investors is needed to ensure that better CSR activities covering all dimensions are applied as part of a firm's business strategy. Consistent and understandable reporting requirements should also support the system to ensure the functioning of the market mechanisms.

4. Conclusions and opportunities for future research

While CSR is a topic of interest for researchers across many fields, "accountants have an important contribution to make to the debate" (Tilt, 2009). CSR research in accounting is definitely more visible within the international academic community than 40 years ago, but it still seems to be a research niche in countries that do not have a long CSR tradition and practice, such as the CEE countries. Some of the areas for future CSR research in this region include: the determinants and consequences of good CSR practices, the role of multinationals and of business rankings and awards in improving local practices, the process of change in integrating the CSR thinking in organizations, CSR disclosures and the impact of the institutional context, the role of academia and professional organizations in promoting good CSR practices, the role of regional and national regulators in establishing adequate CSR regulations and frameworks that promote sound CSR practices in the region, the perception of CSR-related matters by the millennials[2], or the impact of Information Technology advancements on CSR practices. Research should aim to build the business case for CSR and to include the relevant matter of education. As such, research would contribute to the public debate about CSR in particular, and to accounting education, in general.

One way to fostering the development of the CSR concept in CEE countries is to make the business case for CSR. This may be done by disseminating to this audience the results of relevant research bringing evidence of the potential benefits gained by companies if they invest in CSR. Among others, such benefits include enhanced corporate image, increased staff loyalty, or lower costs and risks. Such empirical research should bring evidence of the measurable payoff of CSR initiatives to companies as well as to their stakeholders, and its impact on value creation. Research in this area could employ either empirical methodologies (for a more general picture) or case studies and semi-structured interviews (for an in-depth analysis and promotion of good practices).

CSR is but one disclosure topics, and interest for it in accounting research was enhanced by the IASB's support for non-financial disclosures through initiatives such as the IASB Practice Statement Management Commentary, or the support of the IR project. Research at the border of financial and non-financial disclosures thus emerges (Barbu *et al.*, 2014). Moreover, the implementation of the Directive 2014/95/EU has drawn attention of the accounting environment to the non-financial disclosures and calls for research in this area.

CSR research should also contribute and focus on education. Studies on accounting curricula or students (Jastrzębska & Legutko-Kobus, 2011; Krasodomska, 2013) or accounting professionals (Albu *et al.*, 2011) show significant deficiencies in the CEE region: CSR is under-represented in the accounting curricula of universities and professional bodies, and is not an expected area of work for accountants. The research in the field of CSR education should focus on its relation with accounting and finance. The courses in CSR offered by universities and professional bodies in CEE countries might be analysed in comparison with their western counterparts, and surveys might be used to collect students' and trainers' opinions on this matter. Implications for both academia and professional bodies should be derived and brought to the attention of such important organizations.

References

Albu, N., Albu, C.N., Gîrbină, M.M. & Sandu, M.I. (2011) "The implications of corporate social responsibility on the accounting profession: the case of Romania", *Amfiteatru Economic*, vol. XIII, no. 29: 221-234

Ararat, M., Yurtoğlu, B.B., Suel, E. & Tura, D. (2011) "Sustainable Investments in Turkey 2010", International Finance Corporation, Washington

Aslan, Ü. & Sigalı, S. (2016) "Corporate social responsibility research in accounting: evidence from Turkey", *Accounting and Management Information Systems*, vol. 15, no. 2: 410-419

Barbu, E.M., Dumontier, P., Feleagă, N. & Feleagă, L. (2014) "Mandatory Environmental Disclosures by Companies Complying with IASs/IFRSs: The Cases of France, Germany, and the UK", *The International Journal of Accounting*, vol. 49, iss. 2: 231–247

Burchell, S., Clubb, C. & Hopwood, A.G. (1985) "Accounting in its social context: Toward a history of value added in the United Kingdom", *Accounting, Organizations and Society*, vol. 10, no. 4: 381-413

Carroll, A.B. (1999) "Corporate Social Responsibility Evolution of a Definitional Construct", *Business & Society*, vol. *38*, no. 3: 268-295

Carter, C.R. & Jennings, M.M. (2004) "Role of purchasing in corporate social responsibility: a structural equation analysis", *The Journal of Business Logistics*, vol. 25, no. 1: 145–187

Cohen, J.R., Holder-Webb, L.L., Nath, L. & Wood, D. (2012) "Corporate reporting of nonfinancial leading indicators of economic performance and sustainability", *Accounting Horizons*, vol. 26 (1): 65-90

Dahlsrud, A. (2008) "How corporate social responsibility is defined: an analysis of 37 definitions", *Corporate social responsibility and environmental management*, vol. 15.1: 1-13

Deloitte (2011) *Integrated reporting. A better view?*, Deloitte Global Sustainability and Climate Change Services

Demir, G., Cagle, M.N. & Dalkılıç, A.F. (2016) "Corporate Social Responsibility And Regulatory Initiatives In Turkey: Good Implementation Examples", *Accounting and Management Information Systems*, vol. 15, no. 2: 372-400

Dyczkowska, J., Krasodomska, J. & Michalak, J. (2016) "CSR in Poland: Institutional Context, Legal Framework and Voluntary Initiatives", *Accounting and Management Information Systems*, vol. 15, no. 2: 206-241

Guşe, R.G., Almăşan, A., Circa, C. & Dumitru, M. (2016) "The role of the stakeholders in the institutionalization of the CSR reporting in Romania", *Accounting and Management Information Systems*, vol. 15, no. 2: 304-340

Jastrzębska, E. & Legutko-Kobus, P. (2011) „Kształcenie na rzecz społecznej odpowiedzialności biznesu na uczelniach ekonomicznych" [Education in line with the corporate social responsibility at economic universities] (in:) M. Bernatt, J. Bogdaniecka, T. Skoczny (Eds.), *Społeczna odpowiedzialność biznesu – krytyczna analiza [Corporate social responsibility – critical analysis]*, Uniwersytet Warszawski, Warszawa, 193-211

Karagul, M. (2011) "Ahi-Order Organization from Ottoman Empire Until Today and Its Economical Development Relation", *International Journal of Business and Social Science*, vol. 2, no. 21 [Special Issue – November 2011]: 214-225

KPMG (2013) *KPMG Survey of Corporate Responsibility Reporting 2013*, KPMG International, the Netherlands

Krasodomska, J. (2013) "Corporate Social Responsibility as a factor influencing the development of social accounting and assessment of employers", *eFinanse. Financial internet quarterly*, vol. 9, no. 1: 12- 25

Lungu, C.I., Caraiani, C., Dascălu, C., Turcu, D. & Turturea, M. (2016) "Archival analysis of Corporate Social Responsibility research: the Romanian perspective", *Accounting and Management Information Systems*, vol. 15, no. 2:341-371

Moir, L. (2001) "What do we mean by corporate social responsibility?", *Corporate Governance: The international journal of business in society*, vol. 1(2): 16–22

Paliwoda-Matiolańska, A. (2015) "Corporate Social Responsibility in Poland: is there a place for value creation?" (in:) CSR Trends. Beyond Business as Usual, J. Reichel (Ed.), Centrum Strategii i Rozwoju Impact (CSR Impact), Łódź, 7-28

Surdykowska, S.T. (1999) *Rachunkowość międzynarodowa [International Accounting]*, Zakamycze, Kraków

Tilt, C.A. (2009) "Corporate Responsibility, Accounting and Accountants" (in:) Professionals´ Perspectives of Corporate Social Responsibility, S. O. Idowu, W. L.Filho (Eds.), Springer Science & Business Media, 11-32

Walrod, T. (2016) "Aligning your CSR Program with the Millennials", *Millennials Magazine*, January 29 2016, available online at http://millennialmagazine.com/align-your-csr-program-with-millennials/

Waniak-Michalak, H., Macuda, M. & Krasodomska, J. (2016) "Corporate Social Responsibility and accounting in Poland: a literature review", *Accounting and Management Information Systems*, vol. 15, no. 2:242-303

[1] Karagul (2011) defines an Ahi-order organization as "a system which gathers ethic and art, production and trade and it was started to be observed on the lands of Anatolia starting from 13th century and after the fall of Seljuk State. Ahî-Order Organization aims to establish strong and dependable relations between the rich and poor, producer and consumer and with the citizens and the state and it has tried to establish all of its works on social ethics and social justice system".

[2] A study published in the Millennials Magazine outlines the increased importance of CSR matters to the 80 million American millennials reshaping the work place (Walrod, 2016).

Permissions

All chapters in this book were first published in JAMIS, by Bucharest University of Economic Studies; hereby published with permission under the Creative Commons Attribution License or equivalent. Every chapter published in this book has been scrutinized by our experts. Their significance has been extensively debated. The topics covered herein carry significant findings which will fuel the growth of the discipline. They may even be implemented as practical applications or may be referred to as a beginning point for another development.

The contributors of this book come from diverse backgrounds, making this book a truly international effort. This book will bring forth new frontiers with its revolutionizing research information and detailed analysis of the nascent developments around the world.

We would like to thank all the contributing authors for lending their expertise to make the book truly unique. They have played a crucial role in the development of this book. Without their invaluable contributions this book wouldn't have been possible. They have made vital efforts to compile up to date information on the varied aspects of this subject to make this book a valuable addition to the collection of many professionals and students.

This book was conceptualized with the vision of imparting up-to-date information and advanced data in this field. To ensure the same, a matchless editorial board was set up. Every individual on the board went through rigorous rounds of assessment to prove their worth. After which they invested a large part of their time researching and compiling the most relevant data for our readers.

The editorial board has been involved in producing this book since its inception. They have spent rigorous hours researching and exploring the diverse topics which have resulted in the successful publishing of this book. They have passed on their knowledge of decades through this book. To expedite this challenging task, the publisher supported the team at every step. A small team of assistant editors was also appointed to further simplify the editing procedure and attain best results for the readers.

Apart from the editorial board, the designing team has also invested a significant amount of their time in understanding the subject and creating the most relevant covers. They scrutinized every image to scout for the most suitable representation of the subject and create an appropriate cover for the book.

The publishing team has been an ardent support to the editorial, designing and production team. Their endless efforts to recruit the best for this project, has resulted in the accomplishment of this book. They are a veteran in the field of academics and their pool of knowledge is as vast as their experience in printing. Their expertise and guidance has proved useful at every step. Their uncompromising quality standards have made this book an exceptional effort. Their encouragement from time to time has been an inspiration for everyone.

The publisher and the editorial board hope that this book will prove to be a valuable piece of knowledge for researchers, students, practitioners and scholars across the globe.

List of Contributors

Anna Białek-Jaworska and Anna Matusiewicz
University of Warsaw, Faculty of Economic Sciences

Delroy Chevers, Devon Lawrence, Arlene Laidlaw and Dane Nicholson
The University of the West Indies, Jamaica

Marina Trpeska, Atanasko Atanasovski and Zorica Bozinovska Lazarevska
University Ss Cyril and Methodius, Faculty of Economics-Skopje, Macedonia

Semiu Babatunde Adeyemi, Sunday Obah and Ini Etete Udofia
University of Lagos, Nigeria

Walid Khoufi and Dhouha Khrifech
University of Sfax, Tunisia

Atila Karkacıer and Fatih Coşkun Ertaş
Gaziosmanpaşa University, Tokat, Turkey

Costel Istrate
Alexandru Ioan Cuza University of Iaşi, Romania

Alhassan Musah and Erasmus Dodzi Gakpetor
Dominion University College, Ghana

Fred Kwasi Anokye
University of Ghana, Legon

Cătălin Nicolae Albu
Bucharest University of Economic Studies, Romania

Cagnur Balsari
Dokuz Eylul University, Turkey

Joanna Krasodomskac
Cracow University of Economics, Poland

Index